# Best-Selling Professional Resources for College Instructors!

As the world's leader in education, Allyn & Bacon understands your interest in continual professional development. From the latest advancements in technology for the classroom to special insights for adjunct professors, these books were written for you!

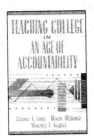     

**Instructing and Mentoring the African American College Student: Strategies for Success in Higher Education**
Louis B. Gallien, Jr., Regent University and
Marshalita Sims Peterson, Ph.D, Spelman College
©2005 / 0-205-38917-1

**Grant Writing in Higher Education:
A Step-by-Step Guide**
Kenneth Henson, The Citadel
©2004 / 0-205-38919-8

**Using Technology in Learner-Centered Education: Proven Strategies for Teaching and Learning**
David G. Brown and Gordon McCray, both of Wake Forest University, Craig Runde, Eckerd College and Heidi Schweizer, Marquette University
©2002 / 0-205-35580-3

**Creating Learning-Centered Courses for the World Wide Web**
William B. Sanders, University of Hartford
©2001 / 0-205-31513-5

**Success Strategies for Adjunct Faculty**
Richard Lyons, Faculty Development Associates
©2004 / 0-205-36017-3

**The Effective, Efficient Professor:
Teaching, Scholarship and Service**
Philip C. Wankat, Purdue University
©2002 / 0-205-33711-2

**Emblems of Quality in Higher Education:
Developing and Sustaining High-Quality Programs**
Jennifer Grant Haworth, Loyola University, Chicago and Clifton F. Conrad, University of Wisconsin, Madison,
©1997 / 0-205-19546-6

**Faculty of Color in Academe: Bittersweet Success**
Caroline Sotello Viernes Turner, Arizona State University and Samuel L. Myers Jr., University of Minnesota
©2000 / 0-205-27849-3

**An Introduction to Interactive Multimedia**
Stephen J. Misovich, Jerome Katrichis, David Demers, William B. Sanders, all of the University of Hartford
©2003 / 0-205-34373-2

**Learner-Centered Assessment on College Campuses: Shifting the Focus from Teaching to Learning**
Mary E. Huba, Iowa State University and Jann E. Freed, Central College
©2000 / 0-205-28738-7

**The Online Teaching Guide: A Handbook of Attitudes, Strategies, and Techniques for the Virtual Classroom**
Ken W. White and Bob H. Weight, both of University of Phoenix Online Faculty
©2000 / 0-205-29531-2

**The Adjunct Professor's Guide to Success:
Surviving and Thriving in the College Classroom**
Richard Lyons, Faculty Development Associates, Marcella L. Kysilka, and George E. Pawlas, both of University of Central Florida
©1999 / 0-205-28774-3

**Teaching Tips for College and University Instructors: A Practical Guide**
David Royse, University of Kentucky
©2001 / 0-205-29839-7

**Advice for New Faculty Members**
Robert Boice, Emeritus, SUNY Stony Brook
©2000 / 0-205-28159-1

**Writing for Professional Publication:
Keys to Academic and Business Success**
Kenneth Henson, The Citadel
©1999 / 0-205-28313-6

**Teaching College in an Age of Accountability**
Richard Lyons, Faculty Development Associates, Meggin McIntosh, University of Nevada - Reno, and Marcella L. Kysilka, University of Central Florida
©2003 / 0-205-35315-0

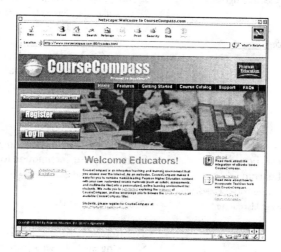

# Instructor's Manual and Test Bank

*for*

Hooyman and Kiyak

# Social Gerontology
## A Multidisciplinary Perspective

Eighth Edition

*Prepared by*

Maria L. Claver
California State University, Long Beach

Boston   New York   San Francisco
Mexico City   Montreal   Toronto   London   Madrid   Munich   Paris
Hong Kong   Singapore   Tokyo   Cape Town   Sydney

ISBN-13: 978-0-205-56630-3
ISBN-10: 0-205-56630-8

Printed in the United States of America

10 9 8 7 6 5 4 3 2 1     11 10 09 08 07

# Table of Contents

# Introduction

Welcome to the Instructor's Manual and Test Bank for the 8th Edition of *Social Gerontology: A Multidisciplinary Perspective*. The purpose of this manual is to provide material that will enrich instruction using this text.

The first half of this text consists of an Instructor's Manual, arranged by chapter. Within each chapter is an outline, followed by a summary of the main points covered in the chapter, a bulleted list of learning objectives, a list of key terms and key people with corresponding textbook page numbers, discussion topic suggestions, classroom activities and student project ideas, suggested films, websites and additional resources. The discussion topics, classroom activities, films, websites and resources are by no means an exhaustive list, but aim to provide both suggestions to get the first-time instructor started as well as fresh ideas for those who have taught this material numerous times.

Listed below are the websites of the film production companies referenced throughout the manual in the Film Suggestion section. Many of the film websites provide links to discussion guides and teaching materials related to the film.

The second half of the manual is a Test Bank, again arranged by chapter, containing 50 multiple choice, true or false, short answer, and essay questions for each chapter. Below each question is the answer, a difficulty rating from 1 to 3 (3 being the most difficult), and page reference to locate the question's content in the textbook. These test questions are provided to assist the instructor with designing quizzes and exams appropriate for the purposes of the course, whether meant to serve as an ungraded check-in or as a graded final exam.

During the process of resource-checking/updating and searching for additional resources, it became clear that there are boundless resources for teaching gerontology and not everything I found could be squeezed into this instructor manual. One resource worth mentioning here is the monthly Teaching Gerontology e-Newsletter, edited by Harry Moody, which provides user-friendly information about recent research findings, interesting materials, and idea-provoking classroom activities. To subscribe, send an email to teachgero@yahoo.com. Back issues of the newsletters are available at: http://www.hrmoody.com/newsletters.html.

The Teaching Tips for First-Time Instructors guide included at the end of this instructor's manual has proven to be very useful to me and my colleagues, as well. It is my hope that the information contained in this guide provides not only content to make it possible to teach this course well, but inspiration for new and innovative approaches to teaching social gerontology.

Maria L. Claver

Websites for Films
American Foundation for the Blind: www.afb.org
Fanlight Productions: www.fanlight.com
Filmakers Library: www.filmakers.com
Films for the Humanities and Sciences: www.films.com
First Run/Icarus Films: www.frif.com
Insight Media: www.insight-media.com
New Day Films: www.newday.com
Terra Nova Films: www.terranova.org
WHMT/PBS Video Productions: www.whmt.org
Wise Owl Productions, Inc.: www.wiseowlproductions.com
Women Make Movies: www.wmm.com

# Sample Syllabus for Social Gerontology

**Semester:**                          **Office location:**
**Time:**                              **Office Hours:**
**Location:**                          **Telephone:**
**Instructor:**                        **E-mail:**

## Required Text

Hooyman, Nancy R. and H. Asuman Kiyak. 2007. *Social Gerontology: A Multidisciplinary Perspective.* Boston: Allyn & Bacon.

## Course Objectives

By the end of the course, the student will be able to:

- define social gerontology and discuss its origins and current areas of focus;
- summarize the biological and physiological changes related to aging;
- explain the cognitive changes that are linked with aging as well as the theories that explain such changes and adaptations;
- demonstrate an understanding of the social context older adults experience, such as their living arrangements, employment, family supports and discrimination; and
- discuss the social policies and social problems affected older adults in the U.S.

## Assessment of Student Learning

1. Course Grade: Your grade in this class is based on two exams worth 100 points each and a series of projects worth a total of 300 points. The total possible points for this course is 500 points. The final grade distribution is as follows:

   500-450 A
   449-400 B
   399-350 C
   349-300 D
   299-250 F

2. Examinations: Of the two exams in this course, one will be a midterm exam and one will be a final exam. Check the schedule of readings for the date of the midterm exam; the final exam will be given at the time assigned by the university. Each of the exams will include a mix of multiple choice, true-false and essay questions. Exams will cover all readings, class discussions, lectures, projects, and videos assigned for that portion of the semester.

3. Projects: There will be one 20-point assignment for each of the 15 weeks of class. (20 points x 15 weekly projects = 300 course project points) The instructions for each assignment will be provided in enough time to allow the student to complete the project.

## Policies and Procedures

1. Academic Honesty: Please do not cheat or plagiarize. In the event that it is discovered that you have cheated or plagiarized, I will follow the procedures laid out in the student code of conduct. Failing individual projects and exams as well as failing the course are possible. If you are uncertain about plagiarism or are having difficulties in this course, please see me.

2. Extra Credit Options: There may be the opportunity for extra credit throughout the semester. Such opportunities will be announced in class and will come with written instructions.

3. Attendance and Participation: Class attendance is expected. If you must miss class, please obtain a copy of the notes from another student. All exams must be taken at the time and date scheduled. Only extreme and documented excuses will qualify the student for a make-up exam. Please see me if a make-up exam is necessary. When the class is discussing the course material, please keep comments relevant and sociologically aware.

## Schedule of Class Readings, Discussions, and Exams*

| Week | Date | Topic | Reading |
|------|------|-------|---------|
| 1 | 1 | *Part 1: The Field of Social Gerontology* <br> Introduction to Social Gerontology | Chapter 1 |
| 2 | 3 | Aging in Other Countries and Across Cultures in the United States | Chapter 2 |
| 3 | | *Part 2: The Biological & Physiological Context of Aging* <br> Social Consequences of Aging | Chapter 3 |
| 4 | | Managing Chronic Diseases and Promoting Well-Being | Chapter 4 |
| 5 | 4 | *Part 3: The Psychological Context of Social Aging* <br> Cognitive Changes with Aging | Chapter 5 |
| 6 | 5 | Personality and Mental Health in Old Age | Chapter 6 |
| 7 | 6 | Love, Intimacy, and Sexuality in Old Age | Chapter 7 |
| 8 | 2 | **Midterm Exam (Chapters 1-7)** <br><br> *Part 4: The Social Context of Aging* <br> Social Theories of Aging | Chapter 8 |
| 9 | 7 | Social Supports and Challenges of Informal Caregiving | Chapters 9 & 10 |
| 10 | 8 | Living Arrangements and Social Interactions | Chapter 11 |
| 11 | 9 | Productive Aging | Chapter 12 |
| 12 | 10 | Death, Dying, Bereavement, and Widowhood | Chapter 13 |
| 13 | 3 | The Resiliency of Elders of Color and Older Women | Chapters 14 & 15 |
| 14 | 11 | *Part 5: The Societal Context of Aging* <br> Social Policies to Address Social Problems | Chapter 16 |
| 15 | 12 | Health and Long-Term Care Policy and Programs | Chapter 17 |
| 16 | | **Final Exam (Chapters 8-17)** | |

*This is a tentative schedule. The instructor reserves the right to make changes to this schedule as needed. Any changes will be announced in class and it is the student's responsibility to know about these changes.

# CHAPTER 1: THE GROWTH OF SOCIAL GERONTOLOGY

## Chapter Outline

I. The Field of Gerontology
    A. Social Gerontology
    B. What is Aging?
    C. An Active Aging Framework
    D. A Person-Environment Perspective on Social Gerontology
    E. Why Study Aging?
II. Growth of the Older Population
    A. Changes in Life Expectancy
    B. Maximum Life Span
III. The Oldest-Old
    A. Ages 85 and Older
    B. Centenarians
    C. Population Pyramids
IV. Support Ratios
V. Population Trends
    A. Ethnic Minorities
    B. Geographic Distribution
    C. Educational and Economic Status
VI. Impact of Demographic Trends
VII. Longevity in Health or Disease?
VIII. How Aging and Older Adults Are Studied
    A. Development of the Field
    B. Historical Forces
IX. Formal Development of the Field
    A. Major Research Centers Founded
X. Research Methods
    A. The Age/Period/Cohort Problem
    B. Cross-Sectional Studies
    C. Longitudinal Studies: Design and Limitations
    D. Sequential Designs
    E. Problems with Representative Samples of Older People
XI. Summary and Implications for the Future

## Chapter Summary

Chapter 1 presents an introduction to the field of gerontology, which addresses the social, psychological, physical, and demographic concerns related to aging and introduces the role of the person-environment perspective to study issues relevant to aging. Due to an increasing interest in understanding the process of aging and the changing demographics of the world, including the United States, gerontology is a growing field. More and more people in the U.S. are living beyond age 65 or even 85, with these "oldest old" as the fastest growing age group among Americans. The population of older adults in the U.S. is also becoming more ethnically diverse, although elders of color generally have a lower life expectancy due to health and economic disparities. The growth of the older population has raised questions as to whether our nation is prepared to meet the health care and social service needs of this group and their families.

Given the growth in the number of older adults, society needs to address the public policy issues related to aging, including assessing the appropriateness of current policy and exploring innovative policy to meet the changing needs of older adults. Researching policy and social issues related to aging poses some challenges to gerontologists. The important question centers on being able to distinguish age differences from cohort differences. Improvements in gerontological research, such as the use of longitudinal studies and sequential designs, have been made, but more exploration is needed.

## Learning Objectives

*After reading chapter 1 the student should be able to:*
1.1 Define aging, gerontology, social gerontology, and geriatrics
1.2 Describe the active aging framework and the person-environment perspective
1.3 Understand the reasons for studying social gerontology and the development of the field
1.4 Discuss the important demographic trends affecting the U.S.
1.5 Illustrate life expectancy, life span and longevity in terms of health and disease
1.6 Explain the research methods and designs for studying older adults as well as the importance of representative sample for social gerontological research

## Key Terms and Key People

*Active Aging*: a model of viewing aging as a positive experience of continued growth and participation in family, community, and societal activities, regardless of physical and cognitive decline (p. 7)

*Active* versus *Dependent Life Expectancy*: a way of describing expected length of life; the term active denoting a manner of living that is relatively healthy and independent, in contrast to being dependent on help from others (p. 28)

*Ageism*: negative attitudes, beliefs, and conceptions of the nature and characteristics of older persons that are based on age that distort their actual characteristics, abilities, etc. (p. 4)

*Aging*: changes that occur to an organism during its life span, from development to maturation to senescence (p. 5)

*Baltimore Longitudinal Study of Aging*: a federally funded longitudinal study that has examined physiological, cognitive, and personality changes in healthy middle-aged and older men since 1958, and in women since 1978 (p. 31)

*Cohort*: a group of people of the same generation sharing a statistical trait such as age, ethnicity, or socioeconomic status (for example, all African American women between the ages of 60 and 65 in 1999) (p. 6)

*Competence Model*: a conception or description of the way persons perform, focusing on their abilities vis-à-vis the demands of the environment (p. 9)

*Compression of Morbidity*: given a certain length of life, a term referring to relatively long periods of healthy, active, high-quality existence and relatively short periods of illness and dependency in the last few years of life (p. 28)

*Cross-Sectional Research*: research that examines or compares characteristics of people at a given point in time and attempts to identify factors associated with contrasting characteristics of different groupings of people (p. 29)

*Environmental Press*: features of the social, technological, or natural environment that place demands on people (p. 9)

*Geriatrics*: clinical study and treatment of older people and the diseases that affect them (p. 3)

*Gerontology*: the field of study that focuses on understanding the biological, psychological, social, and political factors that influence people's lives (p. 3)

*Life Expectancy*: the average length of time persons, defined by age, sex, ethnic group, and socioeconomic status, in a given society are expected to live (p. 13)

*Life Course:* a broader concept than individual life span development that takes account of cultural, historical, and societal contexts that affect people as they age (p. 8)

*Longitudinal Research*: research that follows the same individual over time to measure change in specific variables (p. 13)

*Maximum Life Span*: biologically programmed maximum number of years that each species can expect to live (p. 15)

*Person-Environment (P-E) Perspective*: a model for understanding the behavior of people based on the idea that persons are affected by personal characteristics, such as health, attitudes, and beliefs, as they interact with and are affected by the characteristics of the cultural, social, political, and economic environment (p. 8)

*Resilience:* capacity to overcome adversity, in part due protective personal, family, community and societal factors (p. 8 )

*Selective Dropout:* elders who drop out of longitudinal studies tend to be sicker, less educated, and more isolated (p. 35)

*Senescence:* gradual decline in all organ systems, especially after age 30 (p. 5)

*Sequential Research Designs*: research designs that combine features of cross-sectional and longitudinal research designs to overcome some of the problems encountered in using those designs (p. 35)

## Discussion Topics

- Distinguish between different types of aging. To what extent would one expect consistency among these types of aging?

- Distinguish between gerontology and geriatrics; define social gerontology.

- What historical and cultural factors have differentially influenced the cohort of people who are currently aged 65 to 75 and those aged 35 to 45?

- Distinguish among the young-old, the old-old, and the oldest-old in terms of social and health characteristics.

- Discuss the benefits of studying social gerontology from a person-environment perspective, focusing on the competence model.

- Discuss your own reasons for learning about older adults and the aging process, and the benefits you expect to gain from your learning experience.

- Describe some factors that are responsible for increased life expectancy at birth, and factors that may significantly extend life expectancy beyond age 65 for future cohorts.

- What are the economic, political, and social implications of the increasing rectangularization of the survival curve in the U.S.?

- Discuss the geographic distribution of the older U.S. population and implications for policies in states with higher and lower than average proportions of older persons in their population.

- What evidence is there for potential biological differences between centenarians and others who survive to their 70s and 80s?

- Compare your own experiences as members of a birth cohort with those from the cohorts of the 1920s and 1930s.

- Describe the age/period/cohort problem in social gerontological research. What research designs have been developed to overcome some of these problems? What are the strengths and weaknesses of each design?

- Discuss the advantages and disadvantages of conducting longitudinal research in aging.

## Classroom Activities and Student Projects

*Activity 1.1   Attend a Conference*
Find out if there is a state, regional, or local gerontological society/organization meeting in your area and have your students attend one of their conferences. Another option would be for you and your students attend a sociological or psychological conference which has a section on aging. Have the students attend a session and write 3–5 page papers about what they heard about aging.

*Activity 1.2   Analyze a Census Brief*
The Census Bureau produced a series of briefs based on the Census 2000 findings.  One brief is entitled *The 65 and Older Population 2000:  Census 2000 Brief* and can be accessed at http://www.census.gov/prod/2001pubs/c2kbr01-10.pdf.   Have the students download this document and bring it to class.  This document contains a wealth of demographic data on older adults in the United States, including statistics on age, gender, residential location, etc.  Ask the students what conclusions can be made from reading this document.

*Activity 1.3   Matching Game*
List characteristics of the research approaches (e.g., longitudinal research, cross-sectional research) on note cards and have students match the characteristic with the type of research it describes. Have two teams compete to see who can complete the task first.

*Activity 1.4   Scavenger Hunt*
Assign groups of students a decade ranging from 1910 – 2000 and ask them to bring facts about the decade to the following class meeting. Have each group present what they learned about the decade and apply it to the corresponding cohort.

## Suggested Films
*These films are not available through Allyn & Bacon.*

*"2000"* (1999)
Magic Hour Films APs, 29 minutes, $49 VHS
This charming film shows the interaction of the very young with the very old. Each scene reveals something of the unique bond shared by children and older adults. Forty people meet in pairs. The age of each pair totals 100 (e.g., a one-year old with a 99-year old).

*Age* (2002)
Insight Media, 30 minutes, $139 VHS
This film presents the terminology that serves as the foundation of social gerontology, such as age cohort and life expectancy and discusses societal implications of an aging population.

*Angelus Plaza:  A New Look at Old Age* (2001)
Filmakers Library, 27 minutes, $250 VHS/DVD
This film portrays three active, lively older adults who, despite the usual physical complaints of old age, demonstrate a new definition of later life.

*Myths and Realities of Aging* (1993)

Insight Media, 60 minutes, $99 VHS

This video examines ageism in its many forms. It features experts and elders who describe how people learn about aging and debunk common myths, including the idea that most people over the age of 60 are ill or sexually inactive.

*Oldtimers* (1993)

First Run Icarus Films, 17 minutes, $175 VHS

This film profiles a community of older adults who meet at a local bar in San Francisco and discuss their experiences of living alone.

*Surfing for Life* (2001)

David Brown, 56 minutes, $49 VHS/$51 DVD

This film profiles 10 older surfers as inspirational models of healthy and successful aging. Discussion guide at www.surfingforlife.com

## Suggested Websites

*The Gerontological Society of America (GSA)*

http://www.geron.org/

This site provides a wealth of information on the organization, its conferences, and its resources.

*The Federal Interagency Forum on Aging Related Statistics (FIFARS)*

http://www.agingstats.gov/

Many federal agencies are part of FIFARS, which provides tables and statistics on many issues related to older adults, such as education, poverty, and health.

*Baltimore Longitudinal Study of Aging*

http://www.grc.nia.nih.gov/branches/blsa/blsa.htm

This site is home to the BLSA, which is the longest study of aging and is sponsored by the National Institute on Aging. Information about the study as well as its data can be accessed here.

*The New England Centenarian Study*

http://www.bumc.bu.edu/Departments/HomeMain.asp?DepartmentID=361

This site is home to the New England Centenarian Study, which is sponsored by the Boston University Medical College and has been studying centenarians for a decade. Information about the study, its findings, and as case studies of centenarians can be accessed here.

*Okinawa Centenarian Study*

http://www.okicent.org/cent.html

This site is home to the Okinawa Centenarian Study, which studies centenarians in Japan and is based on data from the last century. Information about the study can be accessed here.

## Additional Resources

Altpeter, Mary and Victor W. Marshall. 2003. "Making Aging "Real" for Undergraduates." *Educational Gerontology*. 29:739–756.

Clark, Philip G. 2002. "Values and voices in teaching gerontology and geriatrics: Case studies as stories." *The Gerontologist*. 42:297–307

Hirshorn, Barbara. 1991. "Introducing the Demography of Aging: Relating Population Processes to the Aging Society." *Teaching Sociology* 19: 231–236.

# CHAPTER 2:
# HISTORICAL AND CROSS-CULTURAL ISSUES IN AGING

## Chapter Outline

I. Worldwide Trends
     A. Demographic Changes
     B. Economic Implications for Industrialized Countries
II. The Impact of Modernization
     A. Resources Held by Older Adults
     B. Modernization Theory
     C. Impact of Modernization on Filial Piety
     D. Modernization and Intergenerational Relations
III. A Cross-Cultural View of Elders' Roles in Contemporary Societies
     A. Immigrants from Traditional Cultures
     B. Living Arrangements of Older Immigrants
     C. Financial Dilemmas of Immigrant Elders
IV. Summary and Implications for the Future

## Chapter Summary

Chapter 2 addresses worldwide demographic changes with an emphasis on the increase in absolute and relative size of older populations in many countries. It presents a discussion of aging and older adults from a variety of contemporary cultures. Although the aging of populations can present economic and social challenges, the conclusion from these diverse examples is that societies appear to be reconciling older adults' contribution to society and the reverence given to them. For example, Japan has enacted legislation to provide long-term care for the elderly due to its increasing number of older adults and the effects of modernization. Cross-cultural similarities include having family members serve as primary caregivers and linking elders' societal participation to the level of respect they receive. While control of resources becomes a means of interaction for societal members at any age, it becomes more significant in one's later years. One example of an exchange of resources is the intergenerational exchange of caregiving experienced by older adults who immigrate to the U.S.

In the U.S., the number of older immigrants has grown dramatically, and older immigrants primarily come from Asian and Latin American countries. They tend to be less educated, less likely to speak English, less likely to have health care coverage and use health and social services and more likely to receive government benefits. Although older immigrants tend to reciprocate care received from adult children with the provision of childcare for grandchildren, they tend to lose autonomy and opportunities for active aging.

## Learning Objectives

*After reading chapter 2 the student should be able to:*
2.1   Identify the role of older people in non-western cultures
2.2   Discuss the changes in social roles of older persons
2.3   Describe societal norms regarding aging and older adults' expectations of society
2.4   Contrast perspectives regarding the impact of modernization on the relationship between older persons and the larger society

## Key Terms and Key People

*Filial Piety*:  a sense of reverence and deference to elders that encourages care for one's aging family members (p. 53)

*Modernization Theory*:  advances in technology, applied sciences, urbanization, and literacy which in this context are related to a decline in the status of older people (p. 51)

*Skipped Generation Households:* often because of economic necessity, the middle generation moves out of the home and grandparents assume responsibility for the day-to-day care of grandchildren (p. 54)

*Social stratification*:  the division of large numbers of people into layers according to their relative power, property, and prestige; applies to both nations and to people within a nation, society, or other group (p. 50)

## Discussion Topics

- What specific aspects of modernization contribute to a change in older people's social status? In addition to modernization, what other reasons explain changes between generations in American society?

- What factors may influence the differential social status of older people in different societies at the same stage of modernization?

- To what extent can older people maintain power in a social system through control of knowledge and property?

- Describe any gender differences that may arise in the ability of older people to control resources. Give examples of such control in the U.S. and other countries.

- It has been suggested that the study of aging in other cultures is of intrinsic interest but has no relevance to an understanding of old age in our own society. Argue the pros and cons of this proposition.

- What influence does the physical and cognitive status of an older person have on society's response toward older people in general?

- Discuss how cultural values of reciprocity and filial piety have blended with economic and political factors to maintain the status of older persons in Japan.

## Classroom Activities and Student Projects

*Activity 2.1 Presentations on Culture*
Have each student select either a contemporary or historical culture and research that culture's ideas about aging. Topics for the students to address include power, prestige, filial responsibility, modernization, and status and roles of older adults in that culture. The students then give a class presentation on their findings. The students could also be asked to write a paper documenting their findings.

*Activity 2.2 Biography*
Have each student select an autobiography written by an older adult who was greatly influenced by his or her culture and shares these experiences in his or her writings. This allows students to see the interplay between culture and individual lives. The students can then write a 3–5 page paper in which they summarize the autobiography, make connections between culture and the individual, and illustrate the beliefs about aging that had an impact on the life of the author.

## Suggested Films
*These films are not available through Allyn & Bacon.*

*Aging in Japan: When Traditional Mechanisms Vanish* (1990)
Films for Humanities and the Social Sciences, 45 minutes, $89.95 VHS/DVD
This film explores the role of older adults in Japan in both a historical and contemporary context.

*Busy Forever*
Filmmakers Library, 52 minutes, $295 VHS/DVD
The unexpected pace at which Japanese are aging is creating concern regarding the ratio of working people to non-working (or dependent) people. The trend has been for older Japanese workers to stay in the workforce long after the traditional retirement age. This film shows us some of the people who are working well into their 70s and 80s.

*For Better or Worse* (1993)
Terra Nova Films, 55 minutes, $149 VHS/DVD
This film presents five culturally diverse couples who have each been together more than 50 years talking about their relationships and life experiences.

*Murray Avenue: A Community in Transition*
New Day Films, 28 minutes, $99 VHS/DVD
A tender portrait of an old, vital, Jewish neighborhood. Pittsburgh's Jewish identity is depicted in this portrait of three vital, traditional community gathering spots: a butcher's shop, a bakery, and a newsstand.

*Old Men* (1999)
First Run Icarus Films, 94 minutes, $440 VHS
This film profiles the life of older men in China. Through the details of their daily routine, we observe the physical and psychological aches that accompany old age, and we witness the solace that can be found in tradition and companionship.

## Suggested Websites

*AARP*
http://news.aarp.org/UM/T.asp?A910.52851.3591.11.903449
See an interactive global map, "Aging Everywhere," that contains information such as age dependency ratios, life expectancy at birth, and links to speeches and research on a variety of topics.

*The Population Reference Bureau*
http://www.prb.org
Browse by the topic "Aging" and open a variety of articles based on Census Bureau data about older adults in the U.S. and around the world. Also try the Quick Link "Graphics Bank", then "Aging" for Powerpoint presentations and slides on populations and health.

*U.S. Census Bureau*
http://www.census.gov/ipc/www/idbpyr.html
This site allows you to obtain population pyramids (graphs that show the distribution of population by age and sex) for any country in the world.

## Additional Resources

Brogden, Michael. 2001. *Geronticide: Killing the Elderly.* Jessica Kingsley Publishers.

Cruikshank, Margaret. 2002. *Learning to Be Old: Gender, Culture, and Aging.* Rowan and Littlefield.

Gilleard, Paul and Paul Higgs. 2001. *Cultures of Aging.* Prentice Hall.

# CHAPTER 3:  THE SOCIAL CONSEQUENCES OF PHYSICAL AGING

## Chapter Outline

I.  Biological Theories of Aging
    A.  Wear and Tear Theory
    B.  Autoimmune Theory
    C.  Cross-Linkage Theory
    D.  Free Radical Theory
    E.  Cellular Aging Theory
    F.  Endocrine & Immunological Theory
II. Can Aging Be Reversed or Delayed?
    A.  Growth Hormones
    B.  Caloric Restrictions
    C.  Anti-Aging Compounds
III. Research on Physiological Changes with Age
    A.  Aging in Body Composition
    B.  Changes in Organ Systems
    C.  Changes in Sleep Patterns with Aging
IV. Changes in Sensory Functions
    A.  Changes in Vision
    B.  Environmental Modifications
    C.  Changes in Hearing
    D.  Changes in Taste and Smell
V.  Implications for the Future
VI. Summary

## Chapter Summary

    Chapter 3 presents an overview of the age-related physiological changes that occur throughout the human life span.  Most of the age-related changes are gradual.  Some begin in early adulthood, while other changes do not appear until late adulthood.  While some signs of old age are visible, such as graying hair and a slower walk, numerous others are not visible. These include changes to the internal organs, which are measured by functional capacity. Age-related changes do not necessarily imply that one's quality of life has diminished.  Often the changes are so gradual that the individual has made adaptations for them.  Health care practitioners and family members can support older adults by providing a social support system and helping the older adult to obtain assistive devices.

    Age-related physical changes vary greatly between individuals as such changes are dependent on heredity, lifestyle, and nutrition.  Exercise is a key component of maintaining physical abilities into one's later years.  Studies indicate that sleep patterns change with normal aging, but that the most severe sleep disturbances are linked to physical and psychiatric disorders.  Changes related to one's senses do not happen in a constant pattern across older adults.  Changes in vision can occur either quite rapidly or very slowly and can affect social interaction.  Changes in hearing typically begin before changes in vision.  Hearing aids can mediate these changes, but older adults may be apprehensive about using them.  Changes in taste acuity are negligible, where as changes in smell are more prominent.  Older adults should thus be encouraged to participate in activities that enhance their taste and olfactory functions.  There is still much to learn about normal physiological changes with aging, especially in the areas of taste, smell, and pain perception. Most importantly, research is needed to distinguish normal changes from those related to disease.

## Learning Objectives

*After reading chapter 3 the student should be able to:*
3.1 Explain the major theories of biological aging
3.2 Summarize the research on reversing the effects of aging
3.3 Describe the effects of aging on body composition
3.4 Identify the impact of age-related changes on different organ systems and the implications of these changes for older people's ability to interact with their social and physical environment
3.5 Discuss the ways in which the environment can be modified to help accommodate the biological changes experienced by most older people

## Key Terms and Key People

*Accommodation*:  ability of the lens of the eye to change from rounded to flat, in order to see objects that are closer or farther from the lens (p. 96)

*Age-Related Macular Degeneration (AMD)*:  loss of visions in the center of the visual field caused by insufficient oxygen reaching the macula (p. 98)

*Atherosclerosis*:  accumulation of fats in the arteries and veins, blocking circulation of the blood (p. 84)

*Atrophic Gastritis*:  chronic inflammation of the stomach lining (p. 88)

*Autoimmune Theory*:  the hypothesis that aging is a function of the body's immune system becoming defective, producing antibodies against itself (p. 72)

*Cataract*:  clouding of the lens of the eye, reducing sight and sometimes leading to blindness; requires surgical extraction of the lens (p. 97)

*Cellular Aging Theory*:  the hypothesis that aging occurs as cells slow their number of replications, based on the observation that cells grown in controlled laboratory environments are only able to replicate a finite number of times (p. 73)

*Cross-Linkage Theory*: the hypothesis that aging is a function of the reduction of collagen with age, causing loss of elasticity in most organ systems (p. 72)

*Dementia*:  diminished ability to remember, make accurate judgments, etc. (p. 89)

*Diastolic Blood Pressure*:  the level of blood pressure during the time that chambers of the heart are filling with blood (p. 84-85)

*Endocrine and Immunology Theory:* focuses on loss of sex hormones and T-cells as the cause of many normal age-related declines and chronic diseases associated with aging (p. 74)

*Estrogen:* a female sex hormone that declines significantly with aging; can be replaced alone (ERT) or in combination with progesterone, another female sex hormone (HRT) (p. 88)

*Free Radical Theory:* a special case of the cross-linkage theory of aging that posits that free radicals, highly reactive molecules, may produce DNA mutations (p. 73)

*Functional (or Reserve) Capacity:* the ability of a given organ to perform its normal function, compared with its ability to function under conditions of illness, disability, and aging (p. 83)

*Glaucoma:* a disease in which there is insufficient drainage or excessive production of aqueous humor, the fluid in the front portion of the eye (p. 95-96)

*Glucose:* a type of sugar found in plants and animals, serves as a major energy source and circulates in blood (p. 89)

*Hyperthermia:* body temperatures several degrees above normal for prolonged periods (p. 80)

*Hypothermia:* body temperatures several degrees below normal for prolonged periods (p. 80)

*Kinesthetic System:* the body system that signals one's position in space (p. 82)

*Kyphosis:* stoop-shouldered or hunched condition caused by collapsed vertebrae as bone mass is lost (p. 82)

*Master Athletes:* individuals who have continued to participate in competitive, aerobic exercise into the later years (p. 78)

*Melanin:* skin pigmentation (p. 79)

*Menopause:* one event during the climacteric in a woman's life when there is a gradual cessation of the menstrual cycle because of the loss of ovarian function; considered to have occurred after 12 consecutive months without a menstrual period (p. 88)

*Neurons:* nerve cells in the brain (p. 89)

*Orthopedic Injuries:* injuries to the bones, muscles, and joints (p. 81–82)

*Osteoporosis:* a dramatic loss in calcium and bone mass resulting in increased brittleness of the bones and increased risk of fracture; more frequently found in white, small-stature women (p. 81)

*Otosclerosis:* loss of hearing caused by hardening of stapes and inability to vibrate, not normal aging (p. 101)

*Periodic Limb Movement Disorder (PLMD):* neuromuscular disturbance resulting in uncontrolled movement of legs during sleep (p. 91)

*Prebycusis:* age-related hearing loss (p. 101)

*Prolongevity:* research aimed at increasing average life expectancy by reducing burden of disease but not disrupting fundamental aging processes (p. 77)

*Renal Function*: kidney function, defined by the rate at which blood is filtered through the kidneys (p. 87)

*Senescence*: biological aging, i.e., the gradual accumulation of irreversible functional losses to which the average person tries to accommodate in some socially acceptable way (p. 71)

*Sleep Apnea*: five-to-ten second cessation of breathing which disturbs sleep in some older persons (p. 91)

*Sleep Hygiene*: behaviors associated with sleep; e.g., location, lighting, regular versus irregular bedtime, use of drugs that promote or hinder sleep (p. 91)

*Systolic Blood Pressure*: the level of blood pressure during the contraction phase of the heart (p. 84-85)

*Telomerase*: the enzyme responsible for rebuilding telomeres (p. 74)

*Telomerase Inhibitors*: chemicals produced by the organism that block the production of telomerase (p. 74)

*Telomeres*: excess DNA at the ends of each chromosome, lost as cells replicate (p. 74)

*Tinnitus*: high-pitched ringing in the ear (p. 101)

*Urinary Incontinence*: diminished ability to retain urine; loss of bladder control (p. 87)

*Varicosities*: abnormal swelling in the veins, especially the legs (p. 84)

*Vital Capacity*: the maximum volume of oxygen intake through the lungs with a single breath (p. 84)

*Wear and Tear Theory*: one of the biological theories of aging; states that aging occurs because of the system simply wearing out over time (p. 72)

# Discussion Topics

- Several biological theories of aging have emerged over the past 40 years. Provide a critical analysis of each theory in terms of how it helps our understanding of the aging process and its potential for reversing that process.

- Discuss the potential benefits of human growth hormones and caloric restriction for extending the life span and active life expectancy.

- In what ways could specific changes in body composition influence an older person's reactions to medications and alcohol?

- Discuss some physiological and environmental risk factors for hypothermia in older people. What environmental interventions could be provided to alleviate these risks?

- Discuss the problem of hyperthermia in older people. What are the individual and environmental risk factors involved? How can hypothermia affect the older person's cognitive functions?

- In what ways can research on master athletes help us understand differences between normal (or usual) versus ideal (or successful) aging?

- Compare normal, age-related changes in different organ systems. Which systems show the greatest change? Which show the least? Suggest environmental interventions to alleviate the impact of some of these changes on the older person.

- Discuss the impact of biological factors versus lifestyle on declines in physiological functions such as musculoskeletal and cardiovascular. How can lifestyle changes reverse or alleviate some of the declines?

- Describe some examples of age-related changes in sleep patterns, and suggest how older people can achieve good sleep hygiene.

- Provide three examples of normal, age-related changes in visual functioning and three examples of pathological aging. To what extent can environmental interventions aid the older person undergoing these changes?

- There are numerous structural changes in the eye and the ear with aging that may influence older people's visual and auditory functioning. Describe these structural changes, and explain to what extent these changes versus changes in central processes may affect visual and auditory functioning.

- Describe some communication techniques and environmental interventions that may be used by professionals working with older people who have hearing and vision impairments.

- There is some debate about the role of structural changes versus social behavior in older people's complaints about their taste and olfactory acuity. Present evidence for each set of factors regarding their impact on older people's enjoyment of food and fragrances.

- Discuss the importance of using more refined measurement techniques to assess age-related changes in taste and olfaction.

- To what extent are complaints of pain an indication of changes in tactile sensitivity versus personality and social expectations among older persons?

## Classroom Activities and Student Projects

*Activity 3.1 Geriatrics Physician as a Guest Speaker*
Ask a geriatric physician or a family practitioner who specializes in the health care of older adults to speak to the class about his or her experiences and the needs of older patients. Potential topics might include reversing or delaying aging, normal biological changes related to aging, and chronic and acute conditions facing older adults.

*Activity 3.2 Simulating Biological Changes*
Check out "Sociology of Aging Age Related Impairments: A Simulation Exercise" by Monika Deppen Wood, MA (http://crab.rutgers.edu/~deppen/teach.htm) for an excellent exercise in which students use everyday household supplies to replicate many of the changes that happen in the later years of life. In completing this in-class exercise, students will experience first hand the limitations of certain conditions such as glaucoma and arthritis and confront the challenges of caregiving.

## Suggested Films
*These films are not available through Allyn & Bacon.*

*Aging: The Natural Process* (2001)
Insight Media, 37 minutes, $319 DVD
Explores natural changes that occur in the human body as it ages and describes actions that can be taken to maximize and maintain functionality.

*The Aging Process* (1991)
Films for the Humanities and Sciences, 19 minutes, $89.95 VHS/DVD
This film explores the role of biology on the aging process as well as the role of exercise and nutrition.

*Profiles in Aging and Vision* (1998)
American Foundation for the Blind, 33 minutes, $39.95 VHS
This film illustrates the potential eye conditions that older adults might face and the resources that can be implemented when facing these conditions.

*Menopause* (1996)
Fanlight Productions, 60 minutes, $199 VHS
The years of menopause are a period of profound change in many women's lives. This documentary explores many myths about menopause as well as presents a thorough discussion of the experiences and symptoms that may be encountered during this time.

*The Older Adult World* (2004)
Insight Media, 27 minutes, $329 DVD
Designed to allow viewers to see and experience the world as an older adult, this program looks at the natural, age-related changes that affect the daily lives of elderly adults. It explores changes in vision, hearing, manual dexterity, and taste.

## Suggested Websites

*Biology Center by the American Federation for Aging Research*
http://www.infoaging.org/
The Biology Center (click on "Biology of Aging") provides facts on aging such as aging on a cellular level and neurobiology.

*The National Women's Health Information Center*
http://www.4women.gov/Menopause/
This page of the 4Woman.gov site contains information on "Menopause & Hormone Therapy."

*The National Women's Health Information Center*
http://www.4women.gov/mens/groups/older.cfm
This page of the 4Woman.gov site addresses "Older Men's Health" and contains information on hernias, incontinence, arthritis, etc.

## Additional Resources

Berger, Kathleen Stassen and Ross Thompson. 2000. *The Developing Person Through the Life Span*. New York: Worth Publishers.

Ferrini, Armeda and Ferrini, Rebecca. 2007. *Health in the Later Years, 4th ed.* Columbus, OH: McGraw-Hill.

Komesaroff, Paul A., Philipa Rothfield, and Jeanne Daly. 1997. *Reinterpreting Menopause: Cultural and Philosophical Issues*. London: Routledge.

Masoro, Edward J. and Steven N. Austad. 2001. *Handbook of the Biology of Aging, 5th ed.* Burlingon, MA: Academic Press.

# CHAPTER 4:
# MANAGING CHRONIC DISEASES AND PROMOTING WELL-BEING IN OLD AGE

## Chapter Outline

I. Defining Health
    A. Health Status and Disability
    B. ADLs and IADLs
II. Quality of Life in Health and Illness
III. Chronic and Acute Diseases
    A. Interactive Effects
    B. Causes of Death in Later Years
    C. Common Chronic Conditions
        1. Heart Disease and the Cardiovascular System
        2. Strokes and Other Cerebrovascular Problems
        3. Cancer
        4. Arthritis
        5. Osteoporosis
        6. Chronic Obstructive Pulmonary Disease/Respiratory Problems
        7. Diabetes
        8. Problems with the Kidneys and Urinary Tract
        9. Problems with the Intestinal System
        10. Oral Diseases
        11. HIV/AIDS in the Older Population
        12. Accidents among Older People
        13. Older Drivers
IV. Falls and Their Prevention
V. Use of Physician Services by Older People
    A. Use of Other Health Services
VI. Health Promotion with Older People
    A. The Relationship of Health Practices to Health Outcomes
    B. Exercise as Part of Health Promotion
    C. Improving the Effectiveness of Health Promotion Programs
    D. Limitations of Health Promotion
VII. Implications for the Future
VIII. Summary

## Chapter Summary

Although older adults are at a higher risk for more diseases than younger people, most rate their own health as satisfactory. Health status refers not only to an individual's physical condition, but also to functional ability in various social and psychological domains. Thus, health affects one's social environment and psychological well-being. Older adults' quality of life is inextricably linked to their health status. Chapter 4 presents an overview of the chronic and acute conditions commonly faced by older adults. The top three causes of death in older adulthood are heart disease, cancer, and stroke, all chronic conditions. Other common chronic conditions facing older adults include arthritis, osteoporosis, chronic obstructive pulmonary disease (respiratory problems), diabetes, problems with the kidneys and urinary tract, problems with the intestinal system, oral diseases, and HIV/AIDS. Chronic diseases affect older adults differently based on gender and ethnic minority status. According to mortality statistics, older people may seem less likely to die of accidents (the fourth leading cause of death for older adults) than younger adults; however the cause of death is often masked by the true incidence of death. Many states are requiring older drivers to comply with additional driving laws as an approach to preventive health care. With the growth of the older population there has been an increased demand on the health care system.

Older adults use physician services more frequently than other age groups for acute problems, but not as often as expected for outpatient medical, dental, mental health services or preventive care. Health promotion uses multi-disciplinary perspectives to advocate for optimal well-being and quality of life for older adults. A major goal is the elimination or postponement of chronic disease, in particular. As baby boomers age, we can expect a more informed cohort of healthcare consumers, higher demand from the healthcare system and a self-care and wellness focus. Healthy People 2010 goals focus on increasing the quality of years of healthy life for all Americans and eliminating health disparities among segments of the population.

## Learning Objectives

*After reading chapter 4 the student should be able to:*
4.1   Define health, quality of life, ADLs, and IADLs
4.2   Identify the social and psychological factors that affect perceptions of health and use of health services
4.3   Distinguish among chronic diseases that occur most frequently in older adults
4.4   Discuss HIV/AIDS as a chronic condition in older adults as well as the role of accidents, falls, and driving fatalities and their prevention
4.5   Summarize the use of health services, including prescription drug use, by older adults
4.6   Explain the concept of health promotion and its benefits in old age

## Key Terms and Key People

*Acute Condition*:  short-term disease or infection, often debilitating to older persons (p. 118)

*Acute Myocardial Infarction*:  loss of blood flow to a specific region of the heart, resulting in damage of the myocardium (p. 125)

*Activities of Daily Living (ADL)*: summary of an individual's performance in personal care tasks such as bathing or dressing, as well as such home-management activities as shopping, meal preparation, and taking medications (p. 115)

*Arteriosclerosis*:  loss of elasticity of the arterial walls (p. 124)

*Atherosclerosis:* accumulation of fats in the arteries and veins, blocking circulation of the blood (p. 124)

*Benign Hypertrophy of the Prostate*:  enlargement of the prostrate gland in older men, without signs of cancer or other serious disease; may cause discomfort (p. 139)

*Chronic Condition*: long-term (more than three months), often permanent, and leaving a residual disability that may require long-term management or care rather than cure (p. 119)

*Comorbidity*: simultaneously experiencing multiple health problems, both chronic and acute (p. 121)

*Diabetes Mellitus*: a disease that impairs the ability of the pancreas to produce insulin, a hormone that enables glucose from the blood to cells, and accumulates in the blood (p. 136)

*Diagnosis Related Groups (DRGs)*: a system of classifying medical cases for payment on the basis of diagnoses; used under Medicare's prospective payment system (PPS) for inpatient hospital services (p. 148)

*Disability*: an impairment in the ability to complete multiple daily tasks (p. 115)

*Diverticulitis*: a condition in which pouches or sacs (diverticula) in the intestinal wall become inflamed and infected (p. 140)

*Edentulous*: the absence of natural teeth (p. 141)

*Frailty*: severe limitations in ADL (p. 116)

*Good Health*: more than the mere absence of infirmity, a state of complete physical, mental, and social well-being (p. 114)

*Health Promotion*: a model in which individuals are responsible for and in control of their own health; includes a combination of health education and related organizational, political, and economic changes conducive to health (p. 150)

*Health Status*: the presence or absence of disease as well as the degree of disability in an individual's level of functioning (p. 115)

*Hiatus Hernia*: a condition in which a small portion of the stomach slides up through the diaphragm (p. 141)

*Hypokinesia*: the degeneration and functional loss of muscle and bone due to inactivity (p. 154)

*IADL (Instrumental Activities of Daily Living)*: daily activities involving use of the environment (p. 115)

*Immunity*: resistance to environmental carcinogens, viruses, and bacteria (p. 121)

*Incontinence*: the inability to control urine and feces—of two types: urge incontinence, where a person is not able to hold waste products long enough to reach a toilet, and stress incontinence, where leakage occurs during physical exertion, laughing, sneezing, or coughing (p. 139)

*Osteoarthritis*: gradual degeneration of joints that are subject to physical stress (p. 129)

*Osteopenia*: a significant loss of calcium and reduced bone density not associated with increased risk of fractures (p. 131)

*Quality of Life*: going beyond health status alone, this concept considers the individual's sense of competence, ability to perform activities of daily living, and satisfaction with social interactions, in addition to functional health (p. 117)

*Rheumatoid Arthritis*: a chronic inflammation of the membranes lining joints and tendons, characterized by pain, swelling, bone dislocation, and limited range of motion; can occur at any age (p. 129)

*Sarcopenia*: atrophy of skeletal muscle mass, generally resulting from a sedentary lifestyle and some chronic diseases (p. 146)

## Discussion Topics

- Describe how age and gender influence ADLs and IADLs.

- What are some of the implications of current research findings for the relationship between behavioral factors and chronic diseases?

- Describe ethnic and gender differences in chronic diseases.

- What are some risk factors for arteriosclerosis?  Describe some behavioral methods to prevent these risk factors.

- In what ways can osteoarthritis affect an older person's ADLs and subjective health ratings?

- For what chronic conditions has HRT been shown to have some benefits?  What are some potential iatrogenic problems that HRT can cause?

- In what ways has the oral health of newer cohorts of elders improved when compared to older cohorts?  What factors influence oral health status in old age?

- Describe the major causes of AIDS in older men and women.  How would you design an education program on AIDS for this population versus a younger audience?

- What are some risk factors for auto accidents in older people and how can these be prevented?

- Discuss how socio-cultural factors (demographics, cultural values) influence
    1. evaluations of health
    2. health status
    3. health behavior
    4. utilization of health care services

- If you were developing a health promotion program to encourage older people to visit physicians for preventive purposes, what approach would you utilize? Briefly describe the major components of your health promotion program.

## Classroom Activities and Student Projects

*Activity 4.1: Health Promotion Speaker*
Invite a guest speaker to class from a local senior center or health center who operates a health promotion program in your community. Ask the speaker to discuss the history of the program, its goals and objectives, and the program's results. An alternative to this activity would be to take the class to the center and have the students speak directly with the program participants.

*Activity 4.2: Constructing a Health Promotion Program*
Optimal health is more than just the absence of disease. Have the students work in groups to construct a health promotion program. The program should focus on promoting optimal health for older adults. Each group should select a specific condition facing older adults, such as macular degeneration, presbycusis, or arthritis. The program should address the specific causes of the condition, the potential for social stigma, and adaptations that can be made to alleviate the condition, as well as the proposed program's structure, goals, objectives, and potential results.

## Suggested Films
*These films are not available through Allyn & Bacon.*

*Age is No Barrier* (1992)
Filmakers Library, 25 minutes, $295 VHS/DVD
For the past five years, U of Agers, a Canadian gymnastics team has traveled throughout Canada, dazzling audiences with their gymnastic prowess. Turning cartwheels, climbing ropes, exercising on parallel bars, they are living proof that strength and agility can be maintained late in life. Fitness is the key to wellness and life-long independence.

*The Doctor Is In: Factors in Healthy Aging* (1990)
Films for the Humanities and Sciences, 28 minutes, $89.95 VHS/DVD
This episode of *The Doctor is In* explores the predictors of healthy aging and uses various examples, including a research project on Harvard graduates, to illustrate the roles of biology and the environment.

*The Doctor Is In: Aging: Gifts of Aging* (1990)
Films for the Humanities and Sciences, 29 minutes, $149.95 VHS/DVD
This episode of *The Doctor Is In* highlights the lives of five older adults as they thrive in their later years.

*It's an Age Thing: Driving* (2003)
WMHT/PBS Video Productions, 30 minutes, $19.95 VHS/DVD
This film is episode 2 in the series "It's an Age Thing" and discusses senior driving programs and ways to talk to an older adult about driving safety.

## Suggested Websites

*Disease Center by the American Federation for Aging Research*
http://www.infoaging.org/
This site (click on "Healthy Aging" link) provides information on many of the chronic conditions, such as heart disease, diabetes, and cancer, older adults face.

*Healthy Aging for Older Adults*
http://www.cdc.gov/aging/
This site is sponsored by the National Center for Chronic Disease Prevention and Health Promotion and provides links to information and statistics on aging and health promotion.

*Growing Stronger: Strength Training for Older Adults*
http://www.cdc.gov/nccdphp/dnpa/physical/growing_stronger/index.htm
This site is sponsored by the National Center for Chronic Disease Prevention and Health Promotion and provides information on strength training for older adults.

## Additional Resources

Cousins, Sandra O'Brien. 2000. "'My Heart Couldn't Take It': Older Women's Beliefs About Exercise Benefits and Risks." *The Journals of Gerontology.* 55B:283–295.

Nichols, Janice, et al. 2002. *Aging with HIV: Psychological, Social, and Health Issues.* Burlingon, MA: Academic Press.

Stokols, Daniel. 1996. "Translating Social Ecological Theory into Guidelines for Community Health Promotion." *American Journal of Health Promotion.* 10:282–297.

# CHAPTER 5:  COGNITIVE CHANGES WITH AGING

## Chapter Outline

I.  Intelligence and Aging
    A.  Problems in the Measurement of Cognitive Function
    B.  Longitudinal Studies of Intelligence
II. Factors That May Influence Intelligence in Adulthood
III. The Process of Learning and Memory
IV. The Information Processing Model
    A.  The Importance of Learning and Memory in Everyday Life
    B.  Executive Function in Older Adults
V.  Factors That Affect Learning in Old Age
    A.  The Importance of Attention
    B.  Practical Implications of Attention Changes with Aging
    C.  Environmental and Personal Factors
VI. Age-Related Changes in Memory
    A.  Tip-of-the-Tongue States
VII. Improving Cognitive Abilities in Old Age
    A.  Cognitive Retraining
    B.  Memory Mediators
VIII. Wisdom and Creativity
IX. Implications for the Future
X.  Summary

## Chapter Summary

Chapter 5 presents a summary of the research on cognitive changes in later life.  Most of the research has been conducted on intelligence; however, this research presents methodological challenges in its definition of intelligence.  Another methodological concern is distinguishing age changes from age differences.  Longitudinal studies are being conducted to overcome this challenge.  However, even longitudinal studies face challenges of selective attrition and terminal drop. In addition, studies have investigated learning and memory functioning in older adults.  These studies have found that aging appears to affect accessing secondary memory but not the capacity of primary or secondary memory.  In general, some types of memory (e.g., semantic and procedural memory) do not decline whereas others (e.g., episodic memory) do.  Significant changes to memory, intelligence, and learning are not inevitable, and older adults and their caregivers can boost the learning process.   For example, improving physical conditions under which older adults are learning as well as helping the older adult relax will facilitate the learning process.  Those who perform well on intelligence and memory tests have higher levels of education, good sensory functioning, maintain physical activity and good nutrition and have employment and leisure activities that require complex problem solving skills. Fewer research studies have been conducted on wisdom and creativity, yet findings seem to indicate that wisdom increases in later life and a second peak occurs for creativity.  More research is needed in these areas.

## Learning Objectives

*After reading chapter 5 the student should be able to:*
5.1   Discuss the research related to cognitive functions and normal aging
5.2   List the means of measuring the components of intelligence in older adults
5.3   Identify the individual and environmental factors that influence intelligence
5.4   Explain how we learn and how aging affects the learning process
5.5   Define attention and discuss its importance for learning
5.6   Describe the environmental factors that affect how older people learn
5.7   Explain how aging affects the ability to retrieve information from secondary memory
5.8   Illustrate tip-of-the-tongue states as an example of difficulty in retrieval
5.9   Discuss the current understanding of wisdom and creativity in old age
5.10   Summarize cognitive retraining and other ways to help older adults improve their learning and memory skills

## Key Terms and Key People

*Attentional Control*: ability to allocate one's attention among multiple stimuli simultaneously (p. 187)

*Classic Aging Pattern*: this decline observed with aging on some performance scales of intelligence tests versus consistency on verbal scales of the same tests (p. 176)

*Cognitive Retraining*: teaching research participants how to use various techniques to keep their minds active and maintain good memory skills (p. 193)

*Crystallized Intelligence*: knowledge and abilities one gains through education and experience (p. 175)

*Disuse Theory*: the view that memory fades or is lost because one fails to use the information (p. 192)

*Divided Attention:* ability to focus on multiple stimuli simultaneously (p. 187)

*Echoic Memory*: auditory memory; a brief period when new information received through the ears is stored (p. 182)

*Execution Function:* cognitive skills required to organize one's learning function (p. 186)

*External Aids*: simple devices, such as list making, used by older people to keep track of the time or dates, etc. (p. 196)

*Fluid Intelligence*: skills that are biologically determined, independent of experience or learning, similar to "native intelligence," requiring flexibility in thinking (p. 175)

*General Slowing Hypothesis*:  physiological changes that cause slower transmission of information through the nervous system with aging (p. 189)

*Iconic Memory*:  visual memory; a brief period when new information received through the eyes is stored (p. 182)

*Information Processing Model*:  a conceptual model of how learning and memory take place (p. 184)

*Intelligence*: the theoretical limit of an individual's performance (p. 175)

*Intelligence Quotient (IQ)*:  an individual's relative abilities in making judgments, in comprehension, and in reasoning (p. 175)

*Interference Theory*:  the view that memory fades or is lost because of distractions experienced during learning (p. 192)

*Mediators*:  visual and verbal links between information to be memorized and information that is already in secondary memory (p. 195)

*Mnemonics*:  the method of using verbal cues such as riddles or rhymes as aids to memory (p. 195)

*Perceptual Speed*: time, in milliseconds, required to perceive and react to a stimulus (p. 183)

*Primary Mental Abilities*:  the basic set of intellectual skills, including mathematical reasoning, word fluency, verbal meaning, inductive reasoning, and spatial orientation (p. 175)

*Recall*:  the process of searching through secondary memory in response to a specific external cue (p. 191)

*Recognition*: matching information in secondary memory with the stimulus information (p. 191)

*Secondary (Long-Term) Memory*:  permanent memory store; requires processing of new information to be stored and cues to retrieve stored information (p. 183)

*Selective Attention*:  being able to focus on information relevant to a task while ignoring irrelevant information (p. 187)

*Sensory Memory*: the first step in receiving information through the sense organs and passing it on to primary or secondary memory (p. 182)

*Spatial Memory*: the ability to recall where objects are in relationship to each other in space (p. 191)

*Terminal Decline Hypothesis*:  the hypothesis that persons who are close to death decline in their cognitive abilities (p. 181)

*Tip-of-the-Tongue States*:   difficulty retrieving names from secondary memory but often spontaneously recalled later (p. 192)

*Vigilance/Sustained Attention*:  keeping alert to focus on a specific stimulus over time (p. 187)

*Visual Mediators*:  the method of locations; memorizing by linking each item with a specific location in space (p. 195)

*Working (Primary) Memory*: the active process of holding newly acquired information in storage; a maximum of 7± 2 stimuli before they are processed into secondary memory or discarded (p. 182)

## **Discussion Topics**

- Discuss examples of changes in crystallized and fluid intelligence with aging.  In what ways could methodological problems result in exaggerating any real declines in these two types of intelligence?

- Describe the components of the WAIS.  Which subtests measure crystallized versus fluid intelligence?  Why has this become the most widely used measure of intelligence in older adults?

- Discuss the advantages and disadvantages of longitudinal research designs to study intelligence in old age.

- To what extent do changes in sensory processes and physiological functioning affect older people's sensory, primary, and secondary memory?

- Discuss the process of "meta-memory" (i.e., the individual's own perception of memory abilities) and how this might influence older people's performance on tests of memory.

- In what ways can the learning environment be enhanced to improve learning ability and retention of newly acquired information in the older learner?  What factors can disrupt older people's acquisition of new information?

- Studies of learning among younger people have found an inverse-U function between anxiety and performance, such that a moderate level of anxiety is associated with optimal learning. To what extent does this model apply to older learners?

- In what ways have older persons been found to compensate for declines in information processing and perceptual-motor speed?

- Discuss problems of measuring wisdom and creativity. Despite the lack of adequate objective measures, what influences people's subjective judgments of an individual as wise or creative?

- Discuss why there might be differences in the peak age of creativity in music, art, literature, science, and math.

## Classroom Activities and Student Projects

*Activity 5.1: A Memory Exercise*
Have your students complete the memory exercise on page 185 of the text which suggests that the student go to the grocery store and use the method of loci to remember what to buy. Ask the students write a 2-page reaction paper about their experiences. In their reaction paper, the students should include how long it took them to shop and remember the items they needed, whether they forgot to buy particular items, and what they saw as the advantages or disadvantages of the method of loci.

*Activity 5.2: Wisdom and Creativity Discussion*
Ask the student to define "wise." Make a list on the board of their responses. In addition, have the students name specific, (sometimes) famous individuals who exemplify their ideas. Repeat this procedure with the concept of "creative." Come to conclusions about age, reverence, and creative and wise endeavors.

## Suggested Films
*These films are not available through Allyn & Bacon.*

*Aging Successfully: The Psychological Aspects of Growing Old* (1997)
Insight Media, 31 minutes, $249 DVD
This film profiles Paul and Margaret Baltes' SOC model and the tests that are given to older adults to assess cognitive abilities.

*Overview of Aging: Typical Patterns in Aging* (1999)
Insight Media, 39 minutes, $279 VHS
This film reviews the patterns of change that occur in the body and pays special attention to changes that take place in the brain.

*The Aging Mind* (1998)
Insight Media, 28 minutes, $279 DVD
This DVD explains how to determine whether memory loss is the result of age or due to depression, vitamin deficiency, or Alzheimer's disease. It differentiates between normal and pathological aging and emphasizes that poor health is not a natural result of growing older.

*View From the Inside: Older Adults (1995)*
Insight Media, 21 minutes, $149 DVD
This film explores older adulthood from the perspective of older adults and portrays the realities of the positive and negative features of aging.

## Suggested Websites

*AARP*
http://news.aarp.org/UM/T.asp?A910.52851.3474.5.903449
Get a collection of PowerPoint slides on "Aging and Creative Productivity"

*Neurobiology of Aging Information Center of The American Federation for Aging Research*
http://www.infoaging.org/
This site highlights the important cognitive changes that relate to aging, especially those changes related to memory and intelligence. Click on "biological aging" tab and then scroll down to the Neurobiology of Aging Information Center link.

*American Psychological Association (APA)*
http://www.apa.org/topics/topicaging.html
This site is the home to the APA's web page on aging, which presents links, information, and research on aging from a psychological perspective.

## Additional Resources

Anderson-Hanley, Cay. 1999. Experiential Activities for Teaching Psychology of Aging. *Educational Gerontology*. 25:449–456.

Belsky, Janet K. 1999. *The Psychology of Aging: Theory, Research, and Interventions*. Florence, KY: Wadsworth Publishing.

Birren, James E. and K. Warner Schaie. 2001. *Handbook of the Psychology of Aging, 5th ed.* Burlingon, MA: Academic Press.

Small, Gary. 2002. *The Memory Bible: An Innovative Strategy for Keeping Your Brain Young.* New York, NY: Hyperion.

# CHAPTER 6:  PERSONALITY AND MENTAL HEALTH IN OLD AGE

## Chapter Outline

I.  Defining Personality
II. Stage Theories of Personality
       A.  Jung's Psychoanalytic Perspective
       B.  Erikson's Psychosocial Model
       C.  Empirical Testing of These Perspectives
       D.  Dialectical Models of Adult Personality
III. Trait Theories of Personality
       A.  Emotional Expression and Regulation
IV. Self-Concept and Self-Esteem
V.  Stress, Coping, and Adaptation
       A.  Some Useful Definitions
       B.  Aging and Life Events
       C.  What Determines Stress Responses in Old Age?
       D.  Adaptations in the Later Years
VI. Successful Aging
       A.  Critique of Successful Aging Paradigm
VII. Psychological Disorders among Older Persons
       A.  Depression
       B.  Suicide Among Older People
       C.  Dementia
       D.  Delirium
       E.  Alzheimer's Disease
       F.  Characteristics of Alzheimer's Disease
       G.  Behavioral Treatments and Environmental Interventions
       H.  Parkinson's Disease
       I.  Alcoholism
       J.  Drug Abuse
       K.  Paranoid Disorders and Schizophrenia
       L.  Anxiety
      M. Older Adults Who Are Chronically Mentally Ill
VIII. Psychotherapy with Older Persons
       A.  Use of Mental Health Services
IX. Implications for the Future
X.  Summary

# Chapter Summary

Chapter 6 presents the theories and research that relate to personality development. Historically, personality theories have focused on the idea that personality develops early in one's life course and then stabilizes; however, theorists such as Erikson and Jung proposed that personality development continues into later adulthood. The Baltimore Longitudinal Study tested trait theories of personality and found stability in personality from middle adulthood to later adulthood and consistency with age differences when comparing the young and the old. Older adults need to regenerate their self-esteem as they change social roles.

When researchers employ cross-sectional designs it appears as though there are age differences in coping styles, yet when longitudinal studies are implemented, coping styles appear to be stable over the life course. In general, many elders display resilience in coping with life challenges. Access to social support, cognitive skills and personality play a role in coping style. Successful aging is defined as maintaining physical and cognitive abilities, continuing social interaction, and coping with life events.

Measuring mental disorders among older adults poses challenges, but it can be noted that studies of persons living in long-term care facilities find higher rates of mental disorder than studies of the larger community. Of all of the mental disorders the most frequently diagnosed is depression, which becomes a key risk factor for suicide. White males over the age of 85 are overrepresented in suicide statistics. This is often attributed to the changes in status associated with retirement and higher rates of social isolation. Dementia also presents itself among older adults. Some forms of dementia are reversible, while others are not. Dementias, such as Alzheimer's disease, are not inevitable and are not a part of normal aging. Far fewer older adults have paranoia or schizophrenia, unless they experienced these conditions in middle adulthood. Additionally, alcoholism and drug use are more common among younger adults than they are among older adults.

Psychotherapy has been advocated for older adults as it has been seen as quite effective in terms of both the long-term and short-term effects of mental disorders. However, these types of services are underutilized by older adults. Integrating services that address the mental health needs of older adults into other medical and social service programs can greatly enhance service utilization by older adults.

# Learning Objectives

*After reading chapter 6 the student should be able to:*
6.1 State the normal developmental changes and stability in personality across the life span
6.2 Explain the theories of personality that support change or stability as well as the person-environment interactions that affect personality development
6.3 Illustrate emotional expression and regulation with personality development
6.4 Summarize stability versus change in self-concept and self-esteem with aging
6.5 Identify older people's responses to life events and stressors
6.6 Note the predictors and critiques of successful aging and active aging/resilience
6.7 Outline the major psychological disorders and dementias in old age
6.8 Evaluate the extent to which older people use mental health services

*Active and Passive Mastery*:   interactions with one's social environment that are more controlling and competitive, versus more affiliative and docile (p. 213)

*Adaptation*:   ability to change personal needs, motivations, behaviors, and expectations to fit changing environmental demands or conditions (p. 221)

*Anxiety Disorder*:   functional psychological disorder often triggered by external stress; accompanied by physiological reactivity such as increased heart rate and sleep disorders (p. 251)

*Archetypes*:   masculine and feminine aspects of personality, present in both men and women (p. 210)

*Benign Senescent Forgetfulness*:   mild age-related decline in memory and learning ability; not progressive as in dementia (p. 235)

*Cognitive Appraisal*:   the individual's interpretation of an event as stressful, benign, or pleasant; determines individual's response to situation (p. 219)

*Coping (Problem-Focused* versus *Emotion-Focused)*:   conscious responses to stress, determined by nature of stressor, personality, social support, and health (p. 221)

*Defense Mechanisms*:   unconscious responses to stress, determined by nature of stressor, personality, social support, and health (p. 221)

*Delirium*:   a reversible dementia characterized by sudden onset; generally caused by environmental factors (p. 237)

*Dementia*:   progressive, marked decline in cognitive functions associated with damage to brain tissue; may affect personality and behavior; may be reversible or irreversible type (p. 235)

*Depression (Major* versus *Minor* or *Reactive)*:   the most common psychiatric disorder in old are, diagnosed if several behavioral and affective symptoms (e.g. sleep and disturbances) are present for at least two weeks; bipolar disorders are less common in older people than reactive (or minor) and major depression (p. 228)

*Dysthymic disorder*:   a less acute type of depression, but lasting longer than major depression (p. 228)

*Ego Integrity* versus *Despair*:   the eighth and last stage of psychosocial development in Erikson's model; aging individuals achieve wisdom and perspective, or despair because they view their life as lacking meaning (p. 210)

*Electroconvulsive* or *Electroshock Therapy (ECT)*:   a form of therapy for severely depressed patients in which a mild electrical current is applied to one or both sides of the brain (p. 234)

*Generativity*: the seventh stage of psychosocial development in Erikson's model; goal of middle-aged and older persons is to care for and mentor younger generations, look toward future, and not stagnate in the past (p. 211)

*Life Events*: identifiable, discrete life changes or transitions that require some adaptation to reestablish homeostasis (p. 218)

*Life Review*: a form of psychotherapy that encourages discussion of past successes and failures (p. 211)

*Life Structures*: in Levinson's model, specific developmental stages consisting of eras and transitions (p. 213)

*Paranoia*: a psychiatric disorder characterized by irrational suspiciousness of other people (p. 250)

*Pharmacotherapy*: use of medication to treat symptoms of physical or psychiatric disorders (p. 234)

*Psychopathology*: abnormal changes in personality and behavior that may be caused or triggered by genetic predisposition, environmental stress, and/or systemic diseases (p. 227)

*Reminiscence Therapy*: a type of psychotherapy used with depressed, anxious, sometimes confused older adults, stimulating the older person's memory of successful coping experiences and positive events in the past (p. 232)

*Resilience:* the ability to cope with life challenges and maintain one's optimism and psychological well-being (p. 224)

*Schizophrenia:* a psychiatric disorder characterized by thought disorders and hallucinations, psychotic behavior, loss of emotional expression (p. 251)

*Self-Concept*: cognitive representation of the self; emerges from interactions with the social environment, social roles, accomplishments (p. 216)

*Self-Efficacy*: perceived confidence in one's own ability to know how to cope with a stressor and to resolve it (p. 224)

*Self-Esteem*: evaluation or feeling about one's identity relative to an "ideal self"; differs from self-concept in being more of an emotional, not cognitive, assessment of self (p. 217)

*Stage Theories of Personality*: development of individual through various levels, each one necessary for adaptation and for psychological adjustment (p. 209)

*Successful Aging*: achievement of good physical and functional health, cognitive, and emotional well-being in old age, often accompanied by strong social support and productive activity (p. 223)

*Trait Theories*: personality traits that describe individuals in terms of characteristic or "typical" attributes that remain relatively stable with age (p. 214)

## Discussion Topics

- Discuss some differences between stage and trait theories of personality. List some personality characteristics that are described by proponents of each theory.

- Describe how life experiences might influence personality in old age.

- Self-concept is generally established early in life, but is modified through social roles and life experiences. Discuss some experiences of the later years that may alter an older person's self-concept and that may negatively influence their self-esteem.

- Cognitive appraisal has been suggested as a modifier of the perceived stressfulness of a life event. Other researchers have noted that life events are stressful by their very nature. Provide arguments supporting and opposing each position.

- Describe the elements of "successful aging." How would you advise a baby boomer in the best ways to prepare for a successful old age?

- In what ways, if any, is depression manifested in older people? What types of depression are most common in this age group? Which therapeutic interventions appear to be most successful in treating these forms of late life depression?

- What are some risk factors for suicide in old age? Why are some groups of elders at greater risk of suicide than others?

- Discuss some of the new developments in research on dementia, especially the research on causes of Alzheimer's disease. What, if any, implications do these studies have for diagnosing and treating AD patients?

- Discuss the range of therapeutic interventions that could be beneficial to elders with Alzheimer's disease and their family caregivers.

- Describe differences between the effects of Parkinson's disease and AD on older adults.

- Describe why alcoholism is often more difficult to detect in older people than in younger adults, and why therapeutic interventions are critical for older alcoholics.

- Describe characteristics of "drug abuse" in younger versus older persons.

- How can life review be used effectively in older patients?

# Classroom Activities and Student Projects

*Activity 6.1: Journal Article Review*
Assign each student a psychological disorder and then have them access one scholarly psychology article on that disorder. Examples of psychological disorders include depression, dementia, paranoia, and Alzheimer's disease. After each student has read an article on their selected topic, have them write a 2–3 page critique of the article in which they summarize the research findings presented in the article and pose any challenges or questions they may have on the topic. The students can then bring their article and paper to class and take turns briefly highlighting the article that they read.

*Activity 6.2: Coping Skills over the Life Span Discussion*
Ask students to reflect over their own life course. Then ask the students to write a brief essay about one or more life events where their coping skills were demonstrated. In their essay the students should label their coping style according to the classifications in the textbook. Next have the students speak with an older adult in their social environment. In this conversation have the student ask the older adult to recount one or more situations where coping skills were used. The students should write a brief essay summarizing this conversation and classify the older adults' coping style according to the categories in the text. As a final step have the student bring their two essays to class and discuss their findings with their fellow classmates.

# Suggested Films
*These films are not available through Allyn & Bacon.*

*Alzheimer's Care Series* (1997)
Fanlight Productions, 42 minutes, $399 VHS
This three part series presents the behaviors of Alzheimer's patients and the stresses of their caregivers.

*Depression in Older Adults* (1997)
Fanlight Productions, 30 minutes, $185 VHS
This film overviews the causes, consequences, and public policy concerns of depression among older adults.

*The Doctor Is In: Alzheimer's Disease: How Families Cope* (1997)
Films for the Humanities and Sciences, 29 minutes, $129.95 VHS/DVD
This episode of *The Doctor Is In* presents a discussion of the stages Alzheimer's disease (AD) and its effect on the caregivers of someone with AD.

*View from the Inside: Older Adults* (1995)
Insight Media, 21 minutes, $149 DVD
This DVD considers the inner thoughts and feelings of people in their 60s and beyond. Addressing such realities of aging as declining health and loneliness, it offers the positive message that many older adults live happy and independent lives.

## Suggested Websites

*Alzheimer's Association*
www.alz.org
This website gives comprehensive information about Alzheimer's disease and living with Alzheimer's and contains a link for professionals and researchers.

*National Institute on Alcohol Abuse and Alcoholism (NIAAA)*
http://www.niaaa.nih.gov/publications/aa40.htm
This page provides links to access NIAAA's "Alcohol Alert" on "Alcohol and Aging," which documents the prevalence of alcohol abuse among older adults as well as documenting potential treatment options.

*National Institute of Neurological Disorders and Stroke (NINDS)*
http://www.ninds.nih.gov/health_and_medical/pubs/dementias.htm
This page of the NINDS site is entitled "The Dementias: Hope Through Research" and presents a thorough overview of dementias.

*American Medical Association (AMA)*
http://www.ama-assn.org/ama1/pub/upload/mm/433/successful_aging.pdf
This page of the AMA's website provides a two page listing of "Successful Aging Tips."

## Additional Resources

Gurnack, Anne M., Roland Atkinson, and Nancy Osgood. 2001. *Treating Alcohol and Drug Abuse in the Elderly*. New York: Springer Publishing Company.

McGuire, Lisa C., Melissa D. Zwahr. 1999. "Tying it Together: Two Comprehensive Projects for Adult Development and Aging Courses." *Teaching of Psychology*. 26:53–55.

Sheldon, Jane P. 1998. "Addressing Stereotypes and Ageism in a Life Span Development Course." *Teaching of Psychology*. 25:291–293.

# CHAPTER 7: LOVE, INTIMACY, AND SEXUALITY IN OLD AGE

## Chapter Outline

I. Attitudes and Beliefs about Sexuality in Later Life
II. Myths and Reality about Physiological Changes and Sexual Activity
III. Women and Age-Related Physiological Changes
IV. Men and Age-Related Physiological Changes
V. Chronic Illness and Sexuality
VI. Gay, Lesbian, Bisexual and Transgender Partners in Old Age
VII. Psychosocial Factors and Late-Life Affection, Love, and Intimacy
VIII. Facilitating Older Adults' Sexual Functioning
IX. Implications for the Future
X. Summary

## Chapter Summary

Chapter 7 presents information about sexuality and older adults. Older adults may experience physiological changes in the process of aging; however, these changes do not necessarily affect their sexual capacity. For older adults experiencing age-related changes in sexual activity, adaptations can be made to maintain older adults' sexual self-esteem. For example, healthcare practitioners can speak with older adults about broadening the definitions of sexuality and intimacy to include hugging and touching. Health practitioners can assist in this learning by notifying older adults of the side effects of any medications they are receiving. Myths, jokes and stereotypes about older adults and sexuality are often the greatest barriers to older adults participating in sexual experiences. Gerontologists, practitioners and the media can change these myths to convey the message that sex is not only permissible, but desirable in old age. Individuals living in long-term care facilities and cultural diversity need to be considered in conveying an inclusive message.

## Learning Objectives

*After reading chapter 7 the student should be able to:*
7.1 Discuss the prevalent attitudes and beliefs about sex and love in old age that frequently affect an older person's sexuality
7.2 Explain the age-related physiological changes that may alter the nature of men's and women's sexual response and performance, but do not necessarily interfere with their overall experiences of sexuality
7.3 Understand the relationship between chronic illnesses and sexuality
7.4 Note the contemporary social issues related to gay and lesbian relationships
7.5 Note the importance of late-life affection, love, and intimacy
7.6 Identify the implications for families and professionals who work with older people, including in long-term care facilities

## Key Terms and Key People

*Climacteric*:  in women, the decline in estrogen production and the loss of reproductive ability; in men, the decline of testosterone (p. 277)

*Erection*:  the swelling of the penis or clitoris in sexual excitement (p. 281)

*Erectile Dysfunction:* inability to get and sustain an erection (p. 282)

*Hot Flashes*:  a sudden sensation of heat in the upper body caused by vasomotor instability as nerves over-respond to decreases in hormone level during menopause (p. 277)

*Impotence*:  the inability to have or maintain an erection (p. 282)

*Intimacy*:  feelings of deep mutual regard, affection, and trust, usually developed through long association (p. 293)

*Male Menopause*:  a term that suggests a significant change experienced by men as their production of testosterone decreases in later life; although male fertility is maintained, some men experience both psychological and physiological changes (p. 280)

*Menopause*:  cessation of the menstrual cycle (p. 277)

*Orgasm*:  climax of sexual excitement (p. 271)

*Penile Implant*:  a device surgically implanted in the penis to reverse impotence and allow an erection (p. 285)

*Perimenopause*:  unpredictable menstrual cycles—up to ten years before menopause (p. 277)

*Postmenopause*:  when 12 months have passed without a menstrual cycle (p. 277)

*Preorgasmic Plateau Phase*:  in men and women, the phase of lovemaking prior to orgasm and in which sexual tension is at its height (p. 280)

*Prostate Enlargement*:  growth of the prostate, due to changes in prostatic cells with age, which can result in pain and difficult urination (p. 284)

*Prostate Cancer:* the most common cancer among men age 65 and older (p. 284)

*Refractory Period*:  in men, the time between ejaculation and another erection (p. 282)

*Sex*:  in the most narrow sense, a biological function involving genital intercourse or orgasm; in a broader sense, expressing oneself in an intimate way through a wide-ranging language of love and pleasure in relationships (p. 271)

*Sexuality*:  sexual desire, sexual expression, or sexual activity (p. 271)

*Sexupharmaceuticals:* prescribed medications, such as Viagra, to treat men's erectile difficulties (p. 280)

*Urogenital Atrophy*:  reductions in the elasticity and lubricating abilities of the vagina approximately 5 years after menopause (p. 278)

*Viropause:* male menopause (p. 280)

*Widow(er)'s Syndrome*:  a term coined by Masters and Johnson describing sexual dysfunction following a long period of abstinence due to a spouse's illness and/or death (p. 291)

## Discussion Topics

- What are the prevalent attitudes and beliefs about sex and love in old age?  Discuss ways that these are reflected in our society and what consequences they have for older adults.

- Discuss some physiological factors that may influence an older people's sexual activity.

- Discuss some psychological factors that may influence older people's sexual activity.

- How can professionals assist men and women to adapt to age-related changes that will enhance their experiences with intimacy and their sexual functioning and enjoyment?

- Discuss some limitations of the early research on sexuality (e.g. Kinsey's 1938–1948 study, 1954 Duke Longitudinal Study).

- Describe a well-designed study that could accurately determine the frequency and nature of sexual activity in older adults.

- Discuss how peri-menopausal and post-menopausal changes can affect older women's sexual activity and the impact of HRT on this process.

- Describe the impact of various chronic conditions (e.g., arthritis, depression) and their treatment on older people's sexual activity.

- What are some particular issues that older gay men and lesbians face in our society? If you were a health care professional, how would you try to address these issues in working with older homosexual couples?

- In what ways do nursing homes deny the sexuality of residents?  What can nursing home staff do to respect the sexual needs of older residents?

- Discuss reasons why new drugs to treat impotence are selling so quickly.  Why does this reflect about societal norms and expectations regarding older men's sexuality?

## Classroom Activities and Student Projects

*Activity 7.1 Discussion about Older Adults' Sexuality*
Ask your students, "If you were a middle adult sitting in your living room on a Friday night and your 16-year-old daughter and 66-year-old mother both came downstairs to go out on a date, each wearing a short mini-skirt, heels, and a revealing top, which one would you have more of a reaction to? Would this reaction be positive or negative? Why?" This example also works with the hypothetical example of a 16-year old-couple and a 66-year-old couple kissing on a park bench. Explore with the students their thoughts and reactions to these images. Why is there such a negative stereotype about older adults and sexuality? Why are images of sexuality so focused on the young?

*Activity 7.2 Later-Life Mating and Dating*
Dating is a social activity at all ages of life. One place where people are looking for mates is on the Internet. Some dating services target only older adults, while others target individuals of all ages. Have your students look on the Internet for dating websites and evaluate the role of age. Is the website intended strictly for older adults? What kinds of information are given by the participants? Do the websites which target older adults differ from the websites which target all ages? If so, how? Have the students discuss their findings in class.

*Activity 7.3 Personal Ads*
View documentary *Personal Ads*. Divide the students into two groups: One group will write a personal ad for an 18-year-old. The other group will write a personal ad for a 65-year-old. Have a member of each group read the personal ad to the class. What was similar about the ads? What was different? How do these similarities and differences reflect the information contained in this chapter?

## Suggested Films
*These films are not available through Allyn & Bacon.*

*Eager For Your Kisses, Love and Sex at 95 (2006)*
New Day Films, 35 minutes, $189 DVD
After mourning the loss of his wife of fifty years, Bill Cane put an ad in the personals and went ballroom dancing in search of a new companion. He soon embraced a revitalized life full of romance, sex and music.

*Golden Threads* (1999)
Women Make Movies, 56 minutes, $295 VHS
This film presents the life of 93-year-old lesbian activist Christine Burton and covers topics such as sexuality, aging, and life choices.

*Gay and Gray in New York City* (1999)
Fanlight Productions, 22 minutes, $199 VHS
This film presents interviews with many "gay and gray" individuals as well as highlighting two organizations who address the needs of the "gay and gray" community.

*The Personals* (1998)
Fanlight Productions, 37 minutes, $199 VHS/$229 DVD
This Academy-Award winning documentary offers an extraordinary look at the emotional lives of elderly Americans. On stage, a drama group of seniors perform their roles with energy and laughter. Off stage, their lives are often lived alone, and in silence.

*Still Doing It, the Intimate Lives of Women Over 65* (2006)
New Day Films, 54 minutes, $249 VHS/DVD
This film explores the lives of older women. Partnered, single, straight, gay, black and white; nine extraordinary women, age 67-87, express with startling honesty and humor how they feel about themselves, sex, and love in later life and the poignant realities of aging. Outline of film available at: www.stilldoingit.com

*Tonight's the Night* (1995)
Fanlight Productions, 25 minutes, $149 VHS
This film from Canada presents interviews with three older adult couples who discuss their relationships and intimacy.

*Young at Heart* (1987)
Terra Nova Films, 28 minutes, $119 VHS
This is a specially endearing film about a widow and widower, both artists, who meet in their eighties, court and marry. It demonstrates that love and marriage can happen at any age.

## Suggested Websites

*Aging and Human Sexuality Resource Guide*
http://www.apa.org/pi/aging/sexuality.html
This resource guide is distributed through the American Psychological Association's website and provides a wealth of information on sexuality in later life, such as links, statistics, and videos.

*LGBT Aging Project*
http://www.lgbtagingproject.org/index.php
This site is home to the LGBT Aging Project, which is based in Massachusetts and provides information on lesbian, gay, bisexual, and transgendered older adults.

*Sexuality in Later life*
http://www.niapublications.org/engagepages/sexuality.asp
This National Institute on Aging publication details the potential changes to sexual experience in later life as well as the possible effects from medications and treatment options for sexual problems.

## Additional Resources

Healey, Shevy. 1994. "Diversity with a Difference: On Being Old and Lesbian." *Journal of Gay and Lesbian Social Services.* 1:109–117.

Morrow, Deana F. 2001. "Older Gays and Lesbians: Surviving a Generation of Hate and Violence." *Journal of Gay and Lesbian Social Services.* 13:151–169.

Rosenfeld, Dana. 1999. "Identity Work among Lesbian and Gay Elderly." *Journal of Aging Studies.* 13:121–144.

# CHAPTER 8: SOCIAL THEORIES OF AGING

## Chapter Outline

I. The Importance of Social Theories of Aging
    A. Social Gerontological Theory Before 1961
        1. Role Theory
        2. Activity Theory
    B. The First Transformation of Theory
        1. Disengagement Theory
        2. Gerotranscendence Theory
        3. Continuity Theory
    C. Alternative Theoretical Perspectives
        1. Symbolic Interactionism and Subculture of Aging
        2. Age Stratification Theory
        3. Social Exchange Theory
        4. Political Economy of Aging
        5. Life Course Perspective
        6. Life Course Social Capital
    D. The Second Transformation of Theory
        1. Social Phenomenology and Social Constructionism
        2. Critical Theory and Feminist Perspectives
        3. Postmodern Constructions of Aging
        4. The Foucault Effect on Gerontological Theory
II. Summary and Implications for the Future

## Chapter Summary

Chapter 8 presents the major social theories of aging. Each theory has its own perspective on explaining the social experience of aging and no single theory appears to be able to explain all aging phenomena. The earliest theories, such as role theory, activity theory, disengagement theory, and continuity theory, focus on the adjustments that are made between society and the older adult. Alternative theoretical perspectives have been developed that place more emphasis on the macro-structural factors affecting aging. These alternative theories include labeling theory, subculture of aging, age stratification, social exchange theory, political economy theory, and the life course perspective. More recent developments in social gerontological theory have focused on qualitative perspectives and methodologies. Social phenomenology, social construction, critical theory, and feminist perspectives are part of this second transformation of gerontology. As a whole, these theoretical perspectives point to new ways of seeing aging phenomena and new modes of analysis, laying the framework for future research directions. Interdisciplinary studies have also been developed to bring the roles of gender, class, and ethnicity to the forefront of study as well as merge the macro-social and micro-social perspectives.

# Learning Objectives

*After reading chapter 8 the student should be able to:*

1.1 Understand the theoretical question of what is the optimal way from older people to relate to their environments

1.2 Explain the major social theories of aging

1.3 Discuss the important factors related to aging or age-related issues that serve as a guide for further inquiry and possible intervention in the aging process

1.4 Contrast the different lenses through which to view and explain the phenomenon of aging

1.5 Comprehend the framework for discussions of the social aspects of aging that will guide the subsequent chapters

# Key Terms and Key People

*Activity Theory*: a theory of aging based on the hypothesis that (1) active older people are more satisfied and better adjusted than those who are not active, and (2) an older person's self-concept is validated through participation in roles characteristic of middle age, and older people should therefore replace lost roles with new ones to maintain their place in society (p. 309)

*Age Stratification Theory*: a theoretical perspective based on the belief that the societal age structure affects roles, self-concept, and life satisfaction (p. 315)

*Continuity Theory*: a theory based on the hypothesis that central personality characteristics become more pronounced with age or are retained through life with little change; people age successfully if they maintain their preferred roles and adaptation techniques throughout life (p. 312)

*Critical Theory*: the perspective that genuine knowledge is based on involvement of the "objects" of study in its definition and results in a positive vision of how things might be better rather than an understanding of how things are (p. 322)

*Disengagement Theory*: a theory of aging based on the hypothesis that older people, because of inevitable decline with age, become decreasingly active with the outer world and increasingly preoccupied with their inner lives; disengagement is useful for society because it fosters an orderly transfer of power from older to younger people (p. 310)

*Feminist Theory*: the view that the experiences of women are often ignored in understanding the human condition together with efforts to attend critically to those experiences (p. 322)

*Gerotranscendence Theory*: a theory which places greater emphasis on the inner self as people age, they move away from a focus on materialism and productivity to contemplation, spirituality, and a value placed on close interrelationships (p. 311)

*Interactionist Perspective*: a perspective that emphasizes the reciprocal actions of persons and their social world in shaping perceptions, attitudes, behavior, etc., including person-environment, symbolic interaction, labeling, and social breakdown perspectives (p. 313)

*Labeling Theory*; a theoretical perspective derived from symbolic interactionism, premised on the belief that people derive their self-concepts from interacting with others in their social milieu, in how others define us and react to us (p. 313)

*Life Course Capital*: an expansion of the life course perspective that addresses the impact of differential acquisition of resources among different members of a cohort (p. 320)

*Life Course Perspective*: the multidisciplinary view of human development that focuses on changes with age and life experiences (p. 319)

*Opportunity Structures*: social arrangements, formal and informal, that limit or advance options available to people based on such features as social class, age, ethnicity, and sex (p. 317)

*Political Economy of Aging*: a theory based on the hypothesis that social class determines a person's access to resources that dominant groups within society try to sustain their own interests by perpetuating class inequalities (p. 317-318)

*Positivism*: the perspective that knowledge is based solely upon observable facts and their relation to one another (cause and effect or correlation); the search for ultimate origins is rejected (p. 321)

*Postmodern Theory (Deconstructionism)*: the critique of language, discourse, and research practices that constrict knowledge (p. 325)

*Productive Roles*: a concept central to activity theory; activities are volunteer associations, churches, employment, and politics (p. 309)

*Role Theory*: a theory based on the belief that roles define us and our self-concept and shape our behavior (p. 307)

*Social Constructionism*: what is considered to be old varies with economic, cultural, historical and societal context (p. 320)

*Social Exchange Theory*: a theory based on the hypothesis that personal status is defined by the balance between people's contributions to society and the costs of supporting them (p. 316)

*Social Phenomenology and Constructionism*: a point of view in studying social life that places an emphasis on the assumptions and meanings of experience rather than the "objective" facts, with a focus on understanding rather than explaining (p. 320)

*Socialist Feminism:* an extension of feminist theory that attributes women's lower status in old age to capitalist and patriarchal social structures (p. 324)

*Structural Lag*: the inability of social structures (patterns of behavior, attitude, ideas, policies, etc.) to adapt to changes in population and individual lives (p. 316)

*Subculture of Aging Theory*:  a theoretical perspective based on the belief that people maintain their self-concepts and social identities through their membership in a defined group (subculture) (p. 314)

*Symbolic Interactionism*:  a theoretical perspective based on the belief that the interactions of such factors as the environment, individuals, and their encounters in it can significantly affect one's behavior and thoughts, including the aging process (p. 313)

## Discussion Topics

- List several ways that an older person may act that are contrary to normative expectations of behavior by chronological age.  What happens when an older individual violates age norms?

- Describe the three transformations of aging theories.

- Provide alternative arguments in favor of and opposing the concept of older people constituting a distinct subculture.

- Which theory in this chapter is most consistent with your own view of aging?  What evidence supports this theory?

- Which theory described in this chapter could provide you with useful guidelines for working with older people in a community-based setting?  Give examples of practice guidelines that you could derive from this particular theoretical perspective.

- Describe how you could study continuity, social exchange, and social phenomenology theories using both qualitative and quantitative methods.

- What common themes do you see in the ways that both older people and our social institutions attempt to deal with the issue of dependency?

- What theories are reflected in current political attempts to change policies affecting older adults?  How can exchange theory be used to justify reductions in services and benefits for older people?

- Based upon what you know about critical theory and a feminist perspective, explain why women in old age tend to have fewer economic resources than men.

## Classroom Activities and Student Projects

*Activity 8.1: Movie Review and Theory Application*
Have the students each watch a feature length film that portrays older adults and write a 3–5 page paper applying the sociological theories discussed in chapter 8. This exercise allows the students to demonstrate their competence and knowledge of these gerontological theories. Their papers should make links between the theories and the characters and their actions in the movie. For example, do the characters maintain a level of activity similar to their middle adult years (Activity Theory)? Another example would be to discuss the roles of men and women from feminist perspective. Potential suggestions for movies might include *Grumpy Old Men, To Dance with the White Dog, On Golden Pond,* and *Cocoon.*

*Activity 8.2 In-Class Essays*
Write on the board: *According to Sharon Curtin in* Nobody Ever Died of Old Age, *"There is nothing to prepare you for the experience of growing old."* Then give the students 15–20 minutes to write answers to the following questions. Based upon the theoretical perspectives in this chapter, how would you advise younger adults to prepare for this experience? How will you prepare for your own aging? After the time is up, ask the students to read their essays and comment on their classmates' work.

## Suggested Films
*These films are not available through Allyn & Bacon.*

*Age No Problem*
Filmakers Library, 50 minutes, $295 VHS/DVD
This video profiles Vita Needle, a company whose employees are all older adults, who all share in the profits and who all remain active. This heartwarming film affirms the potential of older adults to continue to be productive.

*American Odyssey* (1996)
New Day Films, 34 minutes, $199 VHS
This film profiles one group of older adults who travel in a caravan throughout their retirement and work to socially construct their experiences.

*Kicking High. . . In the Golden Years* (1986)
New Day Films, 58 minutes, $99 VHS
This film profiles six African-Americans as they prepare for a stage production and discuss the activities of their lives.

## Suggested Websites

*Social Gerontology & The Aging Revolution*
http://www.trinity.edu/%7Emkearl/geron.html
This site is part of "A Sociological Tour through Cyberspace," which was developed by Michael Kearl at Trinity University and contains a wealth of information on the sociological approach to aging.

## Additional Resources

Binstock, Robert H. and Linda K. George. 2001. *Handbook of Aging and the Social Sciences.* Burlingon, MA: Academic Press.

Irwin, Sarah. 1999. "Later Life, Inequality and Sociological Theory." *Ageing and Society.* 19:691–715.

Utz, Rebecca L., Deborah Carr, Randolph Nesse, Camille B. Wortman. 2002. "Effect of Widowhood on Older Adults' Social Participation: An Evaluation of Activity, Disengagement, and Continuity Theories." *Gerontologist.* 42:522–533.

# CHAPTER 9:
## THE IMPORTANCE OF SOCIAL SUPPORTS:
## FAMILY, FRIENDS, NEIGHBORS, AND COMMUNITIES

## Chapter Outline

I.   The Nature and Function of Informal Supports
    A.  Impact of Informal Networks and Social Supports on Well-Being
II.  Changing Family Structure
    A.  Growth of the Multigenerational Family
    B.  Defining Multigenerational Families
    C.  Cultural Variations in Multigenerational Families
III. Older Partners
    A.  Marital Satisfaction
    B.  Divorce in Old Age
    C.  Gay, Lesbian, Bisexual and Transgender Partners
IV.  Sibling Relationships
V.   Never-Married Older People
VI.  Childless Older Adults
VII. Other Kin
VIII. Intergenerational Relationships: Adult Children
    A.  Patterns of Intergenerational Assistance
IX.  Grandparenthood and Great-Grandparenthood
    A.  Grandparents as Primary Caregivers of Grandchildren
    B.  Great-Grandparents
    C.  Effects of Divorce on Grandparenthood
X.   Friends and Neighbors as Social Supports
XI.  Interventions to Strengthen or Build Social Supports
XII. Intergenerational Programming
XIII. Relationships with Pets
XIV. Implications for the Future
XV.  Summary

## Chapter Summary

Chapter 9 presents the importance of social supports to older adults and their environment. Contrary to myth, older adults are not socially isolated and typically have family members who participate in their caregiving. This familial caregiving does not imply that older adults live with their family members. One's marital relationship is typically the most important relationship and is frequently studied by gerontologists. More than half of all older adults are married and report satisfaction with their marriages. Fewer studies exist on sibling, grandparent, gay and lesbian relationships, the never-married, and other types of social relations in older adulthood. Adult children also tend to have frequent contact with older adult parents and, like other familial relationships, form an intergenerational exchange pattern over the life course. Regardless of ethnicity or socioeconomic status, the majority of families seek to provide caregiving for family elders rather than utilize long term care facilities. Caregiving, however, is most likely to come from middle-aged females, whether they are family members or not. The needs of these caregivers, in particular, are a growing concern for social and health care providers and policy makers. Grandparents tend to have frequent contact with grandchildren, and grandparents are increasingly taking custodial care of their grandchildren because of the inability or unwillingness of adult children to provide the care. Recent years have seen the development of formal programs to foster intergenerational contact and strengthen ties between older adults and their informal social support networks. Pets are a significant source of support for many older adults. Each of these findings leads to the conclusion that older adults maintain social roles and interaction in their later life and are not socially isolated.

## Learning Objectives

*After reading chapter 9 the student should be able to:*

9.1    Apply the life course perspective and the person-environment model to older adults' informal social support systems in reference to:

   9.1a    social supports, social engagement, and older adults' well-being
   9.1b    multi-generational families
   9.1c    different types of family relationships, such as gay and lesbian families, grandparents and grandchildren, and grandparents as caregivers
   9.1d    friends and neighbors as social support
   9.1e    social support interventions
   9.1 f    intergeneration programming
   9.1 g    pets as social support

## Key Terms and Key People

*Blended Family*:  a family whose membership is comprised of blood and non-blood relationships through divorce or remarriage (p. 338)

*Custodial Grandparents*:  grandparents who are the primary caregivers for grandchildren, when adult children are unable to provide adequate care (p. 356)

*Empty Nest*:  normative for middle-aged parents when adult children leave home for college or employment (p. 343)

*Formal Kinship Care:* placement of children with relatives by the state child welfare system (p. 357)

*Gatekeepers*:  people in formal (e.g., physicians and nurses) or informal (e.g., friends and neighbors) service who, because of regular interactions with older adults, can watch for signs indicating a need for assistance and mobilize help accordingly (p. 366)

*Grandparents' Rights*:  legal rights of grandparents to interact with grandchildren following divorce of the grandchildren's parents; liabilities of grandparent and step-grandparents as custodians of grandchildren in the absence of responsible parents (p. 362)

*Heterosexism*:  assumptions of male-female relationships as the norm; bias against GLBT individuals (p. 348)

*Informal Kinship Care:* relatives, especially grandparents, provide care without any state involvement (p. 357)

*Intergenerational Programs*: services that facilitate the interaction of people across generations; typically young and old (p. 367)

*Intergenerational Stake Hypothesis*: pattern whereby the older generation tends to be more invested in future generations around transmission of values (p. 354)

*Intergenerational Transfers*: exchange of knowledge, finances, and other resources among family members of different generations (p. 352)

*Intimacy at a Distance*: strong emotional ties among family members even though they do not live near each other (p. 352)

*Kinship Care*: the formal placement of children with extended family members (p. 357)

*Multigenerational Family*: a family with three or more generations alive at the same time (p. 337)

*Natural Helpers*: people who assist others because of their concern, interest, and innate understanding (p. 365)

*Non-traditional Families*: new families who assist others because of their concern, interest and innate understanding (p. 338)

*Reciprocal Exchange*: sharing resources and assistance among individuals (p. 334)

*Skipped Generation Household*: where the parent generation is absent (p. 356)

*Social Integration:* encompasses both social networks and support; degree to which a person is involved with others in the larger social structure and community (p. 334)

*Social Networks:* the interrelationships and interactions among individuals that affect the flow of resources and support (p. 334)

*Social Support:* interactions among family, friends, neighbors (informal), and programs (formal) that sustain and encourage individuals (p. 334)

## Discussion Topics

- What are some factors that explain the persistence of myths about the aging family in our culture?

- Describe some cultural values that influence norms of reciprocity between different generations in ethic minority families.

- What are some steps that you could take now to ensure that you will have a strong informal support system in old age?

- Describe the life course of a "typical" marriage that lasts 50+ years. How do marital transitions and roles change over time?

- Assume that you are the director of a retirement community where most residents are age 75 and over. What programs might you develop to foster intergenerational contacts?

- Assume that you are a counselor working with a four-generation family that is experiencing conflicts over caring for a great-grandparent. What would you do to encourage positive intergenerational exchanges? Specifically, what could be done to strengthen the grandchildren-grandparent interactions?

- From the perspective of your discipline, describe an intervention(s) to strengthen an older person's social support system within a high rise apartment building for low-income elders.

- What kinds of services and supports would you recommend for the growing numbers of grandparents who are assuming the primary care of grandchildren?

- Discuss how ethnic minority status, socioeconomic class, gender, and sexual orientation affect family roles and relationships for older people.

- In what ways is the aging family of the future likely to be different from contemporary families? What are the major factors that are likely to change the structure of older families in the future?

- If you were designing a training program on diversity for community home health care staff, what content would you include about families, including gay and lesbian partners?

## Classroom Activities and Student Projects

*Activity 9.1 Analyzing a Census Brief*
Another Census Brief (in addition to the one mentioned in Chapter 1) which relates to the social lives of older adults is *Grandparents Living with Grandchildren 2000: Census 2000 Brief*. This document presents a variety of statistics on the number of grandchildren in the U.S. who live with their grandparents, including information on geographic location, age, gender, etc. The students can download this document at http://www.census.gov/prod/2003pubs/c2kbr-31.pdf and bring it to class for analysis and discussion.

*Activity 9.2 Building an Intergenerational Center*
Based on reading chapter 9, the students should have a familiarity with the benefits of intergenerational reciprocity. Ask the students to form groups and design an intergenerational program for the local community. What services would it provide? What services would it not provide? How would the center work to maintain its focus on intergenerational relations? Where would the center be located and what would it look like?

## Suggested Films
*These films are not available through Allyn & Bacon.*

*Big Mama* (2000)
California Newsreel, 35 minutes, $195 VHS
This Academy Award-winning documentary is about Viola Dees, age 89, also known as Big Mama, who cares for her 12 year old grandson, Walter, whose parents are absent. But is she the best person to raise him?

*Bubbeh Lee and Me* (1996)
New Day Films, 35 minutes, $199 VHS
This film explores the relationship between one grandmother and her grandson as they reflect on life, relationships, and who they are.

*Close Harmony* (1981)
Filmakers Library, 30 minutes, $195 VHS/DVD
This Academy Award winning film is finally available on video for classroom use. A delightfully warm documentary, *Close Harmony* is about a senior citizens' chorus and an elementary school chorus who join for a combined concert.

*Grandparents Raising Grandchildren* (2000)
Fanlight Productions, 22 minutes, $179 VHS
This film profiles three grandparents who are the primary caregivers for their grandchildren.

*It's an Age Thing: Multiple Generations Living Together* (2003)
WMHT/PBS Video Productions, 30 minutes, $19.95 VHS/DVD
This film is episode 8 in the series "It's an Age Thing" and draws on the experiences of multi-generational families to illustrate this growing trend.

## Suggested Websites

*Grandparenting*
http://www.aarp.org/life/grandparents/
This page of the AARP site contains information about grandparenting and the role of grandparents and other relatives raising grandchildren in the family.

*Pets for the Elderly Foundation*
http://www.petsfortheelderly.org/index.htm
The Pets for the Elderly Foundation site provides information about the foundation's services and articles on the role of pets in older adults' lives.

## Additional Resources

Kropf, Nancy P. and Denise Burnette. 2003. "Grandparents as Family Caregivers: Lessons for Intergenerational Education". *Educational Gerontology*. 29:361–372.

Raschick, Michael and Berit Ingersoll-Dayton. 2004. "Costs and Rewards of Caregiving among Aging Spouses and Adult Children." *Family Relations*. 53:317–325.

Stafford, Philip B. 2001. "Teaching the Ethnography of Aging." *Educational Gerontology*. 27:557–567.

*When the Day Comes. . . Women as Caregivers* (1991)
Filmakers Library, 28 minutes, $295 VHS/DVD
This film presents the stories of four women who have served as primary caregivers for loved ones and who discuss the benefits and burdens of caregiving. The caregivers are as in need of social support as those they care for.

## Suggested Websites

*National Alliance for Caregiving (NAC)*
http://www.caregiving.org/
The NAC site provides a report on caregiving in the U.S. and information on caregiving.

*National Center on Elder Abuse (NCEA)*
http://www.elderabusecenter.org/
The NCEA's site provides information, statistics and laws about elder abuse, serving as a clearinghouse for information on this topic.

*National Family Caregiver Support Program (NFCS) Resource Room*
http://www.aoa.dhhs.gov/prof/aoaprog/caregiver/carefam/carefam.asp
This page of the U.S. Department of Health and Human Services' site provides elders and caregivers with key information about the NFCS legislation and ways to access support resources.

## Additional Resources

Biggs, Simon, Chris Phillipson, and Paul Kingston. 1995. *Elder Abuse in Perspective (Rethinking Aging Series)*. Berkshire, UK: Open University Press.

Connidis, Ingrid Arnet. 2001. *Family Ties and Aging*. Thousand Oaks, CA: Sage Publications.

Lechner, Viola W., Margaret Neal. 1999. *Work and Caring for the Elderly: International Perspectives*. New York: Brunner/Mazel Publisher.

# CHAPTER 11: LIVING ARRANGEMENTS AND SOCIAL INTERACTIONS

## Chapter Outline

## Chapter Summary

Chapter 11 discusses the various options older adults have for living arrangements and the effect of the environment on physical and psychological well-being for older adults. Throughout this discussion the main theme is that there is no "good" or "bad" living environment. Each type of environment has strengths and weaknesses, benefits and dangers and the needs, preferences and abilities of the older adult predicts the appropriateness of the housing. The goal is to decrease the environmental press, or demands placed on the older adult by the environment. For example, although today's older adults are far less likely than previous generations to live in rural communities, one significant concern is the ability for older adults who reside in rural communities to access quality housing and services.

Regardless of community size, as people age, their neighborhood becomes more significant as their living space becomes more constricted. Thus, neighbors become an especially important source of support. While older adults fear crime more than any other age group, they are least likely to be victimized. Frequently the role of long term homeownership makes relocating quite a challenge for older adults. Older adults' homes may be in need of renovations, yet the older adults may be unable to make or pay for these repairs. However, the older adult may benefit a great deal by relocating to a residence with other older adults and services nearby.

As individuals live longer, there becomes an increased need for housing that can address the ever changing needs of its residents by offering a range of services. A relatively small number of individuals need 24-hour skilled nursing, and for these individuals nursing homes are the most beneficial form of living arrangement. For older adults needing less frequent nursing care or assistance, assisted living and foster care are beneficial options. Home care is an option for older adults who wish to reside in a private residence, and the cost is partially reimbursed by Medicaid and Medicare. Adult day care provides many older adults with caregiving during the day while primary caregivers may be at work. Structural changes, such as the reduction of the number of single room occupancy residences, have led to some older adults becoming homeless. Homeless older adults often lack health care and other basic necessities. A recent growing concern is the number of older adults in prisons because of chronic disease management and escalating costs of care as well as the inability of the prison environment to provide for the needs of an aging inmate.

## Learning Objectives

*After reading chapter 11 the student should be able to:*
11.1 Discuss the person-environment theories that describe adaptation to aging
11.2 Outline the impact of the natural and built environment on older persons' social functioning
11.3 Illustrate the influence of an aging population on community planning and housing
11.4 Describe the new options in long-term care for frail elders
11.5 List the services to help elders remain independent in the community and the new technology to help *aging in place*
11.6 Explain the housing policies affecting older adults as well as the impact of federal budget cuts, SRO housing, and homelessness
11.7 Discuss the need for geriatric facilities and services in prisons

## Key Terms and Key People

*Adult Day Care (ADC)*: a community facility that that frail older people living at home can attend several hours each day; when based on a health rehabilitation model, it provides individualized therapy plans; those based on a social model focus on structured social and psychotherapeutic activities (p. 455)

*Adult Foster Care* or *Adult Family Home*: a private home facility, licensed by the state, in which the owner of the home provides housekeeping, personal care and some delegated nursing functions for the residents (p. 452)

*Aging in Place*:  continuing to live in a private home or apartment, even when declining competence reduces P-E congruence and more assistance with ADL is needed (p. 436)

*Assisted Living*:  a housing model aimed at elders who need assistance with personal care, e.g., bathing and taking medication, but who are not so physically or cognitively impaired as to need 24-hour attention (p. 449)

*Assistive Technology*:  a range of electronic and computer technologies whose goal is to assist people with disabilities to remain independent and perform as many ADL as possible without assistance from others (p. 456)

*Co-Housing:* a community of families or elders who share some activities in a common house but live independently (p. 436)

*Community Residential Care (CRC)*:  a general label for residential long-term care options other than nursing homes; includes adult foster care, adult family homes, and assisted living (p. 449)

*Continuous Care Retirement Community (CCRC)*:  a multilevel facility offering a range from independent to congregate living arrangements, including nursing home units; generally requires an initial entry fee to assure a place if long-term care is needed in the future (p. 443)

*Culture Change:* new models of nursing home care that attempt to humanize these facilities and make them more home-like and less institutional (p. 447-448)

*Eden Alternative*:  a new paradigm for nursing home care that encourages active participation by residents by allowing them to care for plants and animals (p. 448)

*Elder-Friendly (Livable) Communities*: cities, suburbs, and towns that offer transportation, social and health services and safe and adaptable housing to help other residents age in place (p. 433)
*Gerontechnology*: a new field of research and practice aimed at using technology to improve older adults' independence (p. 456)

*Green House:* an expansion of the Eden Alternative that focuses on smaller groups of residents served by a core group of workers who perform multiple tasks (p. 448)

*Home Health Care*: a variety of nursing, rehabilitation, and other therapy services, as well as assistance with personal care and household maintenance, that are provided to people who are homebound and have difficulty performing multiple ADL (p. 453)

*Intentional Communities:* a group of families or elders with common values (e.g., political, religious, lifestyle) who live independently but share meals, activities, and some expenses (p. 436)

*Long-Term Care*:  a broad range of services geared to helping frail older adults in their own home and community settings; can include nursing homes, nutritional programs, adult day care, and visiting nurse services (p. 444)

*Medicaid Waivers*: exceptions to state Medicaid rules that allow use of Medicaid funds for services that are traditionally not covered by Medicaid, such as chore services and adult family homes (p. 451)

*Naturally Occurring Retirement Community (NORC)*: a neighborhood or larger area occupied mostly by older people, but without having been planned specifically for this population (p. 436)

*Negotiated Risk*: agreement between facility administration and a resident, family, or guardian that the resident in a CRC setting will maintain autonomy but will assume risks if problems such as falls and accidents result from such independence (p. 450)

*Nursing Homes*: facilities with three or more beds staffed 24 hours per day by health professionals who provide nursing and personal-care services to residents who cannot remain in their own homes dues to physical health problems, functional disabilities, and/or significant cognitive impairments (p. 444)

*Pioneer Network:* a coalition of nursing home administrators and LTC advocates focused on improving quality of care and residents' quality of life by making organizational changes (p. 448)

*Resident-Centered Care:* a model of long-term care in which frail elders have the right and ability to determine their own needs and how these should be met (p. 447)

*Single-Room-Occupancy (SRO) Hotels*: older buildings in urban centers that have been converted to low-cost apartments; often these are single rooms with no kitchen, minimal cooking and refrigeration facilities, and bathrooms shared with other units (p. 461)

*Telehealth*: transmitting a patient's health status and vital signs via computer or telephone lines directly to a health provider (p. 457)

*Universal Design*: designing a product or building or landscape to make it accessible to and usable by the broadest range of users (p. 456)

*Universal Worker:* nursing home staff who perform multiple services, including meal preparation, personal care, and housekeeping, rather than specializing in one task (p. 448)

# Discussion Topics

- What aspects of person-environment congruence are most important in selecting housing for an older person who must relocate from his own home to a long-term care facility?

- Describe the advantages and disadvantages of suburban living for older people.

- Discuss some options available to an older person who does not wish to move to retirement housing, but prefers to stay in the large mortgage-free home in which she has lived for 40 years but can no longer maintain.

- What services and programs should be developed in a NORC in order to support elderly residents of that community and prevent a move to a long-term care facility?

- Describe the prevalence of crimes against older people, comparing by gender, race, and income level. What factors may account for discrepancies between perceived versus objective prevalence rates?

- Provide some guidelines for designing a multilevel facility for older people that would be suitable for both a healthy and active 65-year-old and an 85-year-old with dementia.

- Discuss the pros and cons of assisted living facilities as an option for an older person who has problems with multiple ADLs.

- Design a congregate housing project which admits 65- to 75-year-old residents and allows them to live successfully as they age in place.

- Describe some trends in long-term care that have resulted in older people receiving services in settings other than nursing homes. What societal and policy factors have influenced these changes?

- If financial constraints were not a problem, what types of assistive technology might be used in an older persons' homes to help them age in place?

- Describe the impact of the loss of SRO housing on problems of homelessness among older Americans.

## Classroom Activities and Student Projects

*Activity 11.1  Field Trip to Nursing Home or Assisted Living Facility*
Contact a local nursing home or assisted living facility to ask for a tour of their organization. Ask if the tour guide could discuss life in the facility and find out if it would be possible for the students to talk directly with the residents. Ideally, if students could visit both a nursing home and an assisted living facility, this would be a significant opportunity for them to compare and contrast the benefits of each type of residence as well as ascertain which type of living situation would be appropriate for particular older adults and their needs.

*Activity 11.2  Shopping for Technology*
Send the students out on a shopping trip via the Internet for products which older adults could purchase to modify their home. For each item found, the students should note the price, ease of purchasing, ease of installation or assembly, and benefits of use. Is the item something that an older adult can realistically obtain and use? Are there social class concerns with such products?

## Suggested Films
*These films are not available through Allyn & Bacon.*

*I'm Pretty Old* (1993)
Fanlight Productions, 20 minutes, $135 VHS
This film presents several nursing home residents talking about their living arrangements.

*More than Skin Deep* (2001)
Fanlight Productions, 25 minutes, $149 VHS
This film explores the connections between self-esteem and aging by focusing on six nursing home residents, who go to a beauty shop.

*Pink Sunset Villa* (2004)
Filmakers Library, 50 minutes, $295 VHS/DVD
This gentle film, made in Holland, shows us the evolution of a home being built for senior gays and lesbians. It introduces us to the graying men and women as they prepare to distill their possessions and their memories for the move to spacious cheery apartments in the new residence.

*Sunset Hall* (2003)
Capital Entertainment, 138 minutes
This is a funny and intimate documentary drama that will make you think differently about growing old. Set against the backdrop of a retirement home for political progressives, the film goes inside the world of two women, Irja (81) and Lucille (95), whose feisty engagement with life draws them together inextricably.

*94 years and One Nursing Home Later* (1999)
Terra Nova Films, 33 minutes, $139 VHS
This film builds on the experiences of the producer's family to explore the role of family relationships as family member's social roles change throughout the life course. Website: www.94years.com

## Suggested Websites

*Assisted Living Federation of America (ALFA)*
http://www.alfa.org/
ALFA is the national organization of assisted living. On this site ALFA provides information on laws, resources, and conferences related to assisted living.

*Eldercare Locator*
http://www.n4a.org/locator.cfm
This page, which is sponsored by the National Association of Area Agencies on Aging, provides and overview of and contact information for the Eldercare Locator program.

*Nursing Homes*
http://www.medicare.gov/Nursing/Overview.asp
This page, which is part of the Medicare site, provides information on nursing homes in the U.S., including a "nursing home compare" tool and a list of nursing home residents' rights.

## Additional Resources

Crane, Margaret. 1999. *Understanding Older Homeless People: Their Circumstances, Problems, and Needs (Rethinking Aging).* London: Taylor and Francis Group.

Diamond, Timothy. 1995. *Making Gray Gold: Narratives of Nursing Home Care (Women In Culture and Society).* Chicago: University of Chicago Press.

Vaillant, George E. 2002. *Aging Well: Surprising Guideposts to a Happier Life from the Landmark Harvard Study of Adult Development.* New York: Little, Brown and Company.

# CHAPTER 12: PRODUCTIVE AGING: PAID AND NONPAID ROLES AND ACTIVITIES

## Chapter Outline

I.  What Do We Mean By Productive Aging?
II. Retirement
        A. Timing of Retirement
        B. Satisfaction with Retirement
        C. The Importance of Planning
III. Employment Status
        A. More Older People Seek Employment
        B. Barriers to Employment
        C. Creating New Employment Opportunities
IV. Economic Status: Sources of Income in Retirement
        A. Social Security
        B. Asset Income
        C. Pensions
        D. Earnings
V. Poverty Among Old and Young
        A. Poverty Differentials Over Time
        B. Poverty Differentials by Gender
        C. Poverty Differentials by Ethnic Minority Status
        D. Poverty Differentials by Age and Living Status
        E. Public Assistance
VI. Patterns and Functions of Nonpaid Roles and Activities
        A. Leisure
        B. Religious Participation, Religiosity, and Spirituality
        C. Benefits of Religious Participation and Religiosity
        D. Value of Spiritual Well-Being
        E. Civic Engagement
        F. Membership in Voluntary Associations
        G. Volunteer Work and Organizations
        H. Educational Programs
        I. Political Participation
        J. Voting Behavior
        K. Senior Power
VII. Implications for the Future
VIII. Summary

## Chapter Summary

Chapter 12 presents the challenges older adults face as they enter retirement in a society that predominantly emphasizes paid employment as a means to productivity. More older adults are working past the traditional age of retirement. Deciding when to retire is a complex decision often resting on financial, psychological, and physical well-being. This planning often begins many years before the individual actually retires. Once retired, not all older adults experience the same situation. Many older adults continue working, while others embrace leisure time and volunteering. For a minority of older adults, one's later years are fraught with financial concerns and may lead to an income below the poverty line. For some, dissatisfaction with retirement causes poor health or loss of identity and self-esteem. Regardless, this is frequently a time of adjustment to new roles in terms of employment, parenting, grandparenting, marriage, and other social relations. Participation in leisure pursuits, civic engagement and education is often a means to build and strengthen informal social support networks, influence wider social policies, serve others and substitute new roles for the old. Various factors influence this participation including gender, ethnic minority status, health, social class and education level. Religiosity and spirituality do not appear to decline in later life and appear to be an effective way of coping. Voting appears to increase in later life. Some argue that older adults form a unified political bloc that can influence politicians and policy. In general, organizational participation seems to be constant across one's life course.

## Learning Objectives

*After reading chapter 12 the student should be able to:*
12.1 Define and critique the concept of productive aging
12.2 Describe retirement as a status and a social process that affects economic well-being, roles, and activities in old age
12.3 Explain the employment status, socioeconomic status, and sources of income of older adults
12.4 Summarize the activity patterns common among older adults
12.5 Discuss the role of religiosity and spirituality in coping for older adults

## Key Terms and Key People

*Age Discrimination in Employment Act (ADEA):* federal law that protects workers age 45 and over from denial of employment strictly because of age (p. 490)

*American Association of Retired Persons (AARP):* national organization open to all adults age 50 and over, offering a wide range of informational material, discounted services and products, and a powerful lobby (p. 522)

*American Society on Aging (ASA):* association of practitioners and researchers interested in gerontology (p. 524)

*Assets:* an individual's savings, home equity, and personal property (p. 494)

*Association for Gerontology in Higher Education (AGHE):* the only national membership organization devoted primarily to gerontological education (p. 524)

*Civic Engagement:* active participation in one's community by voting, volunteering, joining community groups (p. 509)

*Civic Ventures:* provides resources for civic engagement and awards to innovators and agencies working for the common good (p. 509)

*Displaced Homemaker:* widowed or divorced women under age 60 who do not yet quality for Social Security benefits but may lack the skills for employment (p. 493)

*Elderhostel:* program in which older adults can take inexpensive, short-term academic courses associated with colleges and universities around the world (p. 517)

*Employment Retirement Income Security Act (ERISA):* 1974 legislation to regulate pensions (p. 495)

*Experience Corps:* trains adults age 55 and older to serve in inner-city schools (p. 515)

*Feminization of Poverty:* variety of factors that lead to higher proportion of poverty among women than men (p. 499)

*Foster Grandparents Program:* volunteer program pairing seniors with children who have special needs (p. 516)

*Generations United:* a national intergenerational coalition (p. 521)

*Gerontological Society of America (GSA):* an association of researchers, educators, and practitioners interested in gerontology and geriatrics (p. 524)

*Gray Panthers:* a national organization founded by Maggie Kuhn that encourages intergenerational alliances around social issues (p. 524)

*National Association of Retired Federal Employees (NARFE):* national organization of adults retired from the federal government; primarily involved in political and social issues (p. 522-523)

*National Council of Senior Citizens (NCSC):* mass-membership organization involved in political action for older adults (p. 522)

*National Council on the Aging (NCOA):* national organization of over 2000 social welfare agencies concerned with aging that provides technical consultation and is involved in federal legislation activities (p. 524)

*Older Women's League (OWL):* a national organization, formed by Tish Sommers and Laurie Shields, concerned about issues affecting older women (p. 524)

*Retired Senior Volunteer Program (RSVP):* federal program in which older adults volunteer in schools, hospitals, and other social agencies (p. 516)

*Retirement*: the period of life, usually starting between age 60 and 65, during which an individual stops working in the paid labor force (p. 477)

*Senior Community Services Employment Program (SCSEP)*: programs sponsored by government or business that encourage the employment of older workers (p. 490)

*Senior Companion Program*: a volunteer program in which seniors assist other seniors (p. 515)

*Senior Learning Programs*: academic programs specially designed for older adults, or programs of tuition waivers that allow older adults to take college courses at no cost (p. 517)

*Senior Net*: national educational program that teaches older adult computer skills and provides opportunities for on-line communication (p. 518)

*Social Security*: federal program into which workers contribute a portion of their income during adulthood and then, beginning sometime between the ages of 62 and 65, receive a monthly check based on the amount they have earned and contributed (p. 478)

*Spirituality*: believing in one's relationship with a higher power without being religious in the sense of organized religion (p. 507)

*Supplemental Security Income (SSI)*: federal program to provide a minimal income for low-income older people (and other age groups with disabilities) (p. 500)

*Vesting of Pension Benefits*: amount of time a person must work on a job in order to acquire rights to a pension (p. 495)

## Discussion Topics

- Discuss the concept of productive aging. What are ways that older people can continue to play meaningful roles in our society? What are barriers to such roles?

- What are some factors that influence the employment and retirement patterns of older men and women?

- If you were the Director of Personnel in a corporation that wanted to maximize older workers' skills, what steps would you recommend to your company (e.g., changes in policies, programs, benefits, etc.)?

- What are the primary barriers to the employment of older individuals? What are some strategies to overcome these barriers?

- In planning for or thinking about your own retirement, what factors do you consider to be most important? What would you like to do upon retirement? What steps can you take now to assure satisfaction with your retirement?

## Learning Objectives

*After reading chapter 13 the student should be able to:*
13.1  Summarize attitudes toward death in our culture
13.2  Discuss the dying process and its meaning to the dying person
13.3  Understand the conditions for care of the dying and pain management
13.4  Contrast the perspectives of the right to die (active and passive euthanasia)
13.5  Identify the increasing ethical, medical, and legal issues raised by whether to continue life-sustaining technologies
13.6  Note the legal options of advance directives available to individuals
13.7  Define bereavement, grief, and mourning
13.8  Reflect on the experience of widowhood

## Key Terms and Key People

*Active Euthanasia:*  positive steps to hasten someone else's death, such as administering a lethal injection; assisted suicide, perhaps by a physician (p. 558)

*Advance Directive:*  documents such as living wills, wills, and durable power of attorney for health care decisions that outline actions to be taken when an individual is no longer able to do so, often because of irreversible illness (p. 562)

*Anticipatory Grief:*  grief for a loved one prior to his or her death, usually occurring during the time that the loved one has a terminal illness, that may allow survivors to prepare; may be a barrier to adaptation (p. 572)

*Assisted Suicide/Physician Assisted Suicide (PAS):*  considered active euthanasia when a physician actively aids with a person's death, typically through the use of drugs (p. 558)

*Bereavement:*  state of being deprived of a loved one by death (p. 569)

*Bereavement Overload:*  an experience of older adults who are exposed to the increased frequency of family and friends' deaths and become desensitized to the impact of death (p. 507–575)

*Bioethics:*  discipline dealing with procedural approaches to questions about death, dying, and medical decision making (p. 568)

*Compassion and Choices:*  national organization supporting the right to die (p. 568)

*Conservatorship:*  person designated by a court to manage the affairs, either personal or fiscal or both, of persons unable to do so for themselves (p. 567)

*Death with Dignity:*  dying when one still has some independence and control over decisions about life (p. 553)

*Durable Power of Attorney*: legal document that conveys to another person designated by the person signing the document the right to make decisions regarding either health and personal care or assets and income, or both, of the person giving the power; it is a durable power that does not expire, as a power of attorney normally does, when a person becomes incompetent (p. 567)

*Dying Person's Bill of Rights*: affirms dying person's right to dignity, privacy, informed participation, and competent care (p. 546)

*Dying Process*: stages as advanced by Kübler-Ross; five stages experienced by the dying person: (1) denial and isolation, (2) anger and resentment, (3) bargaining and an attempt to postpone, (4) depression and a sense of loss, and (5) acceptance (p. 543)

*Euthanasia*: the act or practice of killing (active euthanasia) or permitting the death of (passive euthanasia) hopelessly sick or injured individuals in a relatively painless way; mercy killing (p. 554)

*Grief Process*: intense emotional suffering caused by loss, disaster, misfortune, etc.; acute sorrow; deep sadness (p. 569)

*Grief Reaction*: emotional and cognitive process following the death of a loved one or other major loss (p. 570)

*Guardianship*: person who establishes legal control over another person's body as well as finances (p. 567)

*Hastened Death:* viewed as a more socially acceptable term than *euthanasia* because it speeds up the inevitable (p. 554)

*Hemlock Society*: national organization that promotes the right to die for terminally ill persons, calls for legalizing assistance for those who decide to take their own lives, and publishes information on nonviolent painless methods to commit suicide (p. 568)

*Hospice*: a place or a program of care for dying persons that gives emphasis to personal dignity of the dying person, reducing pain, sources of anxiety, and family reconciliation when indicated (p. 548)

*Informed Consent*: written or oral document that states indications and reasons for treatment, its benefits, risks, and alternatives (p. 554)

*Living Will*: legal document in which an individual's wishes about medical treatment are put in writing should he or she be unable to communicate at the end of life; directs physicians and hospitals to withhold life-sustaining procedures, take all measures to sustain life, or whatever seems appropriate to the person executing the document (p. 562)

*Medical Power of Attorney*: similar to "durable power of attorney," but focuses on a health care surrogate to make decisions about medical care (p. 567)

*Mourning*: culturally patterned expression of grief at someone's death (p. 569)

*Palliative Care*:  treatment designed to relieve pain provided to a person with a terminal illness for whom death is imminent (p. 546)

*Passive Euthanasia*:   voluntary elective death through the withdrawal of life-sustaining treatments or failure to treat life-threatening conditions (p. 556)

*Patient Self-Determination Act*:  federal law requiring that health care facilities inform their patients about their rights to decide how they want to live or die; for example, by providing them information on refusing treatment and on filing advance directives (p. 562)

*Right to Die*:  the belief that persons have a right to take their own lives, especially if they experience untreatable pain, often accompanied by the belief that persons have a right to physician assistance in the dying process (p. 546)

*Self-Neglect*:  a process by which a person voluntarily makes decisions that are equivalent to choosing to die (e.g., refusing help, not eating) (p. 557)

*Surrogate Decision Maker*:  person legally designated to act according to patient's known wishes or "best interest" (p. 566)

*Uniform Health Care Decision Act:* mandates compliance with patients' health care decisions (p. 565)

## Discussion Topics

- What are ways in which our society seeks to deny or avoid death?  How do these influence your own attitudes toward death?

- What are some strengths and limitations of Kübler-Ross' stage model of dying?

- Discuss ways that psychosocial factors interact with the biological process of dying.

- What are some issues for people to consider when preparing for death?  What can you do in your own life to prepare for your own death?

- What is your own position on euthanasia?  With regard to older people?  With regard to youth?  What would you want for yourself if you were terminally ill?  What would you include if you were writing a living will?

- What can human service professionals do to protect the rights of dying patients and to ensure a "good death"?  Discuss ways that these goals may be in conflict with one another.

- Given increased life expectancy and life-prolonging medical techniques, discuss both the ethical and legal issues related to dying.

- If you were a health care professional working in a nursing home, what kinds of services would you develop to help older residents and their relatives cope with dying, death, and bereavement?

- Discuss the characteristics of an ideal hospice program.

- Discuss cultural and individual characteristics that might influence how an older man or woman copes with the death of a spouse to whom they were married 50 years.

## Classroom Activities and Student Projects

### Activity 13.1 Obituary Analysis
Have the students each bring to class an obituary section from a newspaper. In addition to local newspapers, encourage the students to select obituary sections from around the country and around the world. Then ask the students to work in groups of 2–4 to evaluate the obituaries of older adults, based on their age, cause of death, occupation, gender, sexual orientation, family relationships, size of the community they resided in, size of the obituary, prestige level of the newspaper, etc. Once the small groups have completed their analysis, have each group present their findings to the class and prompt the class to come to some conclusions about the presentation of the life and death of older adults through obituaries.

### Activity 13.2 Death and Controversies Debate
Many controversies surround the medical and legal aspects of death and dying. Assign the students to work in teams to debate some of the current controversies, such as physician assisted suicide and the right to die. Encourage the students to include religious views, U.S. Supreme Court cases, and public policy issues in each side of the debate. For example, one team could present the argument in favor of physician assisted suicide and another team could present the argument against physician assisted suicide. After each team presents their arguments, allow time for rebuttal and class discussion. Video taping the debate is an optional idea for future learning.

### Activity 13.3 Around the Room Conversation
Make 5 signs, each containing one of the following terms: strongly agree, somewhat agree, neutral/not sure, somewhat disagree, strongly disagree and post them around the classroom. Read a statement about a death and dying issue and ask students to stand beneath the sign that most closely represents their opinion. Tell students they are permitted to change their position at any time during the discussion. Have students discuss why they are standing beneath the sign they chose. Topics that work well with this activity are euthanasia, the death penalty, and remarrying after widowhood.

### Activity 13.4 Death Rituals & Culture Presentations
Assign groups of students a culture (e.g., Native American, Jewish, Asian American) to research regarding death rituals. Have each group present information about their culture, using music, photographs, role play and artifacts to teach the class about death beliefs and practices.

## Suggested Films

*These films are not available through Allyn & Bacon.*

*Care for the Dying (The Series)* (2000)
Terra Nova Films, 4 tapes, each tape 20–37 minutes, $159 single VHS/$499 four tape set VHS
This four tape series explores the issues and decisions that older adults need to discuss and make as they approach the final stages of their life.

*Facing Death* (2002)
First Run Icarus Films, 57 minutes, $248 VHS
This remarkably intimate film was produced in 2002, when Küblerr-Ross lived secluded in the desert, and was awaiting - as she says - her own death, on the verge of the transition she researched so passionately.

*A Family Undertaking* (2003)
Fanlight Productions, 56 minutes, $229 VHS/$249 DVD
This video documentary explores the complex psychological, cultural, legal and financial issues surrounding an important and growing new trend: the home funeral movement.

*Full Circle* (1997)
Terra Nova Films, 29 minutes, $165 VHS
This film tells the story of a middle-aged woman bringing her elderly mother home to die.

*The Self Made Man* (2006)
New Day Films, 57 minutes, $250 VHS/DVD (with extra features – 64 minutes)
This film, about a 77-year old man diagnosed with a terminal disease who decides to take his own life, explores "rational suicide," the "right-to-die" and the difficult end-of-life choices faced by an aging population.

*To Live Until I Die* (1999)
Fanlight Productions, 56 minutes, $229 VHS
This film presents the lives of six terminally ill older adults in its exploration of living and dying.

## Suggested Websites

*End of Life Choices (The Hemlock Foundation)*
http://www.hemlock.org/
This site serves the Hemlock Foundation's home page and provides information on the organization and their work to promote "freedom of choice at the end of life."

*Aging with Dignity*
http://www.fivewishes.org
This site presents its Five Wishes advance directive, which addresses the personal, emotional, and spiritual issues that people say matter most to them during times of serious illness.

*Hospice Foundation of America (HFA)*
http://www.hospicefoundation.org/
This site defines and describes hospice as well as serving to announce HFA's teleconferences and other resources.

*The National Hospice and Palliative Care Organization (NHPCO)*
http://www.nhpco.org
The NHPCO site provides information on hospice, including statistics, answers to frequently asked questions, videos, and discussion of public policy.

## Additional Resources

Dickinson, George E. and David Field.  2002.  "Teaching End-of-Life Issues: Current Status in United Kingdom and United States Medical Schools." *American Journal of Hospice and Palliative Care.*  19:181–186.

Palmore, Erdman.  1987.  "Cross-Cultural Perspectives on Widowhood." *Journal of Cross-Cultural Gerontology.*  2:93–105.

Van Baarsen, Berna.  2002.  "Theories on Coping with Loss: The Impact of Social Support and Self-Esteem On Adjustment to Emotional and Social Loneliness Following a Partner's Death in Later Life." *Journals of Gerontology:  Series B:  Psychological and Social Sciences.*  57B: S33–S42

# CHAPTER 14: THE RESILIENCE OF ELDERS OF COLOR

## Chapter Outline

I.  Defining Ethnicity and Culture
> A.  Defining Minority and People of Color
> B.  The Dramatic Growth of Populations of Color

II.  Research History
> A. Ethnic Minorities in Gerontology

III. Older African Americans
> A.  Economic Status
> B.  Health
> C.  Social Supports and Living Situations

IV. Older Latinos
> A.  Economic Status
> B.  Health
> C.  Social Supports and Living Situations

V. Older American Indians
> A.  Economic Status
> B.  Health
> C.  Social Supports and Living Situations

VI. Older Asians/Pacific Islanders
> A.  Economic Status
> B.  Health
> C.  Social Supports and Living Situations

VII. Implications for Services

VIII. Implications for the Future

IX.  Summary

## Chapter Summary

Today's population of older adults is increasingly diverse. Chapter 14 presents the challenges faced by elders of color and the resiliency elders of color have in confronting these challenges.  Ethnogerontology, the study of the causes, processes, and consequences of race, national origin, and culture on individual and population aging, questions whether elders of color face double jeopardy because of the intersection of their age and their race.  Elders who are African American, Latino, American Indian, or Asian/Pacific Islander face variations in the aging process, yet share much similarity.  In general, elders of color experience shorter life expectancies, greater financial challenges, and a lack of adequate housing and health care.  It must be noted that there is much variation within each group and that two groups in particular (Japanese Americans and Chinese Americans) have longer life expectancies than do whites. The crossover effect describes recent findings that after age 75, there is a narrowing in differences in health status and life expectancy between ethnic groups.  Many elders, especially immigrants to the United States, experience considerable resilience to challenges they face despite barriers to social programs, such as language difficulties, isolation and poverty.  However, in some instances barriers to social programs exist, such as language difficulties, isolation, and poverty.

## Learning Objectives

*After reading chapter 14 the student should be able to:*
14.1 Define ethnicity, minority status, and people of color
14.2 Discuss the research history on ethnic minorities
14.3 Explain the challenges faced by older African Americans, Latinos, American Indians, and Asians/Pacific Islanders
14.4 List barriers to service for elders of color
14.5 State the implications for culturally competent services

## Key Terms and Key People

*Crossover Effect*:  the lower death rates among African Americans, Asian Americans, and American Indians after age 75 (p. 596)

*Cultural Competence*:  having the knowledge and skills to work effectively with ethnic minorities (p. 625)

*Double Jeopardy Hypothesis*:  the hypothesis that aging persons of color are in jeopardy in our society due to both growing old and being part of an ethnic minority (p. 596)

*Ethnogeriatrics*:  cross-cultural geriatric care that recognizes cultural difference in response to health and disease (p. 625)

*Ethnogerontology*:  study of causes, processes, and consequences of race, national origin, and culture on individual and population aging (p. 596)

*Fictive Kin*:  foster parents of children, close friends, or neighbors who function in the absence of blood relatives or when family relationships are unsatisfactory (p. 604)

*Health Disparities*:  socioeconomic and racial/ethnic inequalities in health, mortality, and other adverse conditions across the life span (p. 597)

*Healthcare Disparities*:  differences in access, quality, or rate of utilization of a health care service, where ethnic minorities have a substantially lower utilization rate (p. 597)

*Indian Health Service*:  federal program that provides health care for Native Americans and Alaskans of all ages through hospitals and community clinics (p. 615)

*Law of Primogeniture*:  the exclusive right of the eldest so to inherit his estate that was traditional among Asian families (p. 624)

*Multiple Hierarchy Stratification*:  the theory that social class, in addition to ethnic minority status, can jeopardize older minorities (p. 596)

## Discussion Topics

- What are the major problems facing ethnic minority elders in our society? What do you perceive to be some solutions to these problems? Barriers to these solutions?

- What are some strengths of older persons of color who have grown up in an earlier era of racial discrimination in the U.S.?

- Apply social exchange theory to an analysis of the status of ethnic minority elders in our society. Cite examples that illustrate the centrality of control over valued resources to their status.

- Older persons are not a homogeneous population. Identify dimensions along which ethnic minority elders differ from and are similar to the older population in general. Drawing upon your own discipline's research and practice perspective, what are some implications of these dimensions for both research and the delivery of services?

- Describe some similarities and differences in family and living arrangements between older African Americans, Hispanics, and American Indians.

- To what extent has immigration affected the aging experiences of Hispanics and Asian Americans in the U.S.?

- Suggest directions for future research on ethnic minority elders. What are some of the difficulties of conducting such research?

- Describe your own ethnic and cultural experiences and how those might affect your own aging process and that of other members of your family.

## Classroom Activities and Student Projects

*Activity 14.1 Ethnicity Discussion*
Ask the students to describe their own perceptions of the older population of a specific ethnic minority group. To what extent are these stereotypes? To what extent are these based on personal experiences? Do they have any research support for their perceptions?

*Activity 14.2 Building a Multi-Cultural Senior Center*
Assign the students to groups and assign each group to represent the needs of one cultural group in the community. Then, ask the students if they were designing a multicultural senior center, describe typical programs and how they would differ from more traditional centers and from programs for a specific ethnic group. Bring the class together and have each group argue for the needs of their culture.

## Suggested Films

*These films are not available through Allyn & Bacon.*

*The Latino Family* (1993)
Films for the Humanities and Sciences, 28 minutes, $89.95 VHS/DVD
This film profiles three generations of a Mexican-American family to illustrate the traditions and stamina of Latino families. It shows how the traditional roles of the Latino elderly are being altered by their families' needs.

*Legacy*
Terra Nova Films, 30 minutes, $165 VHS
This film profiles Native American elders who speak about historical and contemporary relations between the U.S. government and Native American tribes.

*Wind Grass Song: The Voice of Our Grandmothers* (1989)
Women Make Movies Productions, 20 minutes, $225 VHS
This film presents interviews with women of diverse ethnicities who are age 85–101 and live in Oklahoma.

## Suggested Websites

*Aging in the Hispanic Community*
http://www.pbs.org/americanfamily/aging.html
This site is part of the PBS series entitled "American Family," which is a drama series that presents the life of a Hispanic family.

*Michigan Center for Urban African American Aging Research (MCUAAR)*
http://mcuaaar.iog.wayne.edu/
This site of the MCUAAR serves to mentor and recruit researchers who specialize in research on African American elders.

*National Indian Council on Aging (NICA)*
http://www.nicoa.org/
This site of the NICA provides advocacy, publications, and policies on aging for American Indian and Alaska native elders.

*National Asian Pacific Center on Aging (NAPCA)*
http://www.napca.org/aboutus/aboutus/mission.aspx
This site illustrates the advocacy, education, and empowerment that NAPCA provides for older Asian Pacific Americans.

## Additional Resources

Becker, Gay, Yewoubdar Beyene, Edwina Newsom, Nury Mayen. 2003. "Creating Continuity through Mutual Assistance: Intergenerational Reciprocity in Four Ethnic Groups." *Journals of Gerontology: Series B: Psychological and Social Sciences.* 58B:S151–S159.

Burnette, Denise. 1999. "Social Relationships of Latino Grandparent Caregivers: a Role Theory Perspective." *Gerontologist.* 39:49–58.

Torres-Gil, Fernando and Karra Bikson Moga. 2001. "Multiculturalism, Social Policy and The New Aging." *Journal of Gerontological Social Work.* 36:13–32.

# CHAPTER 15: THE RESIILIENCE OF OLDER WOMEN

## Chapter Outline

I. Rationale for a Focus on Older Women's Needs
    A. Older Women's Economic Status
    B. Social Security and Gender Inequities
    C. Inequities for Women: Privatizing Social Security
    D. Proposals to Reduce Gender Inequities in Social Security
    E. Private Pensions and Gender Inequities
II. Older Women's Health Status
    A. Health Insurance and Gender Inequities
    B. Higher Incidence of Chronic Health Problems
    C. Osteoporosis
    D. Menopause
III. Older Women's Social Status
    A. Widowhood
    B. Limited Opportunities to Remarry
    C. Informal Networks and Social Support
IV. Implications for the Future
V. Summary

## Chapter Summary

Chapter 15 presents a discussion of the lives of older women. Older women significantly outnumber the number of older men in the U.S. and typically live longer than men. Therefore, the concerns of older women often become the key issues of aging. These issues include a lack of access to health care and long-term care, and a lack of financial resources. In many instances, older women are cared for by other women as women are frequently the primary caregivers in the family and in long-term care facility settings. This gender-based caregiving of both the young and the old throughout one's life course can have its repercussions on the older female as she lacks financial resources in her later years due to a lack of or a broken pattern of external employment in her lifetime. Women who live alone, who are of an ethnic minority, or who are over age 75 face the greatest financial challenges. Conversely, many women have overcome many of the challenges of aging through social support provided through friendship. Increased attention to the needs and strengths of older women is partly due to the efforts of national groups such as the Older Women's League.

## Learning Objectives

*After reading chapter 15 the student should be able to:*
15.1 Discuss the economic conditions faced by older women as well as their health and social status and how these factors interact
15.2 Illustrate the strengths and resilience of older women
15.3 List the program and policy options to reduce older women's vulnerability to poverty, poor health, and social isolation

## Suggested Websites

*Aging and Women Getting Older*
http://www.4woman.gov/faq/
This page of the 4Women.gov site contains answers to frequently asked questions about women and aging and provides links to information on common conditions faced by older women.

*National Center on Women and Aging (NCWA)*
http://heller.brandeis.edu/national/index.html
This site provides an overview of the work of the NCWA, which includes empowering and advocating for older women in regard to income security, health, and caregiving.

*Woman Sage*
http://womansage.com/
This site provides information on women and aging, such as issues related to health, money, travel, relationships, and caregiving.

## Additional Resources

Stephenson, Peter H., Nuala K. Wolffe, Rory Coughlan and Sharon D. Koehn. 1999. "A Methodological Discourse on Gender, Independence, and Frailty: Applied Dimensions of Identity Construction in Old Age." *Journal of Aging Studies*. 13:391–401

Sugar, Judith A., Jamie L. K. Anstee, Stephan Desrochers, and Edina E. Jambor. 2002. "Gender Bias in Gerontological Education: The Status of Older Women." *Gerontology and Geriatrics Education*. 22:43–55.

Tunaley, Jillian R., Susan R. Walsh, Paula Nicolson. 1999. "'I Am Not That Bad for My Age': The Meaning of Body Size and Eating in the Lives of Older Women." *Ageing and Society*. 19: 741–760.

# CHAPTER 16: SOCIAL POLICIES TO ADDRESS SOCIAL PROBLEMS

## Chapter Outline

I. Variations among Policies and Programs
II. Factors Affecting the Development of Public Policies
    A. Values Affecting Social Policy
    B. Economic Context
III. The Development of Public Policies for Older People
    A. 1930 to 1950
    B. 1960 to 1970: Program Expansion
    C. 1980 to 1990: Program Reduction
    D. 1990s: Diversity and Deficit Spending
    E. Era of the Market and Personal Responsibility
IV. Income Security Programs
    A. Social Security
    B. Future of Social Security
    C. Supplemental Security Insurance
V. Private Pensions and Income Tax Provisions
    A. Private Pensions
    B. Income Tax Provisions
VI. Social Services
VII. Policy Dilemmas
    A. Age-Based vs. Need-Based Programs
    B. Politics of Productivity vs. Politics of Entitlement
    C. Intergenerational Inequity Framework
    D. Critique of The Intergenerational Inequity Framework
    E. Interdependence of Generations Framework
VIII. Who is Responsible?
    A. Reductions in Government Support
IX. Implications for the Future
X. Summary

## Chapter Summary

Chapter 16 presents the history and contemporary challenges of the social policies which address the social problems facing older adults. Older adults are not a homogeneous group; they are quite a diverse group based on gender, socioeconomic status, race and residential community size. This diversity is often a considerable barrier to uniting older adults as a political resource.

Cultural values and beliefs greatly influence the availability of social programs. In the past, age entitlement programs were based on the public value that all older adults were deserving of public assistance. Most of the funding for age-based programs since the 1960s has been Medicare and Old Age and Survivors and Disability Insurance of Social Security (OASDI). More recently, such age-based entitlement programs have been called into question due to the expanding nature of the programs and the improvements made in the standard of living of older adults. There has been a resulting public sentiment that age-based entitlement programs should be reduced or restructured, such as through means-testing or privatization.

When compared to European countries, the U.S. has lagged behind in its development for policies that address the needs of older adults. In 1935 the Social Security Act was the first major policy addressing the concerns of the older population. Subsequently, in 1965 the passage of the Medicare legislation also substantially affected the older population in the U.S. Since the 1960s there has been a series of pieces of legislation which have addressed older adults' needs. For example, policies have addressed nutrition, respite care, low-income home energy, and volunteer programs. Debate about whether social programs for older adults should be age-based or need-based has led to the development of various social organizations that posit that older adults are benefiting at the cost of younger age groups. Organizations such as Generations United advocate for the interdependence of generations by claiming that assistance from young to old and old to young is a benefit for all who are involved. Older adults are not likely to come together as a unified group in support of age-based programs. Rather, their increasing diversity suggests that specializing group alliances will develop, resulting in policies that benefit both older adults and future generations. A challenge to a significant number of older adults is the cost of health care, especially home and community based long term care.

## Learning Objectives

*After reading chapter 16 the student should be able to:*
16.1  Define policy and differentiate the types public policies
16.2  List the factors that affect public policy development
16.3  Provide an overview of the history of aging policies from prior to the 1960s to today
16.4  Explain Social Security benefits, the fiscal challenges, and proposed reforms, including privatization and proposals to reduce gender inequalities
16.5  Discuss the direct social services funded through the Administration on Aging (AOA) and Title XX
16.6  Describe the major policy dilemmas and implications for future directions

## Key Terms and Key People

*Age-Based Programs*: programs only available to people of a certain age (p. 677)

*Aging Network*: the system of social services for older adults funded by the Older Americans Act (p. 698)

*Area Agencies on Aging*: offices on aging at the regional and local levels that plan and administer services to meet the needs of older adults within that area established and partially funded through the Older Americans Act (p. 699)

*Cash Substitute*: a benefit given in a form other than cash, such as a voucher, which may be exchanged for food rent, medical care, etc. (p. 677)

*Cash Transfer*: a benefit paid by cash or its equivalent (p. 677)

*Categorical*: in this context, a manner of dealing with public problems by addressing the problems of specific groups of persons rather than attempting solutions that are comprehensive or dealing with problems as they affect the entire population (p. 679)

*Contributory Plans*: programs providing benefits that require the beneficiary to contribute something toward the cost of the benefit (p. 677-678)

*Cost of Living Adjustments (COLA)* : changes in benefits designed to maintain steady purchasing power of such benefits (p. 683)

*Direct Benefit*: a benefit given directly, in the form of either a cash payment or of some commodity such as food or housing (p. 677)

*Eligibility Criteria*: factors that determine the ability of programs to deliver to benefits to people (p. 677)

*Entitlement Programs*: government programs organized in such as way that appropriations from a legislative body are not required; rather, eligibility on the part of the applicants triggers receipt of benefits regardless of the total cost of the program (p. 675)

*Generational Investment*: investments made by one generation for the benefit of another, such as the payment of Social Security taxes by the working population for the benefit of retirees, the services provided by older persons for the care of children, and the payment of property taxes that benefit school children (p. 704)

*Generational Justice:* older adults receiving benefits based on age is morally justifiable since all adults can eventually benefit from age-based programs (p. 702)

*Indirect Benefit*: a benefit given through tax deductions or exemptions or other indirect means (p. 677)

*Interdependence of Generations Framework*: recognition of intergenerational transfers that occur across the life span (p. 704)

*Intergenerational Inequity*: the view that one generation or age group receives benefits that are disproportional to those received by another (p. 702)

*Need-Based (or Means-Based) Entitlement Programs*: social programs delivered to persons who meet defined criteria of eligibility based on need or ability to pay for the benefits (p. 677)

*Non-contributory Programs*: programs providing benefits that do not require the beneficiary to contribute toward the cost of the benefit (p. 678)

*Older Americans Act*: federal legislation for a network of social services specifically for older people (p. 677)

*Politics of Entitlement*:  political preferences, especially as applied to elders, for the allocation of resources based on notions of older persons as needy, worthy, and deserving of public support (p. 701)

*Politics of Productivity*:  political preferences, especially as applied to elders, for the allocation of resources based on a recognition of the diversity of the aging population (some are well-off, others are poor; some are capable of continued productive work, while others are ill or disabled) (p. 701)

*Privitization*:  changes in Social Security that would divert payroll taxes to private investment accounts (p. 692)

*Selective Benefits*:  benefits available on an individually determined need or mean basis (p. 678)

*Social Policy*:  government policy designed to address a social problem or issue (p. 676)

*Social Programs*:  the visible manifestations of policies (p. 677)

*Title XX* or *the Social Services Block Grant*:  funding for social services (e.g., homemaking chores, adult day care) based on need, not age (p. 697)

*Universal Benefits*:  benefits available on the basis of social right to all persons belonging to a designated group (p. 678)

## Discussion Topics

- What factors underlie the relatively slow development of social policy for older adults in the United States, and the incremental, residual nature of the policies that have been formulated? How does this contrast with other Western industrialized societies?

- Identify the pros and cons of age-based versus needs-based services.  Which approach—or combination of approaches—do you support and why?

- What do you perceive to be some limitations or gaps of the current Social Security system? What is your position on the advantages and disadvantages of recommendations to privatize Social Security, such as encouraging enrollees to invest part of their payroll taxes in the stock market?

- Debate the arguments expressed by the intergenerational inequity proponents and those of the interdependence of generation's perspective.  What are the strengths and limitations of each argument?  Where do you stand in terms of these arguments?  What is the evidence to support your position?  In your discussion, address the strengths of the "politics of productivity" and the "New Aging" paradigm.

- Describe the range of services offered through the Older Americans Act and the role of Area Agencies on Aging in providing these services. How does the OAA assure widespread access to these programs?

- What is your perspective on the appropriate division of responsibility between the public and private sectors in addressing problems facing older people? Provide a rationale for your point of view.

- What are the primary ways that the social policies of the "New Aging" in the twenty-first century will differ from current public policies?

- Describe the role of private pensions in improving the financial adequacy of only some retirees. How do these pensions perpetuate gender, ethnic, and income inequities into old age?

- Describe and differentiate programs funded by Title XX versus the Older Americans Act.

- Identify one major societal change that you view as necessary to improve the quality of older persons' lives. What are the barriers to this change? What would be a strategy to bring about the needed change?

## Classroom Activities and Student Projects

*Activity 16.1: SSA Guest Speaker*

Invite a speaker from the Social Security Administration to speak about the history, finances, and future of Social Security. Before the speaker arrives, ask the students to write a brief statement on their thoughts on Social Security. They might address such questions as: Do they think Social Security will be there for them when they get older? Where do their ideas on Social Security come from? Then, based on the speaker's presentation, ask the students to write a reaction paper. Their reaction paper should address how the speaker's presentation compares to their ideas about Social Security they wrote in their first essay. Did they learn anything new? Did any of their ideas about Social Security change? If so, how or why?

*Activity 16.2: Journal Article Review*

Assign the students to each read one academic journal article on a social problem affecting older adults. Limitations on the article selection could include selecting an article from a sociological or gerontological journal, an article that was published in the last five years, and an article that investigates a topic related to chapter 16. The students would then need to access, read and summarize the article for a 3–5 page paper.

# CHAPTER 17: HEALTH AND LONG-TERM CARE POLICY AND PROGRAMS

## Chapter Outline

I.  Health and Long-Term Care Expenditures
      A. Factors Underlying Growing Costs
II. Medicare
      A. Medicare-Funded Home Health Care
      B. Efforts to Reduce Medicare Costs
      C. The New Medicare
      D. Medicare Reform and Prescription Drug Coverage
III. Medicaid
      A. Medicaid-Funded Nursing Home Care
      B. Medicaid-Funded Home Health Care
      C. Eligibility for Medicaid Home Health Care and Waiver Program
      D. Medicaid Spend-Down
IV. Private Supplemental and Long-Term Care Insurance
      A. Resultant Inequities
V.  Health and Long-Term Care Reforms
      A. Health Maintenance Organizations
      B. Social Health Maintenance Organizations and Other Innovative Programs
VI. Implications for the Future
VII. Summary

## Chapter Summary

Chapter 17 presents the long-term care programs available to older adults and contemporary issues facing these programs, older adults, and the federal government. Health care costs for older adults have been skyrocketing, which has led to both cost-containment efforts such as greater deductibles and co-payments and the availability of more options for healthcare, such as managed care and HMOs. Medicare is the primary source of funding for the acute health care needs of older adults. It is not a significant source of funding for nursing home care. Medicaid is the primary source of funding for long-term care needs, such as nursing home care. Recently there have been considerable funding cuts to the Medicaid program at the state level and many healthcare agencies limit the number of Medicaid recipients they will care for. Both of these factors have led to challenges for older adults to access long-term care. Additional sources of funding include Title XX and the Older Americans Act, but their funding is limited. For some older adults private insurance provides the necessary funding for long-term care; however, this option is outside the financial reach of the majority of older adults. Health and long-term care financing will continue to be a hotly debated challenge in the coming years.

## Learning Objectives

*After reading chapter 17 the student should be able to:*
17.1 Define acute and long-term care as well as provide their status and expenditures
17.2 Discuss Medicare, home care, cost-reductions, and the 2003 prescription drug bill
17.3 Illustrate the growing need for long-term care, especially home care
17.4 Discuss Medicaid, community-based services, and nursing home care
17.5 Comprehend private long-term insurance, its costs, and its limitations
17.6 List cost-containment initiatives, especially Medicare managed care
17.7 Explain state innovations under Medicare and Medicaid

## Key Terms and Key People

*Capitated Payments*: payments for services based on a predetermined amount per person per day rather than fees services (p. 728)

*Cash and Counseling Programs:* funded by the Robert Wood Johnson Foundation, older adults in three states receive a cash payment to purchase services and products they need (p. 740)

*Centers for Medicare and Medicaid Services (CMS)*: the federal agency that administers the Medicare and Medicaid programs (p. 728)

*Consumer-Directed Care:* under the Medicaid waiver system, older adults can hire personal care attendants, including family members (except for spouses) (p. 740)

*Diagnostic Related Groupings (DRGs):* Medicare payments are fixed prior to admission to hospital or home care, based on diagnostic category, medical condition, and expected length of stay (p. 726)

*Health Maintenance Organizations (HMOs)*: health plans that combine coverage of health care costs and delivery of health care for a prepaid premium, with members typically receiving services from personnel employed by or under contract to the HMO (p. 729)

*Interim Payment System (IPS):* sets stringent caps on cost per home health visit and per beneficiary (p. 728)

*Long-Term Care Insurance*: private insurance designed to cover the costs of facility and sometimes home-based service for people with chronic disabilities (p. 743)

*Managed Care*: policies under which patients are provided health care services under the supervision of a single professional, usually physician (p. 718)

*Medicaid*: a federal and state means-tested welfare program of medical assistance for the categorically needy, regardless of age (p. 735)

*Medicaid Waiver Program:* allows states to provide home care services to elders at risk of nursing home placement "outside" of Medicaid regulations; must be budget neutral (p. 739)

*Medical Savings Account*: proposed Medicare program that will allow beneficiaries to carry private "catastrophic" insurance for serious illness and pay routine costs from a special account (p. 729)

*Medicare*: the social insurance program, part of the Social Security Act of 1965, intended to provide financial protection against the cost of hospital and physician care for people age 65 and over (p. 721)

*Medicare Plus Choice/Medicare Advantage*: starting in 2002, Medicare beneficiaries can choose between traditional Medicare and a Choice Plan that include HMOs (p. 748)

*Medicare Part D:* prescription drug reform legislation; older adults pay for private insurance plan to cover medications; also known as the Medicare Modernization Act (p. 730)

*"Medi-gap" Policies:* private supplemental insurance to help with the catastrophic costs of intensive care, numerous tests, or extended hospitalization (p. 733)

*On Lok*: a comprehensive program of health and social services provided to very frail older adults, first started in San Francisco, with the goal of preventing or delaying nursing home placement (p. 749)

*Parity*: mental health services covered at the same rate as health care services for physical disorders (p. 723)

*Preferred Provider Organizations (PPO)*: networks of independent physicians, hospitals, and other health care providers who contract with an insurance entity to provide care at discounted rates (p. 729)

*Program for All Inclusive Care for the Elderly (PACE)*: federal demonstration program that replicated On Lok's integrated services to attempt to prevent nursing home placement (p. 749)

*Prospective Payment Systems (PPS)*: a system of reimbursing hospitals and physicians based on the diagnostic category of the patient rather than fees for each service provided, as applied to inpatient services (p. 728)

*Social Health Maintenance Organizations (SHMOs)*: prepaid health plans that provide both acute and long-term care to voluntarily enrolled Medicare beneficiaries; only one program is now funded (p. 748)

*Spend Down*: to use up assets for personal needs, especially health care, in order to become qualified for Medicaid (p. 737)

*Subacute Care*: intensive health services to patients after a hospital stay (p. 721)

# Discussion Topics

- The general public increasingly is concerned about the "crisis in health care." What do you perceive to be the primary causes for these increasing costs?

- Describe differences between health services provided under Medicare (Part A versus Part B) and Medicaid.

- How would you respond to arguments that Medicare and Medicaid must be cut and consequently that health care benefits to older people must be limited?

- Describe the basic ways that long-term care services are organized and funded. What are the underlying assumptions and the consequences of these arrangements?

- What kinds of changes, if any, would you recommend be made to Medicare? In this discussion, consider the consequences of efforts to change Medicare, such as DRGs and increased co-payments, as well as proposed changes such as limiting the age of eligibility.

- Discuss the services allowed under Medicare Choice. What impact would you expect this program to have on older adults' use of preventive health services?

- Describe an "ideal" medigap insurance program that would be affordable by a broad range of older adults.

- What kinds of changes, if any, would you recommend be made to Medicaid services in your state?

- Describe the pros and cons of private long-term care insurance.

## Classroom Activities and Student Projects

*Activity 17.1 Congressional Testimony*
Tell your students to presume that they are testifying before Congress on the need for long-term care reform. What would be the major components of their proposed reform with regard to older people? To prepare to answer this question, have the students watch a segment of Congressional testimony on an age-related issue on cable television. After viewing a segment of testimony, have the students develop and role play what they would say if they were the ones testifying before Congress.

*Activity 17.2 Medicare and Medicaid*
Have the students develop a series of questions they have about Medicare and/or Medicaid. Then have the students go onto the Internet to look for answers. What did they find? Did they look at credible sources? Do they now have additional questions? What did others in the class find? How easy or difficult was it for the students to find out this information? Would it be the same for older adults?

## Suggested Films

*These films are not available through Allyn & Bacon.*

*Living Longer...Living Better?* (2000)
Films for the Humanities and Sciences, 29 minutes, $89.95 VHS/DVD
Thanks to recent advances in medicine, longevity is on the rise. But will America's youth-oriented society finally develop the maturity to respect its elders? And will the Medicare and Social Security infrastructures be able to meet the needs of the Baby Boomers?

*Medicine at the Crossroads* (1993)
Terra Nova Films, 60 minutes, $95 VHS
This film profiles the health care systems in India, Ireland, and Arizona to illustrate how social and cultural forces influence health care systems.

*Who Cares: Chronic Illness in America* (2001)
Films for the Humanities and Sciences, 57 minutes, $129.95 VHS/DVD
This film is a Fred Friendly Seminar which discusses the limitations of the health care system, especially as it pertains to chronic illnesses.

## Suggested Websites

*Disability and Aging Issues*
http://www.cms.hhs.gov/Medicaid/consumerag.asp
This site is sponsored the Centers for Medicare and Medicaid Services, the federal agency governing Medicare and Medicaid services, and provides detailed information and links to resources relating to disability and aging issues.

*Medicare*
http://www.medicare.gov/
This site is the official site of the federal Medicare program and provides information on the plan choices and options available to Medicare recipients.

*National PACE Association*
http://www.npaonline.org/
This site is the homepage of the National PACE (Programs of All-inclusive Care for the Elderly) Association and provides details on the organization's work in advocating for older adults' chronic care needs.

*On Lok SeniorHealth*
http://www.onlok.org/
This site provides information on On Lok, a PACE certified program in San Francisco.

## Additional Resources

Jaffe, Dale. 1990. "Teaching Health Care and Aging: Toward a Conceptual Integration." *Teaching Sociology.* 18:313–318.

Murphy, Thomas N. and Mosher-Ashley, Pearl. 1999. "Writing Descriptions of Innovative Aging Programs Facilitates Undergraduate Student Presentations at Professional Conferences." *Gerontology and Geriatrics Education.* 20:79–87.

Pratt, John R. 2004. *Long-Term Care: Managing Across the Continuum, Second Edition.* Boston: Jones and Bartlett Publishers.

# Chapter 1  The Growth of Social Gerontology

1) The rectangular survival curve:
    A) is considered to be the ideal survival curve and is dependent on a fixed maximum lifespan
    B) has become more rectangular over the past century
    C) is not a good representation of changes in worldwide life expectations
    D) both A and B

Answer: D
*Diff: 3        Page Ref: 15–16*

2) The oldest–old subgroup:
    A) is the slowest growing segment of the U.S. population
    B) has about as much education as younger groups
    C) has the same income as younger groups
    D) is the fastest growing segment of the U.S. population

Answer: D
*Diff: 2        Page Ref: 16–17*

3) According to the text:
    A) the "young–old" are those individuals aged 50–65
    B) the "old–old" are those aged 65–75
    C) the "oldest–old" are those aged 85
    D) "old–old" refers to all people age 65+

Answer: C
*Diff: 1        Page Ref: 6*

4) Mary is 60–years–old, drives a Corvette, and has a teenage daughter. She would be considered to have a young:
    A) biological age                          B) chronological age
    C) sociocultural age                       D) psychological age

Answer: D
*Diff: 1        Page Ref: 4*

5) In terms of psychological age, which of the following people is the youngest?
    A) Michelle, a college graduate at age 17        B) Anne, a secretary at age 25
    C) Cathy, a college sophomore at age 48          D) Sarah, a school teacher at age 55

Answer: C
*Diff: 2        Page Ref: 4*

6) The state which has the largest proportion of individuals aged 65 and above is:
    A) Florida            B) Minnesota            C) Utah            D) California

Answer: A
*Diff: 1        Page Ref: 26*

7) The state which has the largest number of individuals aged 65 and above is:
    A) Florida            B) Oregon            C) Washington            D) California

Answer: D
*Diff: 1        Page Ref: 26*

8) The elderly support ratio:
   A) assumes the low birth rate will increase
   B) projects that by 2030 there will be 5 working people per retired person
   C) does not take into account that some older people remain in the work force
   D) decreases as the population ages

Answer: C
*Diff: 3*     *Page Ref: 23*

9) Educational attainment varies widely among the population aged 65 +. Those least likely to have a high school degree are _____, those most likely are _____.
   A) men/women
   B) young-old/oldest-old
   C) Hispanics/non-Hispanic whites
   D) African Americans/non-Hispanic whites

Answer: C
*Diff: 3*     *Page Ref: 26*

10) The term "compression of morbidity" refers to:
    A) fewer people dying from disease
    B) functional decline due to disease is minimized
    C) years of healthy life expectancy
    D) illness affecting only the last few years of life

Answer: D
*Diff: 3*     *Page Ref: 28*

11) The distinction between active and dependent life expectancy is useful in illustrating:
    A) differences between men and women
    B) that not all gains in life expectancy are positive
    C) that most of the gain in life expectancy is a negative gain
    D) the advantages of increased life expectancy for ethnic minorities

Answer: B
*Diff: 2*     *Page Ref: 28*

12) A major problem with the cross-sectional research method is:
    A) respondents become test wise
    B) respondent attrition (loss of subjects) can occur over time
    C) cohort effects may emerge rather than the effects of aging
    D) the message of measurement may change over time

Answer: C
*Diff: 2*     *Page Ref: 33*

13) Regarding the Gerontological Society of America and its publications:
    A) the Journals of Gerontology deal primarily with the psychology of aging
    B) this organization focuses on elders' social welfare
    C) this is a national organization of physicians interested in older patients
    D) this organization includes educators, researchers, and clinicians

Answer: D
*Diff: 2*     *Page Ref: 31*

14) Which of the following institutions and settings have contributed significantly to the study of aging during the 1950s and 1960s?
    A) The Baltimore Longitudinal Study
    B) The Alaska Institute of Aging
    C) The North Dakota Institute on Aging
    D) The New England Centenarian Study
Answer: A
*Diff: 2      Page Ref: 31*

15) A major advantage of longitudinal research designs is that they:
    A) allow for practice effects
    B) eliminate cohort effects
    C) allow a distinction between age and time by testing
    D) compare different groups
Answer: B
*Diff: 2      Page Ref: 33*

16) Which two effects are confounded in cross-sectional research?
    A) age and cohort
    B) age and time-of-measurement
    C) cohort and time-of-measurement
    D) cohort and practice
Answer: A
*Diff: 2      Page Ref: 33*

17) Which two effects are confounded in longitudinal research?
    A) age and cohort
    B) age and time-of-measurement
    C) cohort and time-of-measurement
    D) cohort and practice
Answer: B
*Diff: 2      Page Ref: 33*

18) A valid measure is one that:
    A) yields the same result from repeated measurements
    B) accurately reflects the concept it is intended to measure
    C) is used only in cross-sectional studies
    D) is used only in psychological testing
Answer: B
*Diff: 3      Page Ref: 37*

19) A researcher wants to determine the range of oral disease among the older population by examining the mouths of all 200 residents of a nursing home. The findings cannot be generalized to all older people because:
    A) the sample is not valid
    B) the data are not reliable
    C) the concept is not correctly measured
    D) the sample is not representative
Answer: D
*Diff: 3      Page Ref: 36*

20) Selective dropout from longitudinal studies results in:
    A) poorer test scores with time
    B) healthier and more motivated elders in the final sample
    C) sicker and less educated elders in the final sample
    D) few differences between drop-outs and those who remain
Answer: B
*Diff: 2      Page Ref: 35*

21) In all organ systems normal declines occur:
  A) after age 30
  C) after a physical trauma
  B) in one's 5th decade
  D) after age 60

  Answer: A
  *Diff: 2      Page Ref: 5*

22) Females born in 2005 have an average life expectancy of:
  A) 75.2 years      B) 80.4 years      C) 89.5 years      D) 99.5 years

  Answer: B
  *Diff: 2      Page Ref: 14*

23) What concept captures how earlier life experiences and decisions affect opportunities in later life?
  A) Life course
  C) Active–aging
  B) Person–environment
  D) Environmental press

  Answer: A
  *Diff: 2      Page Ref: 8*

24) Who wrote one of the first textbooks on aging called "The History of Life and Death"?
  A) Roger Bacon
  C) Nathan Shock
  B) Ivan Pavlov
  D) Adolph Quetelet

  Answer: A
  *Diff: 2      Page Ref: 29*

25) The expansion of research in social gerontology in the late 19th century and early 20th century is due to:
  A) the growth of the population over age 65
  B) the need to modify policies for an older population
  C) a mandate by universities and research institutes
  D) both A and B

  Answer: D
  *Diff: 2      Page Ref: 38*

26) In general, the chronological age of most people is consistent with their psychological and biological age.
  Answer: FALSE
  *Diff: 1      Page Ref: 4*

27) More older adults today subsist on incomes below the poverty level compared to the late 1950s.
  Answer: FALSE
  *Diff: 1      Page Ref: 27*

28) Relocating a frail elder to a nursing home is an example of increased environmental press in Lawton and Nahemow's model.
  Answer: TRUE
  *Diff: 3      Page Ref: 9*

29) Personal competence in the person–environment includes family members' assistance to the older person.
  Answer: FALSE
  *Diff: 2      Page Ref: 10*

30) The study of aging is primarily a study of diseases.
    Answer: FALSE
    *Diff: 1      Page Ref: 5*

31) Life expectancy refers to the average years of life one can expect to live, whereas maximum life span refers to the maximum number of years a given species is expected to live.
    Answer: TRUE
    *Diff: 1      Page Ref: 13*

32) Life expectancy after age 80 in the United States is longer than in Japan and Sweden.
    Answer: TRUE
    *Diff: 2      Page Ref: 15*

33) Racial crossover effect describes the tendency for Caucasians to live longer than African Americans.
    Answer: FALSE
    *Diff: 2      Page Ref: 19*

34) Today's cohort of young-old has the same life expectancy, whether they are white or persons of color.
    Answer: FALSE
    *Diff: 1      Page Ref: 14, 24*

35) The proportion of people aged 65 and older among ethnic minority groups will increase in the 21st century.
    Answer: TRUE
    *Diff: 1      Page Ref: 24-25*

36) Surveys of the health status of young-old Americans today provide considerable support for compressed morbidity in the future.
    Answer: TRUE
    *Diff: 2      Page Ref: 28*

37) Cross-sectional research designs are the best method to determine causation.
    Answer: FALSE
    *Diff: 2      Page Ref: 33*

38) Older people who drop out of longitudinal studies tend to be those who score lower on intelligence tests and are more socially isolated.
    Answer: TRUE
    *Diff: 2      Page Ref: 34*

39) Longitudinal studies are currently the most widely used research designs in gerontology.
    Answer: FALSE
    *Diff: 2      Page Ref: 33*

40) Sequential designs are particularly useful in studies of cognitive changes with aging.
    Answer: TRUE
    *Diff: 2      Page Ref: 35*

41) _____ focuses on how to prevent or manage the diseases of aging.
    Answer: Geriatrics
    *Diff: 1      Page Ref: 3*

42) _____ refers to an individual's changing roles and relationships with family and friends, in both paid and unpaid productive roles, and within organizations.

Answer: Social aging
*Diff: 2*     *Page Ref: 4*

43) _____ is the process of optimizing opportunities for health, participation, and security in order to enhance quality of life as people age.

Answer: Active aging
*Diff: 2*     *Page Ref: 7*

44) In 1900 the average life expectancy at birth in the United States was _____ years.

Answer: 47
*Diff: 2*     *Page Ref: 13*

45) Females born in the U.S. in 2005 can expect to reach _____ years.

Answer: 80.4
*Diff: 2*     *Page Ref: 14*

46) Explain the concept of the active aging framework.

Answer: The active aging framework is the process of optimizing opportunities for health, participation, and security in order to enhance quality of life as people age. It shifts our thinking of old age as a time of passivity to one of continued participation in life and that aging is a lifelong process.
*Diff: 2*     *Page Ref: 7*

47) Identify the main reason the older population is growing.

Answer: One of the key factors contributing to the growth of older population is longer life expectancy. In 1900, the average life expectancy was 47 years. By 2005, the average life expectancy was 77.9 years.
*Diff: 2*     *Page Ref: 13-14*

48) What is a centenarian and what have studies found about centenarians and their lives?

Answer: Centenarians are individuals who are over 100 years old. There are a variety of studies on these individuals and they look at both genetic and social factors. Genetic factors determine how well an older person copes with disease, but environmental factors may also influence overall health and functional ability.
*Diff: 2*     *Page Ref: 18-20*

49) What can you tell about a population by looking at its population pyramid?

Answer: A population pyramid tells you about a population age composition and gender composition as well as support ratios. It breaks up the population into 10-year cohorts. As the population ages and fewer children are born, the pyramid becomes more column-shaped.
*Diff: 2*     *Page Ref: 20-23*

50) Discuss the pros and cons of using longitudinal research design for studying gerontological topics.

Answer: Eliminates cohort effects by studying the same people over time, but does not allow a distinction between age and time of testing, cannot separate effects of other variables and has the potential for practice effects. Attrition and resulting selective dropout can compromise a longitudinal study.
*Diff: 2*     *Page Ref: 15-17*

# Chapter 2   Historical and Cross–Cultural Issues in Aging

1) The diverse cultures around the world illustrate that:
   A) the social and economic status among today's elders is very different from earlier periods
   B) the experience of older adults is essentially the same across many cultures
   C) traditional skills and knowledge do not determine the respect and authority conferred to older adults
   D) in most cultures, old age brings with it respect of others
   Answer: A
   *Diff: 3      Page Ref: 50*

2) Which of the following countries has the highest proportion of older adults?
   A) Sweden              B) Greece              C) Italy              D) Germany
   Answer: C
   *Diff: 1      Page Ref: 44*

3) Characteristics of modernization that contribute to the decline of older adults' status in traditional societies include:
   A) literacy                          B) health technology
   C) employment status                 D) both A and B
   Answer: D
   *Diff: 2      Page Ref: 51*

4) The rectangularization of a population structure is due, in part, by:
   A) low birth rate                    B) high birth rate
   C) decreased life expectancy         D) both A and C
   Answer: A
   *Diff: 3      Page Ref: 44*

5) According to modernization theory, which of the following statements is <u>not</u> true?
   A) As we depend less on manual labor and rely more on machines, the aged are maintaining their esteem and influence in society.
   B) Social changes that accompany modernization cause younger and older generations to become increasingly separated.
   C) Urbanization has improved the status of older adults.
   D) both A and B
   Answer: C
   *Diff: 2      Page Ref: 51*

6) A revival of interest in cultural pride resulting in an increased esteem for older adults can be seen in which culture?
   A) African American                  B) European
   C) Chinese                           D) American Indian
   Answer: D
   *Diff: 2      Page Ref: 57*

7) Among the following characteristics, which is the <u>least</u> important one for enhancing older people's status?
   A) knowledge of traditional skills   B) chronological age
   C) information control               D) their social contributions
   Answer: B
   *Diff: 2      Page Ref: 50*

8) Societies in advanced stages of modernization may become more aware of the older population's devalued status through:
   A) religious organizations
   B) politicians
   C) advertising and television
   D) peer pressure
   Answer: C
   *Diff: 2*     *Page Ref: 53*

9) The major premise of modernization theory is that with modernization:
   A) older people's status increases in most societies
   B) there are more opportunities for intergenerational interaction
   C) older people experience a higher quality of life
   D) older people often lose political and social power
   Answer: D
   *Diff: 2*     *Page Ref: 51*

10) In relation to modernization, occupation and education:
   A) have a reversed J-shaped relation
   B) show an increase, but later decline
   C) suggest that after initial stages of modernization, status differences between generations widen
   D) suggest that after initial stages of modernization, the status of older people falls
   Answer: A
   *Diff: 2*     *Page Ref: 52*

11) Which of the following statements about the care of older persons in Japan is true?
   A) Traditionally, Japanese families have cared for their members, and this pattern has not changed significantly.
   B) Japanese families assume no more responsibility for their older relatives than do Western families.
   C) The proportion of older couples living with adult children has declined since 1985.
   D) The old are such a small proportion of the Japanese population that their care is not a significant problem.
   Answer: C
   *Diff: 2*     *Page Ref: 55*

12) Which is true of role changes and suicide among older adults?
   A) Generally, Japanese women aged 75 and older have lower suicide rates than their counterparts in English speaking countries.
   B) In the U.S., suicide rates increase for the 65 and older group when compared to the 40-50 age group.
   C) Suicide rates of older women do not differ by country.
   D) Asian men aged 75 and older have higher suicide rates than any other age group of Asian men.
   Answer: D
   *Diff: 2*     *Page Ref: 52*

13) According to social exchange theory:
   A) as society becomes more modernized, older people lose respect
   B) most societies have a sense of reverence and deference toward elders
   C) it is possible to achieve a balance between costs and contributions made by older adults and the extent of power and respect they command
   D) none of the above

Answer: C
*Diff: 1      Page Ref: 57*

14) Which of the following factors is most important in mitigating the impact of modernization on older people?
   A) expectations of continued financial support by parents
   B) cultural values of respect toward elders
   C) continued participation of elders in the workforce
   D) strong national welfare systems

Answer: B
*Diff: 3      Page Ref: 56*

15) In both contemporary and historic times, elders in most societies have gained power in society because of their:
   A) wisdom
   B) political connections
   C) respect from younger members of society
   D) control of property

Answer: D
*Diff: 3      Page Ref: 50*

16) Values of filial piety and ancestor worship in Japan are based on:
   A) Confucian values                B) Judeo–Christian values
   C) Muslim values                   D) Buddhist values

Answer: A
*Diff: 3      Page Ref: 53*

17) Which is <u>not</u> a reason for the growth of the old–old in developing countries?
   A) immunization                    B) medical care
   C) increasing birth rates          D) improved nutrition

Answer: C
*Diff: 3      Page Ref: 46*

18) Which stages are part of the four–stage life cycle for high–caste men in traditional Hindu law?
   A) student, householder, sage, mendicant
   B) student, merchant, ascetic, mendicant
   C) student, householder, ascetic, mendicant
   D) teacher, householder, ascetic, mendicant

Answer: C
*Diff: 3      Page Ref: 58*

19) According to modernization theory scientific technology:
    A) creates new jobs primarily for the young
    B) increases infant mortality and maternal deaths
    C) reduces the need for literacy and education
    D) increases the number of new jobs for older adults

Answer: A
*Diff: 2*      *Page Ref: 51*

20) In which culture do older women play an especially valuable role?
    A) Aborigine culture in Australia      B) Zulu culture
    C) Chinese culture                     D) both A and B

Answer: D
*Diff: 3*      *Page Ref: 57*

21) The primary caregivers of Japanese elders are:
    A) middle-aged women          B) their grandchildren
    C) middle-aged males          D) younger adult women

Answer: A
*Diff: 3*      *Page Ref: 55*

22) According to Cowgill's modernization theory, the application of health technology includes all of the following <u>except</u>:
    A) reduced infant mortality          B) reduced maternal death
    C) prolonged adult life              D) decreased the number of older persons

Answer: D
*Diff: 2*      *Page Ref: 50*

23) Causes for the decline in the percentage of parents living with children in Japanese culture include:
    A) industrialization
    B) urbanization
    C) increasing number of children since 1950
    D) both A and B

Answer: A
*Diff: 1*      *Page Ref: 54–55*

24) In which country do older adults over age 70 receive free basic medical services?
    A) Japan                    B) the United States
    C) the United Kingdom       D) China

Answer: A
*Diff: 3*      *Page Ref: 54*

25) Older immigrants to the U.S. are:
    A) less likely to be educated
    B) less likely to receive government benefits
    C) less likely to live in poverty
    D) more likely to use health services

Answer: A
*Diff: 2*      *Page Ref: 59*

26) Comparative sociocultural gerontology has been useful in determining aspects of aging that are universal versus aspects of aging that are shaped by culture.

Answer: TRUE
Diff: 2      Page Ref: 50

27) Older women in China are more functionally and economically disadvantaged than older Chinese men.

Answer: TRUE
Diff: 2      Page Ref: 53

28) Elderly Japanese immigrants are more likely to live independently than elderly Mexican immigrants.

Answer: TRUE
Diff: 2      Page Ref: 60

29) The U.S. state with the largest number of non-citizen immigrants is Texas.

Answer: FALSE
Diff: 2      Page Ref: 61

30) The greatest proportion of elderly immigrants to the U.S. between 1991 and 2000 were from South and Central America.

Answer: TRUE
Diff: 2      Page Ref: 58

31) The majority of older immigrants to the U.S. follow their adult children.

Answer: TRUE
Diff: 2      Page Ref: 59

32) The majority of middle aged people in Japan believe that care of older parents is the childrens' responsibility.

Answer: TRUE
Diff: 2      Page Ref: 54

33) The dependency ratio for older retired persons is expected to drop by 2030 in all countries.

Answer: FALSE
Diff: 2      Page Ref: 48

34) In the next 30 years, Mexico will have a higher growth rate in their older population than will the U.S.

Answer: TRUE
Diff: 2      Page Ref: 46

35) Filial piety in traditional cultures results in a desire to live in multigenerational households with aging parents.

Answer: FALSE
Diff: 2      Page Ref: 53

36) Japan has the highest absolute number of older adults.

Answer: FALSE
Diff: 3      Page Ref: 46

37) Early phases of rapid urbanization in many developing countries has led to loss of prestige and support for older adults.

Answer: TRUE
*Diff: 2      Page Ref: 51*

38) As societies move beyond rapid modernization, status differences between generations decline.

Answer: TRUE
*Diff: 2      Page Ref: 52*

39) Despite its advanced industrial status, Japan has maintained strong intergenerational relations by continuing the pattern of retired elders moving in with the oldest son and his family.

Answer: FALSE
*Diff: 2      Page Ref: 55*

40) Modernization Theory was one of the first explanations of the declining status of the old in our society.

Answer: TRUE
*Diff: 1      Page Ref: 51*

41) Modernization theory has been advanced primarily by _____.

Answer: Cowgill
*Diff: 2      Page Ref: 51*

42) _____ values of filial piety and ancestor worship have helped maintain older persons' relatively high status in Japanese society.

Answer:    Confucian
*Diff: 2      Page Ref: 54*

43) The increase in older adults and low birth rate in China have contributed to the population structure taking on a _____ shape.

Answer:    Rectangular
*Diff: 3      Page Ref: 46*

44) Extended families in rural Thailand have adapted to the need for adult children to migrate to the cities by creating _____, where grandparents remain in their rural homes, caring for grandchildren while their adult children work in urban settings.

Answer: skip-generation households
*Diff: 3      Page Ref: 54*

45) Older adults who have come to the U.S. from countries experiencing political strife, war and unrest are called _____.

Answer: refugees
*Diff: 3      Page Ref: 59*

46) Explain Japan's aging crisis.

Answer: Japan is experiencing the most rapid rate of population aging in the world. By 2050, the 65 and older group will comprise 30% of the country's population. Resistance to immigration, which would bring in younger workers, is contributing to the need of economic support of retirees.

*Diff: 3      Page Ref: 45*

47) Discuss the effects of culture and modernization in Japan.

Answer: Japanese culture has traditionally revered older adults, however, the economic demands placed on the nuclear family have challenged this practice. The unprecedented numbers of older people have increased the costs of maintaining older members and have created dilemmas for the younger family members who are responsible for their care.

*Diff: 2      Page Ref: 54*

48) Thoroughly discuss Cowgill's Modernization Theory.

Answer: According to Modernization Theory the decline in status attributed to older adults is due to health technology, scientific technology, urbanization and literacy and mass education. As society becomes more modernized, older people lose political and social power.

*Diff: 3      Page Ref: 51*

49) Discuss "retired husband syndrome."

Answer: In Japan, the medical condition has been observed among women whose husbands have retired by age 60–65 and remain at home full-time, demanding attention from their wives. Women are reporting psychosomatic symptoms related to stress resulting from having to serve their husbands.

*Diff: 3      Page Ref: 55*

50) Define skipped generation households and discuss study findings about older Chinese adults living in three generation households vs. those living in skipped generation households.

Answer: Skipped generation households are those whose grandparents care for grandchildren in the absence of the child's parents. Those living in three generation households reported greater life satisfaction and less depression than those living in skipped generation households.

*Diff: 3      Page Ref: 54*

# Chapter 3 The Social Consequences of Physical Aging

1) A true biological change with aging:
   A) is universal for all members of the species
   B) tends to be progressive and gradual over time
   C) results in a series of diseases of aging
   D) both A and B

   Answer: D
   *Diff: 2      Page Ref: 71*

2) Which of the following theories of aging is an extension of cross linkage theory?
   A) The Free Radical Theory            B) The Wear and Tear Theory
   C) The Autoimmune Theory              D) The Cellular Theory of Aging

   Answer: A
   *Diff: 3      Page Ref: 73*

3) Biological studies of aging using animal models demonstrate that:
   A) DHEA can improve muscle strength and quality of life
   B) caloric restriction promotes health and longevity
   C) low-fat diets from infancy can prolong life
   D) both A and B

   Answer: B
   *Diff: 2      Page Ref: 75*

4) Regarding age-related dangers in body composition:
   A) proportion of fatty tissue increases only slightly from age 25 to 75
   B) muscle mass remains essentially the same as one ages
   C) aging results in increased obesity
   D) changes in body composition affect drug metabolism

   Answer: D
   *Diff: 2      Page Ref: 78-79*

5) With aging, the following changes are found in skin:
   A) secretions by sebaceous and sweat glands deteriorate
   B) there is generally an increase in blood circulation in the skin
   C) older individuals prefer cooler environments than younger persons
   D) the outer skin layer becomes thicker and more elastic

   Answer: A
   *Diff: 2      Page Ref: 79-80*

6) With regard to bone changes and gender:
   A) men tend to lose more bone mass than women as they age
   B) men tend to develop kyphosis more so than women
   C) bone mineral density declines mostly because of estrogen levels declining
   D) bone mineral density declines mostly because of a loss of testosterone

   Answer: C
   *Diff: 2      Page Ref: 81-82*

7) In relation to aging and sensation:
   A) over the life span, the sense of touch remains generally the same
   B) older persons tend to overreport actual pain experienced
   C) older persons can discriminate levels of pain as well as young persons
   D) loss of nerve endings causes a decline in touch sensitivity with aging

Answer: D
*Diff: 2*     *Page Ref: 83*

8) With age, vital lung capacity:
   A) declines very little over the life span of the average person
   B) declines at about half the rate for master athletes when compared to sedentary men
   C) declines more for older women than for older men
   D) declines and thus impairs daily functioning

Answer: B
*Diff: 2*     *Page Ref: 84*

9) Significant elevation of blood pressure is associated with all the following factors <u>except</u>:
   A) diet          B) obesity          C) lifestyle          D) old age

Answer: D
*Diff: 2*     *Page Ref: 85*

10) Regarding urinary functions, increased age results in:
   A) a decrease in bladder function but relatively little change in kidney function
   B) very small percentage of elders (3 to 5 percent) with problems
   C) urinary incontinence among as many as 30 percent in the community
   D) an increase of kidney volume and weight

Answer: C
*Diff: 2*     *Page Ref: 87*

11) Regarding the urinary system with aging:
   A) alcohol and caffeine consumption can prevent urinary incontinence
   B) the renal system declines more than most other organs
   C) dehydration is less of a problem with aging than in youth
   D) changes in the renal system cause drugs to be excreted faster than in young people

Answer: B
*Diff: 2*     *Page Ref: 87*

12) The gastrointestinal system changes in the following way with aging:
   A) secretion of stomach digestive juices decreases
   B) more enzymes are produced in the small intestine
   C) constipation does not afflict most older people
   D) food is passed through the stomach and intestines more rapidly

Answer: A
*Diff: 2*     *Page Ref: 88*

13) The major change in liver functioning with age is:
   A) the liver increases in size
   B) alcohol has less harmful affects than in younger people
   C) jaundice occurs at about the same rate as in younger people
   D) metabolism of medications by the liver declines

Answer: D
*Diff: 2*     *Page Ref: 88*

14) Slower reaction time with aging is most likely due to:
   A) slower response of neurotransmitters
   B) a rapid accumulation of lipofuscin in the brain
   C) a loss of brain mass
   D) anxiety about test taking

   Answer: A
   *Diff: 2       Page Ref: 90*

15) Older people often have more problems seeing under low lighting conditions. This is <u>most</u> likely due to:
   A) inability to modify the opening of the pupil
   B) a slower shift from rods to cones
   C) increased supply of oxygen to the retina
   D) discoloration of the lens of the eye

   Answer: B
   *Diff: 2       Page Ref: 95–97*

16) The structural change with aging that is most associated with hearing loss takes place in:
   A) the pinna          B) the cochlea          C) the stapes          D) the middle ear

   Answer: B
   *Diff: 2       Page Ref: 101*

17) An older person who is experiencing problems with depth perception could improve their home environment by:
   A) using color contrast where different levels meet
   B) using bright patterns on carpets throughout the house
   C) avoiding dark colors
   D) putting signs at the top of every stairway

   Answer: A
   *Diff: 2       Page Ref: 99*

18) Age-related hearing loss is called:
   A) presbycusis          B) tinnitus          C) osteosclerosis          D) ringing

   Answer: A
   *Diff: 3       Page Ref: 101*

19) As we age, our hair:
   A) becomes thinner                    B) becomes thicker
   C) darkens and grows slower           D) gains volume

   Answer: A
   *Diff: 1       Page Ref: 80*

20) The leading cause of blindness worldwide is:
   A) cataract                              B) glaucoma
   C) age related macular degeneration      D) accommodation

   Answer: A
   *Diff: 2       Page Ref: 97*

21) Sleep disturbances can be alleviated by:
   A) decreasing physical exercise
   B) decreasing exposure to natural light during the day
   C) increasing the intake of caffeine
   D) avoiding napping during the day
   Answer: D
   *Diff: 2      Page Ref: 91*

22) Which theory suggests that the human body, like a machine, simply wears out over time?
   A) Wear and Tear Theory              B) Cross–Linkage Theory
   C) Free Radical Theory               D) Autoimmune Theory
   Answer: A
   *Diff: 1      Page Ref: 72*

23) Which concept implies that aging results in a significant decline in the immune system, increasing the older person's susceptibility to infectious disease and risk of death?
   A) immunosenescence                  B) immune system
   C) dementia                          D) electroencephalogram
   Answer: A
   *Diff: 1      Page Ref: 89*

24) It is generally agreed that biological theories must meet four requirements to be viable. Which one of the following is <u>not</u> one of the four requirements?
   A) The process must be universal.    B) The process must be deleterious.
   C) The process must be progressive.  D) The losses must be extrinsic.
   Answer: D
   *Diff: 3      Page Ref: 71–72*

25) When conversing with an older adult who is experiencing hearing loss, you should:
   A) face the person directly and maintain eye contact
   B) sit a little further back and tilt your head to be below eye level
   C) shout loudly
   D) speak in a lower monotonic voice
   Answer: A
   *Diff: 2      Page Ref: 104*

26) According to the cellular aging theory, aging may be attributable to the finite number of cell replications as the organism ages chronologically.
   Answer: TRUE
   *Diff: 2      Page Ref: 73*

27) Theories of biological aging have resulted in adequate knowledge to begin experiments to reverse the aging process.
   Answer: FALSE
   *Diff: 2      Page Ref: 71*

28) If the free radical theory is valid, ingesting vitamin E and beta carotene may slow the aging process.
   Answer: TRUE
   *Diff: 2      Page Ref: 73*

29) Osteoporosis is a normal change in the musculoskeletal system with aging.

Answer: FALSE
*Diff: 2*     *Page Ref: 81*

30) Normal aging is accompanied by a significant increase in systolic and diastolic blood pressure.

Answer: FALSE
*Diff: 2*     *Page Ref: 85*

31) Changes in the size and function of the liver with aging result in greater sensitivity to medications that are metabolized by the liver.

Answer: TRUE
*Diff: 2*     *Page Ref: 88*

32) Older people should increase their intake of caffeine and alcohol in order to inhibit the production of ADH.

Answer: FALSE
*Diff: 2*     *Page Ref: 87*

33) Loss of brain cells with aging is the primary reason for older people's forgetfulness.

Answer: FALSE
*Diff: 2*     *Page Ref: 89*

34) Studies of primates have shown that caloric restriction can improve physical activity and slow down metabolism.

Answer: TRUE
*Diff: 2*     *Page Ref: 76*

35) Changes in circadian rhythms with aging appear to be associated with changes in core body temperatures.

Answer: TRUE
*Diff: 2*     *Page Ref: 91*

36) With aging, the proportion of fat and water in the human body increases.

Answer: FALSE
*Diff: 2*     *Page Ref: 77–78*

37) Glaucoma is both more prevalent and more difficult to treat in African Americans.

Answer: TRUE
*Diff: 2*     *Page Ref: 96*

38) Contrary to earlier studies of taste and aging, recent researchers have found little evidence of taste bud loss with aging.

Answer: TRUE
*Diff: 2*     *Page Ref: 104–105*

39) Changes in kidney size and function with aging cause drugs to be metabolized faster in the older person's body.

Answer: FALSE
*Diff: 2*     *Page Ref: 87*

40) Older adults are less able to discriminate among levels of painful stimuli than younger persons.

Answer: TRUE
*Diff: 2*    *Page Ref: 82*

41) _____ is defined as the normal process of changes over time in the body and its components.

Answer: Senescence
*Diff: 2*    *Page Ref: 71*

42) The enzyme responsible for rebuilding telomeres and in this manner continued cell replication is called _____.

Answer: telomerase
*Diff: 2*    *Page Ref: 74*

43) One true disorder of sleep that occurs with normal aging is _____, which is defined as a 5 - to 10-second cessation of breathing.

Answer: sleep apnea
*Diff: 2*    *Page Ref: 91*

44) Loss of acuity in the center of one's visual field experienced by some older adults is known as _____.

Answer: age-related macular degeneration
*Diff: 2*    *Page Ref: 98*

45) Because of a loss of convergence of images formed in the two eyes, _____ deteriorate with aging.

Answer:    depth and distance perception
*Diff: 2*    *Page Ref: 97*

46) Can aging be reversed or delayed?

Answer: Research is exploring whether aging can be reversed or delayed and current studies focus on growth hormones, caloric restriction, and anti-aging compounds. Growth hormones may lead to increased activity and vigor, but the effects are short-lived. Caloric restriction has been shown in experiments with animals to increase the life-span 30-50%, but it is not generalizable to humans. Anti-aging compounds have been found to benefit animals in lab tests, but again, have not been tested on primates or humans.
*Diff: 2*    *Page Ref: 74-77*

47) What has been learned about vital capacity by studying master athletes?

Answer: Researchers have learned that the maximum volume of oxygen declined by 5.5 percent in master athletes (older people who maintain vigorous exercise programs) and the maximum volume of oxygen declined in sedentary men by 12 percent. Thus, aging plays only a small role in the decline of the respiratory system.
*Diff: 2*    *Page Ref: 84*

48) Differentiate and discuss the different terms related to sensory functions.

Answer: The terms are sensation (taking in information through the sense organs), perception (information received through senses is processed in the brain), sensory threshold (minimum intensity of stimulation required to detect it), recognition threshold (intensity of stimulation needed for recognition), and sensory discrimination (minimum difference necessary for a person to distinguish between two stimuli).
*Diff: 2*    *Page Ref: 93*

49) Explain the difference between glaucoma and cataract.

Answer: Glaucoma, caused by excess pressure in the eye, leads to tunnel vision, whereas cataracts cause fuzzy vision, double vision, problems with glare from bright light and problems with color discrimination, which leads to a clouding of the lens.

*Diff: 2*     *Page Ref: 95–96*

50) Identify potential adaptations that older adults with vision difficulties could make to improve the person-environment fit.

Answer: Facilities should use contrasting colors for signs, avoid creating shiny floors, and avoid placing a single large window at the end of a hall, large print books, audiobooks, playing cards with large letters, magnifying glasses, contrasting color strips on stairs, increasing light, flat versus glossy paint to reduce glare and dimmer switches to control the light levels.

*Diff: 2*     *Page Ref: 99*

# Chapter 4  Managing Chronic Diseases and Promoting Well–Being in Old Age

1) Which of the following represents the most common ADL limitation for older adults?
   A) bathing
   B) eating
   C) walking
   D) making a phone call
   
   Answer: C
   *Diff: 1      Page Ref: 116*

2) Which of the following represents the most common IADL limitation for older adults?
   A) home management
   B) money management
   C) meal preparation
   D) grocery shopping
   
   Answer: D
   *Diff: 1      Page Ref: 116*

3) As people age:
   A) the incidence of acute diseases increases
   B) the incidence of chronic conditions increases
   C) older men are more likely than women to develop chronic diseases
   D) functional health declines significantly
   
   Answer: B
   *Diff: 2      Page Ref: 120*

4) If cardiovascular diseases could be eliminated through better prevention and treatment, the population that could experience the greatest increase in life expectancy would be:
   A) older white women
   B) older white men
   C) non–white women
   D) middle–aged white men
   
   Answer: A
   *Diff: 2      Page Ref: 122*

5) Which of the following has <u>not</u> been found after regular use of HRT among older women?
   A) replenishment of bone density to pre–menopausal levels
   B) improved cholesterol levels
   C) fewer episodes of hot flashes
   D) relief of vaginal dryness
   
   Answer: A
   *Diff: 2      Page Ref: 134*

6) The major risk factor for cardiovascular disease is:
   A) hypotension      B) hypertension      C) atherosclerosis      D) diabetes
   
   Answer: B
   *Diff: 2      Page Ref: 126*

7) Osteoporosis is a major risk factor for:
   A) significant weight loss in older people
   B) problems with bladder control
   C) hip fractures
   D) strokes
   
   Answer: C
   *Diff: 2      Page Ref: 132*

8) Risk factors for falls include all of the following <u>except</u>:
    A) being a past cigarette smoker
    B) being overweight
    C) regularly using sedatives
    D) having had two or more falls in the past year
Answer: B
*Diff: 2        Page Ref: 133*

9) Older people with incontinence:
    A) make up about 50% of men over age 65
    B) should be examined for reversible causes
    C) can generally be treated with medications only
    D) consume more fluids
Answer: B
*Diff: 1        Page Ref: 139–140*

10) Older people with diabetes are more likely than elders without diabetes to:
    A) be Caucasian                    B) be underweight
    C) have a longer life expectancy   D) report ADL limitations
Answer: D
*Diff: 2        Page Ref: 137*

11) Which of the following conditions has <u>not</u> been found to be higher among newer cohorts of elders compared to older cohorts?
    A) edentulousness (total tooth loss)   B) diabetes
    C) hiatus hernia                        D) AIDS
Answer: A
*Diff: 2        Page Ref: 137, 141*

12) Compared to young adults, older persons:
    A) are more likely to cause accidents due to speeding
    B) are less likely to die from injuries sustained in an accident
    C) have more auto accidents per mile driven
    D) have more accidents due to drunken driving
Answer: C
*Diff: 2        Page Ref: 144–145*

13) Risk factors for falls include all of the following <u>except</u>:
    A) inactivity
    B) visual impairments
    C) medications that can cause postural hypotension
    D) overexertion
Answer: D
*Diff: 2        Page Ref: 146*

14) Age–related physiological changes and the effects of many medications are the primary reason why older people:
    A) generally stop driving
    B) prefer driving at night
    C) are at greater risk of injury and death in accidents
    D) prefer driving cars with higher power air bags
Answer: C
*Diff: 3        Page Ref: 145*

15) The best way to prevent falls among older people in their homes is to:
   A) move them to a nursing home
   B) make physical modifications to the home
   C) give them medications to control their balance
   D) encourage slowing down of their activity level

Answer: B
*Diff: 2     Page Ref: 146*

16) In a National Health Interview survey, what % of older adults had not obtained care from a dentist in the previous five years?
   A) about 30%          B) 50%               C) 75%               D) less than 10%

Answer: A
*Diff: 2     Page Ref: 150*

17) All of the following are limitations of health promotion programs with older adults except:
   A) most health promotion efforts have not been well-publicized
   B) most health promotion programs have not included ethnic minorities
   C) interest from Medicare and HMOs has been low
   D) most programs minimize social and economic reasons for individual health practices

Answer: D
*Diff: 2     Page Ref: 158*

18) Older people who take multiple medications:
   A) make up only 10% of the population aged 65 and older
   B) are more likely to be hospitalized for medication complications
   C) are usually very effective in keeping track of their medications
   D) have supplemental medical insurance that completely covers the cost of drugs

Answer: B
*Diff: 2     Page Ref: 149*

19) The greater risk of cancer with age may be due to all of the following except:
   A) the effects of a slow-acting carcinogen
   B) extended preexposure time
   C) improving immune capacity that is characteristics of increased age
   D) prolonged development time necessary for growth to be observable

Answer: C
*Diff: 2     Page Ref: 128*

20) The most common site of fractures are:
   A) vertebrae          B) ankle             C) leg               D) wrist

Answer: A
*Diff: 2     Page Ref: 132*

21) Approximately what percent of persons with AIDS are over age 50?
   A) 11%                B) 25%               C) 35%               D) 48%

Answer: A
*Diff: 3     Page Ref: 142*

22) How many states currently have special license requirements for older drivers?
   A) 5                  B) 21                C) 32                D) 50

Answer: B
*Diff: 2     Page Ref: 144*

23) Which age group is most likely use physician services?
    A) 55–64 year olds
    B) 65–74 year olds
    C) 75–84 year olds
    D) those over age 85

Answer: D
*Diff: 1     Page Ref: 148*

24) The most common OTC (over the counter) medication used by older adults is:
    A) aspirin          B) antacid          C) cold medicine          D) diuretic

Answer: A
*Diff: 2     Page Ref: 149*

25) The primary goal of "Healthy People 2010" for older Americans is to:
    A) improve their quality of life
    B) extend their life expectancy
    C) increase medical services aimed at older adults
    D) improve the health of older women

Answer: A
*Diff: 2     Page Ref: 151*

26) After age 70, men are less likely than women to report limitations with ADLs.

Answer: TRUE
*Diff: 1     Page Ref: 115*

27) Older people with multiple chronic conditions rate their quality of life lower than do their physicians.

Answer: FALSE
*Diff: 2     Page Ref: 118*

28) Adult on-set diabetes is more common among white elders than among African American and Hispanic elders.

Answer: FALSE
*Diff: 2     Page Ref: 137*

29) Hypertension is more common among African Americans than among whites.

Answer: TRUE
*Diff: 2     Page Ref: 126*

30) Co-morbidity has been found in 50 percent of older men, far higher than the rates in women of the same age.

Answer: FALSE
*Diff: 2     Page Ref: 121*

31) COPD is 3–4 times more common among older men than in older women.

Answer: TRUE
*Diff: 2     Page Ref: 136*

32) For drivers aged 65 to 74, motor vehicle accidents are the leading cause of injury-related deaths.

Answer: TRUE
*Diff: 2     Page Ref: 144*

33) The most important treatment for arthritis is to limit any physical activity.
   Answer: FALSE
   *Diff: 2      Page Ref: 130*

34) The symptoms of diabetes are difficult to detect in older people.
   Answer: TRUE
   *Diff: 2      Page Ref: 137*

35) Constipation is a normal part of the aging process.
   Answer: FALSE
   *Diff: 1      Page Ref: 140*

36) Health promotion programs should attempt to improve the general environment as well as individual health practices.
   Answer: TRUE
   *Diff: 2      Page Ref: 158*

37) Recognizing the benefits of exercise for preventing further deterioration of chronic conditions, more than half of today's elders participate in regular physical activities.
   Answer: FALSE
   *Diff: 2      Page Ref: 155*

38) Health promotion programs strictly work toward facilitating less disease among older adults.
   Answer: FALSE
   *Diff: 2      Page Ref: 150*

39) Most driving accidents caused by older adult drivers occur at low speeds.
   Answer: TRUE
   *Diff: 2      Page Ref: 145*

40) Once older adults enter the dental care system, their average number of annual visits is similar to that of younger people.
   Answer: TRUE
   *Diff: 2      Page Ref: 150*

41) More than _____ percent of persons age 70 and over have at least one chronic condition.
   Answer:   80
   *Diff: 2      Page Ref: 119*

42) Heart disease, cancer and strokes accounted for _____ percent of all deaths among people over age 65 and older in 2000.
   Answer:   60
   *Diff: 2      Page Ref: 122*

43) Cancer of the _____ is the most common malignancy in women age 65 and over.
   Answer: breast
   *Diff: 3      Page Ref: 128*

44) _____ is defined as impairments in the ability to complete multiple daily tasks.
   Answer: Disability
   *Diff: 2      Page Ref: 115*

45) _____ results from blockage of an artery supplying blood to a portion of the heart muscle.

Answer: Acute myocardial infarction

*Diff: 3*      *Page Ref: 125*

46) Identify the gender, and ethnic and racial differences in diabetes.

Answer: Diabetes risk is higher for older African Americans, American Indians and Latina women than for older white women, possibly due to higher rates of obesity. African Americans with diabetes are more likely to suffer complications of diabetes such as kidney failure and diabetic retinopathy.

*Diff: 3*      *Page Ref: 113*

47) Compare the ADL and IADL limitations among older men and women.

Answer: Men are less likely to have ADL limitations and show a smaller increase in disability with age. This differs by ethnic minority group.

*Diff: 3*      *Page Ref: 115*

48) What does the term "health status" refer to?

Answer: Health status refers to the presence or absence of disease and the degree of disability in an individual's level of functioning. The concepts that capture this functioning are activities of daily living (ADLs) and instrumental activities of daily living (IADLs).

*Diff: 2*      *Page Ref: 115*

49) Why do older adults rate their health positively?

Answer: Older adults rate their health positively because of their perceived comparisons with peers, their sense of accomplishments, their perceptions of competence, and possessing a broad definition of quality of life.

*Diff: 3*      *Page Ref: 117–118*

50) Discuss the potential reasons for higher rates of accidents among older drivers.

Answer: Reasons for driving accidents among older adults include changes in eye-hand coordination, slower reaction time, hearing impairments, impaired vision (especially at night), slower information processing, declining attention skills, visual–spatial skill problems, and declines in physical strength.

*Diff: 2*      *Page Ref: 145*

# Chapter 5   Cognitive Changes with Aging

1) Measures of fluid intelligence include:
   A) spatial orientation
   C) social judgment
   B) verbal comprehension
   D) word association

   Answer: A
   *Diff: 3        Page Ref: 175*

2) Measures of crystallized intelligence include:
   A) abstract reasoning
   C) word fluency
   B) social judgment
   D) inductive reasoning

   Answer: B
   *Diff: 3        Page Ref: 175*

3) The "Classic Aging Pattern" on the WAIS (Wechsler Adult Intelligence Scale) refers to:
   A) decline in the performance sub-tests beyond age 65
   B) decline in the verbal sub-tests beyond age 65
   C) improvement in mathematical reasoning with aging
   D) improvement in tests of spatial reasoning

   Answer: A
   *Diff: 2        Page Ref: 176*

4) Which of the following conditions is <u>least</u> likely to negatively affect older adults' performance on intelligence tests?
   A) educational level
   C) nutritional deficits
   B) hypertension
   D) constipation

   Answer: D
   *Diff: 2        Page Ref: 180*

5) "Terminal drop" refers to:
   A) an older person who tends to fall due to balance problems
   B) a person approaching death due to a terminal disease
   C) a sharp decline in intelligence test scores shortly before death
   D) a sharp decline in social interactions shortly before death

   Answer: C
   *Diff: 2        Page Ref: 181*

6) In terms of memory and aging:
   A) primary memory refers to an initial temporary stage of memory
   B) secondary memory refers to information of lower priority
   C) iconic memory is a short-term store for verbal information
   D) echoic memory is a long-term store for auditory information

   Answer: A
   *Diff: 2        Page Ref: 182*

7) Which of the following is <u>most</u> likely to affect the performance of a person when taking a mental abilities test?
   A) light levels
   C) time constraints
   B) tone and loudness of test-giver's voice
   D) large print text

   Answer: C
   *Diff: 2        Page Ref: 188*

8) When taking tests, older persons:
    A) commit more errors of commission than omission
    B) commit more errors of omission than commission
    C) are always more cautious than young test-takers
    D) perform worse than young test-takers on perceptual-motor tests
Answer: B
*Diff: 2      Page Ref: 190*

9) Compared to younger test-takers, older individuals perform:
    A) better on tests of free-recall          B) as well on tests of recognition
    C) better on tests of spatial memory       D) as well on tests of recent events
Answer: B
*Diff: 2      Page Ref: 191-192*

10) Suggestions to web designers for improving web pages for older users include all of the
    following except:
    A) avoid using a patterned background behind text
    B) use dark type and graphics on a light background
    C) use bright colors and animation
    D) avoid pop up menus
Answer: C
*Diff: 2      Page Ref: 188*

11) Associating new information with an image has been found to be useful for older people as a:
    A) method of finding their way around a new place
    B) method of enhancing creativity
    C) way of remembering where they have placed their belongings
    D) method of visualizing newly learned words or concepts
Answer: D
*Diff: 2      Page Ref: 195*

12) Researchers who have tested the pros and cons of cognitive retraining programs have found
    that:
    A) reasoning ability can be improved more than spatial orientation
    B) they are effective when combined with memory-enhancing drugs
    C) booster sessions make them ideal for older people
    D) verbal mediators are better than visual methods for older people
Answer: A
*Diff: 3      Page Ref: 193-194*

13) List-making is most helpful for older people who:
    A) have strong vocabulary skills          B) have the least education
    C) have Alzheimer's disease               D) take a lot of medications
Answer: A
*Diff: 2      Page Ref: 196-197*

14) Studies of wisdom in older adults:
    A) reveal increased levels as the person ages
    B) reveal declining levels as the person ages
    C) show high life satisfaction in people who have achieved wisdom
    D) have generally used tests of convergent thinking
Answer: C
*Diff: 2      Page Ref: 198*

15) Studies of creativity:
    A) show that creative young children become creative elders
    B) have examined problem solving skills of artists and scientists
    C) generally have examined the creative output of artists and scientists
    D) generally rely on self-reports of creativity
    Answer: C
    *Diff: 2      Page Ref: 198*

16) Evidence on memory suggests that:
    A) older adults with mild to moderate dementia benefit more from list-making than visual methods of recall
    B) mnemonics can help in learning a list of new words
    C) the method of loci works better for young learners
    D) older people practice many learning techniques
    Answer: B
    *Diff: 2      Page Ref: 195–196*

17) Literature on personal attributes suggests:
    A) wisdom is a characteristic that can be readily define and measured
    B) creativity is the ability to apply unique solutions to new situations
    C) external aids can enhance creativity
    D) aging bring with it wisdom to all
    Answer: B
    *Diff: 2      Page Ref: 197*

18) Which of the following is true regarding creative output?
    A) Creative output is highest from age 30-40.
    B) Creative output from age 70 to 80 is about half that of age 30–40.
    C) The secondary peak of creativity occurs in the 60s.
    D) None of the above
    Answer: D
    *Diff: 2      Page Ref: 199*

19) Which of the following is true regarding studies of intelligence?
    A) Cross-sectional studies entail selective attrition.
    B) Longitudinal studies entail selective attrition.
    C) Older people do better on timed tests.
    D) They can assess age changes and age differences.
    Answer: B
    *Diff: 3      Page Ref: 177*

20) The learning process can be enhanced for older persons by:
    A) reducing time constraints
    B) making the learning task more relevant for them
    C) giving them frequent tests
    D) both A and B
    Answer: D
    *Diff: 3      Page Ref: 189*

21) The most important aspect of memory enhancement may be:
    A) the ability to relax and reduce anxiety and stress
    B) the ability to remember all mnemonics learned
    C) avoiding brightly lit areas
    D) using herbal supplements

Answer: A
*Diff: 2      Page Ref: 196*

22) Which of the following is not one of the criteria used to describe "wise" elders?
    A) subjective knowledge          B) procedural knowledge
    C) lifespan contextualism        D) value relativism

Answer: A
*Diff: 2      Page Ref: 197*

23) Lifespan contextualism:
    A) means considering the contest in which event are occurring and the relationship among
       them
    B) is the opposite of value relativism
    C) is a technique for developing back-up plans
    D) is defined as being able to use decision making strategies

Answer: A
*Diff: 2      Page Ref: 197*

24) The decrement model, which suggest that memory networks deteriorate with aging, is used to
    explain:
    A) tip-of-the-tongue states      B) cognitive retraining
    C) life long learning            D) memory mediators

Answer: A
*Diff: 2      Page Ref: 192*

25) When improving websites for older adults:
    A) avoid using a patterned background behind test material
    B) use many graphic and much animation
    C) give each section of the website a different layout
    D) add many pop-up menus

Answer: A
*Diff: 2      Page Ref: 188*

26) Researchers generally agree that most types of intelligence decline after age 65.

Answer: FALSE
*Diff: 3      Page Ref: 176*

27) Older adults make more errors of omission than errors of commission on tests of paired
    associates.

Answer: TRUE
*Diff: 2      Page Ref: 189*

28) We are able to remember better if information is stored in our primary memory.

Answer: FALSE
*Diff: 2      Page Ref: 183*

29) Allowing older adults more time to take a test makes little difference in how well they perform on the test.

Answer: FALSE
*Diff: 1*      *Page Ref: 189*

30) Cognitive retraining has been found to be effective in helping older adults maintain their memory skills.

Answer: TRUE
*Diff: 2*      *Page Ref: 193*

31) Ginkgo biloba is a popular herbal remedy for memory improvement but has not been found to be useful for dementia.

Answer: TRUE
*Diff: 2*      *Page Ref: 194*

32) Older adults do worse than younger adults on tests of free recall.

Answer: TRUE
*Diff: 2*      *Page Ref: 191*

33) Disuse theory has proven that long-term information deteriorates when it is not used.

Answer: FALSE
*Diff: 2*      *Page Ref: 192*

34) Older people have more problems with spatial memory than do younger people.

Answer: TRUE
*Diff: 2*      *Page Ref: 191*

35) Interference theory has been useful in explaining problems of retrieving information from secondary memory.

Answer: TRUE
*Diff: 2*      *Page Ref: 192*

36) Several long-term studies have found evidence for the benefits of vitamin E, B12 and lecithin for older people's memory.

Answer: FALSE
*Diff: 2*      *Page Ref: 194*

37) Older adults who are most worried about declining memory use external and cognitive aids as a way of coping with the problem.

Answer: TRUE
*Diff: 2*      *Page Ref: 194*

38) Creativity peaks around age 30 and steadily declines with age.

Answer: FALSE
*Diff: 2*      *Page Ref: 199*

39) Achieving wisdom has been found to be associated with life satisfaction in old age.

Answer: TRUE
*Diff: 2*      *Page Ref: 198*

40) Most older people have achieved wisdom because they have been able to reflect on their worldly experiences.

Answer: FALSE
*Diff: 2*     *Page Ref: 198*

41) Teaching research participants how to use various techniques to keep their minds active and maintain good memory skills is known as _____.

Answer: cognitive retraining
*Diff: 1*     *Page Ref: 193*

42) An apparent and rapid decline in cognitive function within 5 years of death is referred to as the _____.

Answer:     terminal decline hypothesis
*Diff: 2*     *Page Ref: 181*

43) Measures of _____ include spatial orientation, abstract reasoning, word fluency and inductive reasoning.

Answer:     fluid intelligence
*Diff: 1*     *Page Ref: 175*

44) _____ are verbal riddles, rhymes and codes associated with the new information.

Answer:     Mnemonics
*Diff: 1*     *Page Ref: 195*

45) The general slowing hypothesis was proposed by _____.

Answer:     Salthouse
*Diff: 3*     *Page Ref: 189*

46) Differentiate between the measures of fluid intelligence and the measures of crystallized intelligence.

Answer: The measure of fluid intelligence include spatial orientation, abstract reasoning, word fluency and inductive reasoning. The measures of crystallized intelligence include verbal meaning, word association, social judgment, and number skills. .
*Diff: 2*     *Page Ref: 175*

47) Discuss the findings of at least one major longitudinal study of aging.

Answer: Answer will vary but may include a discussion of the Seattle Longitudinal Study (found age decrements after 60 on word fluency, numbers, spatial orientation and fluid intelligence), The Iowa State Study (found that there is a general stability in intelligence functioning through middle age, peaking in the late 40s–50s and a decline in some men after age 60), or the New York State Study of Aging Twins (found that performance on non–speed intelligence tests were stable. There was a decrease in hand–eye coordination and fluid intelligence, but there were wide variations).
*Diff: 2*     *Page Ref: 178*

48) Define primary mental abilities and name 5 out of the 7.

Answer: Primary mental abilities are a subset of intellectual skills often measured by most intelligence tests today. They include: number or mathematical reasoning, word fluency, verbal meaning or vocabulary level, inductive reasoning, spatial relations, verbal memory, and perceptual speed.
*Diff: 2*     *Page Ref: 175*

49) Discuss how older adults can use memory mediators to improve their memory.

Answer: Visual mediators (method of loci useful to teach lists of new names, words, or concepts), mnemonics (verbal riddles for new information), and external aids (devices to keep track of time, dates, and important tasks).

*Diff: 2*     *Page Ref: 195–196*

50) Identify the various types of memory, their function and their potential for age –related changes.

Answer: The types of memory include episodic (recalling specific events), explicit (seeing a stimulus in mind in a specific order), flashbulb (remembering personally relevant events), implicit (unintentionally remembering stimuli), procedural (non verbal, motor functions like riding a bike), semantic (words and facts accumulated over time), and source memory (remembering where one heard information).

*Diff: 2*     *Page Ref: 185*

# Chapter 6   Personality and Mental Health in Old Age

1) According to Erik Erikson, the stage of ego integrity refers to:
    A) the stage in young adulthood characterized by falling in love
    B) accepting one's self and one's life as complete and meaningful
    C) a feeling of well-being from having a satisfied relationship with one's partner
    D) none of the above

Answer: B
*Diff: 2        Page Ref: 210*

2) Jung's theory suggests that as people get older:
    A) men exaggerate their masculine characteristics to compensate for their rising age
    B) women develop somewhat more masculine characteristics
    C) both men and women become more masculine
    D) they achieve ego integrity

Answer: B
*Diff: 3        Page Ref: 210*

3) The research of Gutmann, as cited in the text, states that older men are more _____ than younger men.
    A) expressive and nurturing           B) controlling
    C) achievement oriented               D) instrumental

Answer: A
*Diff: 3        Page Ref: 212*

4) The Kansas City Studies, by Neugarten, Havighurst and others, demonstrated that, with aging:
    A) a turning inward and a greater interiority occurs
    B) increased use of denial and sublimation occurs
    C) there is increased tendency toward dialectical features
    D) there is increased tendency toward sex-typed behavior

Answer: A
*Diff: 2        Page Ref: 212*

5) Studies of self-esteem and the aging process show that:
    A) self-esteem in older people is not affected by stressful life events
    B) accepting the aging process and its limitations will not help older persons
    C) life review can help maintain self-esteem
    D) self-esteem declines with aging

Answer: C
*Diff: 3        Page Ref: 217*

6) Research evidence suggests that life events:
    A) are generally negative
    B) can be viewed as "on time" or "off time" events
    C) are not affected by the process of cognitive appraisal
    D) widowhood is an example of an internally created event

Answer: B
*Diff: 1        Page Ref: 218-219*

7) Regarding life events and individual reports:
    A) types of life events common to younger people are about as equally common to older people
    B) older individuals generally report life events to be more stressful than younger individuals
    C) internally created events are generally more stressful than external events
    D) older persons cope better with normative than with non-normative events
Answer: D
*Diff: 2        Page Ref: 219–220*

8) The following are dimensions of coping <u>except</u>:
    A) resigned hopelessness        B) aggression
    C) escape                       D) intrapsychic
Answer: B
*Diff: 3        Page Ref: 222*

9) Forgetting an event that could disturb the feeling of well–being, if brought into consciousness, is called:
    A) coping                       B) adaptation
    C) defense mechanism            D) locus of control
Answer: C
*Diff: 2        Page Ref: 221*

10) Planned behavior in response to a stressful situation is called:
    A) adaptation                   B) defense mechanism
    C) coping strategy              D) accommodation
Answer: B
*Diff: 2        Page Ref: 221*

11) A range of behaviors such as coping, problem solving, goal setting to maintain psychological homeostasis is called:
    A) locus of control             B) successful aging
    C) self–efficacy                D) adaptation
Answer: D
*Diff: 2        Page Ref: 222*

12) In older ages:
    A) control over external events becomes more important
    B) acceptance of change is the most adaptive coping response
    C) the tendency to choose inappropriate coping styles increases
    D) the same coping strategy is chosen, whether or not it is effective
Answer: B
*Diff: 2        Page Ref: 222*

13) Coping strategies:
    A) undergo considerable change as a person ages
    B) undergo no change as a person ages
    C) are generally stable with aging
    D) become more unconscious responses with aging
Answer: C
*Diff: 2        Page Ref: 222*

14) Religious coping styles in response to major life events:
    A) are used minimally (less than 10 percent) by today's older persons
    B) are used by a notable percentage of the older population (20–25 percent)
    C) are used by a large proportion of the older population (50 percent or more)
    D) are used by almost the entire older population (90 percent or more)

Answer: C
*Diff: 3*    *Page Ref: 222*

15) Rowe and Kahn's model of successful aging includes all of the following dimensions <u>except</u>:
    A) financial and economic security          B) physical and functional health
    C) active involvement with society           D) being married

Answer: D
*Diff: 3*    *Page Ref: 223*

16) Rowe and Kahn's model of successful aging includes the following dimension(s):
    A) high cognitive functioning
    B) a significant number of lucky breaks in life
    C) acceptance of social isolation
    D) both A and B

Answer: A
*Diff: 3*    *Page Ref: 223*

17) DSM IV (the Diagnostic and Statistical Manual of Mental Disorders) criteria for major depressive episode include, over a two week period or more:
    A) compulsive behaviors
    B) psychologically induced leg or arm tremor
    C) low energy level or fatigue
    D) blaming others for personal problems

Answer: C
*Diff: 2*    *Page Ref: 230*

18) DSM IV (the Diagnostic and Statistical Manual of Mental Disorders) criteria for major depressive episode include, over a two week period or more, all of the following <u>except</u>:
    A) sleep disturbance                          B) low energy level every day
    C) guilt and worthlessness                    D) anger toward friends and family

Answer: D
*Diff: 2*    *Page Ref: 230*

19) Causes of reversible dementia (delirium) in old age include:
    A) drugs or medication                        B) Korsakoff syndrome
    C) depression                                 D) Alzheimer's disease

Answer: A
*Diff: 2*    *Page Ref: 237–238*

20) Which of the following is true regarding Alzheimer's disease?
    A) It is estimated to affect 10% of all Americans aged 65 and older.
    B) Ginkgo biloba can help in advanced dementia.
    C) There are currently a variety of treatments that can cure Alzheimer's disease.
    D) Behavioral therapy is effective for moderate dementia.

Answer: A
*Diff: 1*    *Page Ref: 238–243*

21) In stages 6 and 7 (advanced dementia) of Alzheimer's Disease what should caregivers do?
    A) visit alternative long-term care facilities that fit the P-E needs of the particular patient
    B) set-up an orientation area in the home
    C) watch for signs of driving problems
    D) encourage increased physical and social activities

Answer: A
*Diff: 3      Page Ref: 245*

22) Predictors of positive aging include all of the following except:
    A) passive acceptance when faced with a crisis
    B) a supportive marriage or a long term partnership
    C) continued involvement with life
    D) mature defense mechanism and active coping mechanisms

Answer: A
*Diff: 2      Page Ref: 225*

23) Risk factors for depression in older adults include:
    A) co-morbidity                          B) married
    C) male gender                           D) financial stability and comfort

Answer: A
*Diff: 2      Page Ref: 229*

24) Seventy-eight percent of suicides among older men were completed with:
    A) a firearm           B) a knife           C) poison           D) medications

Answer: A
*Diff: 2      Page Ref: 235*

25) One form of therapy for older adults which allows them to process grief and loss is known as:
    A) reminiscence therapy                   B) group therapy
    C) cognitive-behavioral therapy           D) life review

Answer: A
*Diff: 2      Page Ref: 232*

26) Most people do not experience major personality shifts as they age.

Answer: TRUE
*Diff: 2      Page Ref: 214*

27) Middle-aged and older adults who are characterized by generativity spend considerable time in reflection about themselves.

Answer: FALSE
*Diff: 2      Page Ref: 211*

28) The dialectical approach to personality development is congruent with the person-environment model presented throughout this text.

Answer: TRUE
*Diff: 1      Page Ref: 213*

29) Self-esteem is affected by role losses with age.

Answer: TRUE
*Diff: 2      Page Ref: 217*

30) Erikson's stages of ego development and Levinson's concept of "life structures" have similar meanings.
Answer: FALSE
*Diff: 2*      *Page Ref: 213*

31) Successful aging is used to describe older adults who have a good income and who live with a family member.
Answer: FALSE
*Diff: 2*      *Page Ref: 223*

32) Depression treatment is effective for about 25% of chronically depressed older adults.
Answer: FALSE
*Diff: 2*      *Page Ref: 232*

33) An older person who tries to hide or mask their depression may be misdiagnosed as having dementia.
Answer: TRUE
*Diff: 2*      *Page Ref: 230*

34) Older women who are widowed, over age 85, and experiencing chronic pain and depression are the group at greatest risk of suicide.
Answer: FALSE
*Diff: 2*      *Page Ref: 234*

35) An irreversible dementia may occur among older adults who are using multiple medications.
Answer: FALSE
*Diff: 2*      *Page Ref: 237*

36) Years ago, families and health care providers referred to marked deterioration in memory as "hardening of the arteries." This remains a correct diagnosis today.
Answer: FALSE
*Diff: 2*      *Page Ref: 236*

37) Anxiety disorders are not diagnosed as frequently in the young as they are in the older population.
Answer: FALSE
*Diff: 3*      *Page Ref: 251*

38) Unfortunately, nothing can be done to help patients with Alzheimer's disease or their family caregivers.
Answer: FALSE
*Diff: 2*      *Page Ref: 247*

39) A majority of those with Alzheimer's disease are cared for in long-term care settings, such as nursing homes.
Answer: FALSE
*Diff: 2*      *Page Ref: 247*

40) When older adults experience signs of mental disorders, they turn first to their family physician rather than a mental health professional.
Answer: TRUE
*Diff: 2*      *Page Ref: 254*

41) The last stage of Erikson's stages of development is _____.

Answer:    ego integrity versus despair
*Diff: 2*      *Page Ref: 211*

42) The underlying characteristics of a person's life at a particular period of time are known as

_____.

Answer:    life structures
*Diff: 1*      *Page Ref: 213*

43) _____ is defined as a combination of physical and functional health, high cognitive functioning, and active involvement with society.

Answer:    Successful aging
*Diff: 1*      *Page Ref: 223*

44) White men aged 85 are at greatest risk for _____.

Answer:    suicide
*Diff: 2*      *Page Ref: 234*

45) The most common therapeutic intervention with depressed older individuals is _____.

Answer:    pharmacological
*Diff: 3*      *Page Ref: 231*

46) discuss the three components of the Model of Successful Aging.

Answer: The model assumes that all three components must exist for successful aging to occur. They include: avoidance of disease and disability, involvement in society, and high cognitive and physical functioning.
*Diff: 3*      *Page Ref: 223*

47) Contrast the three classifications of coping responses and provide examples of each.

Answer: The three classifications of coping responses include general strategies of coping (information search to understanding the situation, direct action to change the situation, inhibition of action, psychological responses to the emotional arousal created by the situation), coping responses to terminal illness (information searching, setting goals, denying/minimizing the problem, seeking emotional support, and rehearsing alternative outcomes) and the dimensions of coping (instrumental, intrapsychic, affective, escape, resigned helplessness).
*Diff: 3*      *Page Ref: 222*

48) Contrast the indicators of Alzheimer's Disease with normal changes in memory.

Answer: Examples of normal changes in memory would include forgetting to set the alarm clock, forgetting a name but remembering it later, and forgetting where the car keys are but finding them after searching. Examples of possibly having AD would include forgetting how to set the alarm clock, forgetting a name and never remembering it, even when told, and forgetting places where one might find the keys.
*Diff: 2*      *Page Ref: 238*

49) Thoroughly discuss Erikson's stage model of development and pay particular attention to the later life stages.

Answer: The model describes psychosocial development throughout the life cycle. The stages relevant to older age are generativity vs. stagnation or ego integrity vs. despair. In generativity vs. stagnation, the goal is to establish a sense of care and concern for the well–being of future generations. The goal in ego integrity vs. despair is to establish a sense of meaning in life.

*Diff: 2*      *Page Ref: 210–211*

50) Summarize the Kansas City Studies.

Answer: Kansas City Studies studied changes in the physiological, cognitive, and personality functions in the same people over several years. They found that older men become more affiliative, nurturant, and sensual as they age and women accept their egocentric and assertive side.

*Diff: 2*      *Page Ref: 212–213*

# Chapter 7  Love, Intimacy, and Sexuality in Old Age

1) Sexual behavior is likely to be influenced by:
   A) physiological changes
   B) the individual's personal sexual history and self–concept
   C) functional ability
   D) all of the above

   Answer: D
   *Diff: 3        Page Ref: 272*

2) Which of the following stereotypes regarding aging and sexuality has been supported by research?
   A) It takes longer to achieve orgasm.
   B) Older men cannot achieve an erection.
   C) Older women cannot have orgasms.
   D) Older people prefer masturbation to intercourse.

   Answer: A
   *Diff: 2        Page Ref: 280–281*

3) <u>Society</u> views sexual activity in older adults as follows:
   A) normal well into the 90s              B) healthy activity for couples
   C) inappropriate                         D) easy to achieve

   Answer: C
   *Diff: 1        Page Ref: 272–273*

4) Regarding sexuality and aging:
   A) according to Kinsey the vast majority of men over age 70 experience sexual dysfunction
   B) sexual experiences become less meaningful and less interesting
   C) few age–related physiological changes prevent continued sexual activity
   D) people's attitudes toward sex become more conservative

   Answer: C
   *Diff: 3        Page Ref: 274*

5) Studies regarding menopause indicate that:
   A) the postmenopausal period is characterized by widely fluctuating emotions
   B) most women undergoing menopause do not experience major psychological problems
   C) menopausal symptoms appear when the menstrual cycle ends
   D) only women who undergo a hysterectomy experience menopausal symptoms

   Answer: B
   *Diff: 2        Page Ref: 277*

6) Menopause is associated with the following:
   A) sexual activity in older women helps maintain vaginal lubrication
   B) HRT cannot protect against lower urinary tract infections
   C) it impedes sexual activity from a physiological perspective
   D) sleep disturbances are rare for postmenopausal women

   Answer: A
   *Diff: 2        Page Ref: 278–279*

7) Studies of attitudes toward menopause suggest that:
   A) most women associate the menopause with appearing unattractive
   B) in many non-Western cultures, menopause is viewed negatively
   C) the major concern for most women is whether or not to use HRT
   D) most women are concerned with depression resulting from menopausal changes

   Answer: C
   *Diff: 2      Page Ref: 279*

8) The following is true about the sexuality of older men:
   A) testosterone loss starts after age 65
   B) approximately 60–80 percent who use Viagra seem to benefit from it
   C) the male climacteric begins about 10 years earlier than menopause in women
   D) sexual enjoyment and desire normally decline dramatically

   Answer: B
   *Diff: 2      Page Ref: 280–282*

9) The following is true about the sexuality of older women:
   A) there is a slower response to sexual stimulation
   B) it takes longer to return to a preorgasmic state
   C) most older women do not want to continue sexual activity
   D) most seek treatment for sexual dysfunction

   Answer: A
   *Diff: 2      Page Ref: 279–280*

10) Which of the following is not true about physiological changes in sexuality with aging?
    A) a reduction of vaginal elasticity and lubrication
    B) a thinning of the vaginal walls
    C) less intense orgasmic contractions
    D) a thickening of vaginal walls

    Answer: D
    *Diff: 2      Page Ref: 278*

11) The following is not true regarding physiological changes in older men's sexuality with age?
    A) Erections may require more direct stimulation.
    B) Erections are slower and less full.
    C) Erections take longer to disappear after orgasm.
    D) Erections have a longer refractory period.

    Answer: C
    *Diff: 2      Page Ref: 281–282*

12) Regarding the prostate in older men:
    A) only a very small percentage of men (5 percent or less) have prostate problems
    B) prostate cancer occurs as often in men age 30–50 as in men aged 65–80
    C) prostate enlargement is most often caused by cancer
    D) prostate cancer has few symptoms in its early stages

    Answer: D
    *Diff: 2      Page Ref: 284*

13) A women's ability to have an orgasm is strongly affected by:
    A) a hysterectomy                  B) a mastectomy
    C) psychological factors           D) changes in the vaginal structures

    Answer: C
    *Diff: 2      Page Ref: 280*

14) With regard to disease and sexuality in older people:
   A) untreated diabetes may cause impotence in men
   B) sexual activity can cause a stroke or heart attack
   C) sexual activity is limited by arthritis
   D) Alzheimer's disease and other dementias should not affect sexuality

   Answer: A
   *Diff: 2      Page Ref: 285–286*

15) Regarding medication and sexuality:
   A) antidepressants may interfere with erectile ability
   B) alcohol consumption improves an erection in men
   C) most treatments for diabetes impair women's sexuality
   D) nitroglycerin can impair sexuality in men

   Answer: A
   *Diff: 2      Page Ref: 285–287*

16) Older gay men today:
   A) have as many gay sexual partners and relationships as younger gay men
   B) gain respect and value in the gay community
   C) are more likely to hide their sexual orientation than younger men
   D) are more likely to be depressed and isolated than heterosexual men

   Answer: C
   *Diff: 2      Page Ref: 289–290*

17) Older lesbians today:
   A) are more open about their sexuality than gay men
   B) have generally practiced serial monogamy
   C) are more depressed and isolated than heterosexual women
   D) are more concerned about loss of attractiveness with aging

   Answer: B
   *Diff: 2      Page Ref: 289*

18) "Widow's or widower's syndrome" can be reduced or eliminated by:
   A) avoiding thoughts about sexual activity
   B) finding an understanding partner
   C) finding a younger partner
   D) medication to treat the condition

   Answer: B
   *Diff: 2      Page Ref: 291*

19) The psychosocial factors which have little influence on sexual activity of older adults include:
   A) past history of sexual activity
   B) the older person's reaction to physical illness
   C) performance anxiety
   D) approval by their adult children

   Answer: D
   *Diff: 2      Page Ref: 292*

20) Regarding physical touch for older people:
    A) most do not enjoy being hugged or touched
    B) older people with dementia have less of a need for hugging and touching
    C) a gentle touch can provide social support
    D) a touch on the hand can arouse the older person sexually

Answer: C
*Diff: 2      Page Ref: 293*

21) More than half of all men over the age of 65:
    A) have some degree of prostate enlargement
    B) have not benefited from oral medications for impotence, such as Viagra
    C) experience impotence at least one out of every four times they have sex
    D) say that better health would improve their satisfaction with their sex life

Answer: A
*Diff: 3      Page Ref: 282-284*

22) Which of the following would not be a component of sex therapy for older adults?
    A) suggesting interventions to build self-esteem
    B) providing opportunities to discuss problems
    C) using a holistic approach that includes exercise and nutrition
    D) emphasizing activities that reduce the amount of intimacy with a partner

Answer: D
*Diff: 2      Page Ref: 294*

23) Psychological factors that affect the ways older people express their sexuality include all of the following except:
    A) a reduced desire for sexual relations
    B) is an individual's reaction to physiological changes
    C) is the reaction of societal attitudes about sex
    D) the availability of a partner

Answer: A
*Diff: 2      Page Ref: 290*

24) Hot flashes during menopause can be relieved by:
    A) wearing breathable clothing, not synthetics
    B) eating spicy food
    C) drinking caffeine and alcohol
    D) sleeping in a warm room

Answer: A
*Diff: 2      Page Ref: 277*

25) Early research on older adults and sexuality was limited by:
    A) small, nonrandom samples
    B) the emphasis on frequency of sexual intercourse
    C) comparisons of younger and older cohorts at the same point in time
    D) all of the above

Answer: D
*Diff: 2      Page Ref: 275*

26) Longitudinal studies of older couples show a marked decline on their sexual activity as compared to their younger selves.

Answer: FALSE
*Diff: 2      Page Ref: 274*

27) The majority of older men do not engage in sexual intercourse.

Answer: FALSE
*Diff: 2      Page Ref: 275*

28) Changes in estrogen levels can occur well before menopause.

Answer: TRUE
*Diff: 2      Page Ref: 277*

29) Due to risks of long term HRT use, the lowest effective dose should be used to treat symptoms of menopause.

Answer: TRUE
*Diff: 2      Page Ref: 279*

30) Most women experience depression and sadness during menopause.

Answer: FALSE
*Diff: 1      Page Ref: 279*

31) Hormonal changes in men occur more slowly than in women.

Answer: TRUE
*Diff: 2      Page Ref: 280*

32) Only a very small percentage of women experience hot flashes during menopause.

Answer: FALSE
*Diff: 2      Page Ref: 278*

33) The majority of older women experience and enjoy orgasms.

Answer: TRUE
*Diff: 2      Page Ref: 276*

34) Unfortunately, nothing can be done to treat impotence among older men because the causes are mostly physiological.

Answer: FALSE
*Diff: 2      Page Ref: 282*

35) Irreversible impotence nearly always results from prostate surgery.

Answer: FALSE
*Diff: 2      Page Ref: 284*

36) Age related physiological changes detrimentally affect sexual functioning.

Answer: FALSE
*Diff: 1      Page Ref: 281*

37) When working with older adults regarding sexual concerns, the focus should be on their ability to maintain genital intercourse in order to experience intimacy.

Answer: FALSE
*Diff: 1      Page Ref: 294*

38) Nursing home staff members are generally sensitive about providing opportunities for older residents to experience intimacy.

Answer: FALSE
*Diff: 2      Page Ref: 292*

39) With aging, the preorgasmic plateau phase increases in length for both men and women.

Answer: TRUE
*Diff: 2*       *Page Ref: 280–281*

40) Age-related changes in vaginal elasticity and lubrication have a significant negative effect on older women's sexual activity and pleasure.

Answer: FALSE
*Diff: 3*       *Page Ref: 278*

41) Viropause is also known as _____.

Answer: male menopause
*Diff: 3*       *Page Ref: 280*

42) Older lesbians, often closeted about their sexual orientation, have been labeled the _____.

Answer: invisible minority
*Diff: 2*       *Page Ref: 289*

43) The three phases of the climacteric are perimenopause, menopause, and _____.

Answer: postmenopause
*Diff: 2*       *Page Ref: 277*

44) A man who has not had sexual intercourse for a long time following the loss or illness of a partner may experience _____.

Answer: widower's syndrome
*Diff: 2*       *Page Ref: 291*

45) Erectile dysfunction or _____ is the chief cause of older men's withdrawing from sexual activity.

Answer: impotence
*Diff: 2*       *Page Ref: 282*

46) Discuss the myths and realities regarding sexual activity in later life.

Answer: Stereotypes frequently portray older adults as asexual and without the physical capabilities or desires to participate in sexual activity; however, this is not true. Older adults are still wanting to and able to participate in sexual experiences though some physical changes do happen either due to biology, disease or medication.
*Diff: 2*       *Page Ref: 273–274*

47) Summarize the effect of the loss of testosterone in men.

Answer: The loss of testosterone in men can lead to a variety of changes including reduced muscle size and strength, increased calcium loss in the bones, and lessened sexual response and interest, decline in immune system response, fatigue and depression, increased relationship problems and arguments with partners about love, sex and intimacy, loss of erection and changes in secondary sexual characteristics.
*Diff: 2*       *Page Ref: 281*

48) Apply continuity theory to the experiences of gay men.

Answer: In support of continuity theory, sexuality appears to be equally important at all phases of a gay man's life. They are just as likely to be involved in the homosexual network.
*Diff: 2*       *Page Ref: 289–290*

49) How do chronic illnesses impact upon sexual activity?

Answer: Chronic illnesses can affect sexual activity as the condition may take all of one's time and focus, as the condition may effect one's well-being and self-perception and the condition may involve much frequent pain. There may be complications of medication, especially from antihypertensive drugs.

*Diff: 2*     *Page Ref: 283*

50) Discuss the importance of staff sensitive to older adult's sexuality if they reside in a staffed facility.

Answer: Staff attitudes may be the greatest barrier to the expression of sexuality for older adults residing in long-term care facilities. Staff and health care practitioners should be sensitive to the needs of their patients including conversations about sexuality and sexual experiences and respectful of privacy and autonomy.

*Diff: 2*     *Page Ref: 292*

# Chapter 8   Social Theories of Aging

1) Regarding theories and concepts of aging:
   A) theories before the 1960s focus on societal forces that influence aging
   B) "age norms" have little to do with "role theory"
   C) disengagement theory has been supported by empirical research
   D) most early theories ignored environmental and lifestyle influences

Answer: D
*Diff: 2      Page Ref: 306–310*

2) Which of the following is <u>not</u> a component of role theory?
   A) role losses                    B) role discontinuity
   C) role additions                 D) role exit

Answer: C
*Diff: 1      Page Ref: 307–308*

3) Activity theory attempted to show:
   A) the more active an older person, the greater his/her life satisfaction and self-concept
   B) leisure and relaxation should be emphasized in old age
   C) societies dictate how active a retired person should be
   D) older people should reduce their activity levels

Answer: A
*Diff: 2      Page Ref: 309*

4) Disengagement attempted to show that:
   A) it is normal for older people to be depressed as they disengage from society
   B) it is adaptive for the well-being of older persons to disengage
   C) successful aging requires gradual disengagement
   D) older people who remain active will experience social rejection

Answer: B
*Diff: 2      Page Ref: 310*

5) Continuity attempted to show that, as people age,:
   A) they substitute similar roles for those roles which they lost
   B) they have problems maintaining their typical ways of adaptation
   C) life satisfaction is greater if men continue to work
   D) they are more influenced by the environment

Answer: A
*Diff: 2      Page Ref: 312*

6) Age stratification theory suggests that older people:
   A) recognize and understand the world view of younger generations
   B) today may be quite different from older persons of the past
   C) vary in their individual responses to aging
   D) are part of a social structure that devalues them

Answer: B
*Diff: 2      Page Ref: 315*

7) The subculture of aging theory argues that:
   A) older people are abandoned by younger groups
   B) older people identify themselves as distinct from other groups
   C) society devalues older adults
   D) disengagement by older persons is normal

Answer: B
*Diff: 2      Page Ref: 314*

8) According to age stratification theory, the generation that retired in the year 2000 may differ from those who retired in the 1950s, in that new retirees:
   A) may view leisure as unhealthy for successful aging
   B) may be more planful and proactive of aging and the dying process
   C) are financially worse off than previous cohorts
   D) are less likely to be parents and grandparents

Answer: B
*Diff: 3      Page Ref: 316*

9) Regarding "structural lag":
   A) societies today have difficulty accommodating to and utilizing retired elders
   B) employers today recognize the resources and skills of older workers
   C) new federal policies encourage workers to move in and out of the workforce
   D) organizations have many opportunities for healthy retired volunteers

Answer: A
*Diff: 2      Page Ref: 316*

10) Social exchange theory states that:
   A) older people exchange goods and services with other older people
   B) most older people exchange material goods and services with younger generations
   C) elders must exchange their material resources for emotional support
   D) elders generally have fewer resources to exchange

Answer: D
*Diff: 2      Page Ref: 316-317*

11) The political economy of aging is a recent model of social aging that is most closely related to:
   A) social exchange theory            B) age stratification theory
   C) structural lag                    D) symbolic interactionism

Answer: A
*Diff: 1      Page Ref: 317*

12) The life course perspective differs from role theory in that this perspective:
   A) considers individual personality as part of roles
   B) places people in their family context
   C) includes the impact of time, period, and cohort on aging
   D) focuses on the individual's developmental achievements and losses

Answer: C
*Diff: 2      Page Ref: 319*

13) The following is consistent with the concept of the "life course perspective":
    A) it focuses on improvements in function and world outlook with aging
    B) the uniqueness of the individual in adapting to a changing environment
    C) adult development is dynamic and interactive
    D) human development is linear and incremental
    Answer: C
    *Diff: 2*        *Page Ref: 319*

14) The following statement is consistent with the concept of social phenomenologists and social constructionists:
    A) standard measures and tests that are available can help understand reality
    B) criteria for evaluating a nursing home would be similar for patients, family and staff
    C) there is no such thing as "reality"
    D) individuals construct their own meanings of "reality"
    Answer: D
    *Diff: 3*        *Page Ref: 320–321*

15) In contrast to other theories, the best method for testing empirically a concept in social phenomenology is to use:
    A) standardized psychological tests          B) qualitative or ethnographic methods
    C) observation checklists                    D) clinical assessments by geriatricians
    Answer: B
    *Diff: 2*        *Page Ref: 321*

16) Critical theorists have been most influenced by:
    A) age stratification theory               B) the life course perspective
    C) social exchange theory                  D) social constructionism
    Answer: D
    *Diff: 1*        *Page Ref: 322*

17) Critical theorists are most concerned about:
    A) defining a useful role for older persons in Western society
    B) creating positive models of aging
    C) reflecting on the losses of aging
    D) bringing a positivist tradition into social gerontology
    Answer: B
    *Diff: 2*        *Page Ref: 322–323*

18) Gerotranscendence theory:
    A) focuses on the need for contemplation in old age
    B) focuses on the historic and cultural context of aging
    C) represents a shift in the elder's perspective to a materialistic view of the world
    D) reflects Western cultural ideals of wisdom and purpose
    Answer: A
    *Diff: 2*        *Page Ref: 311*

19) Which of the following social gerontological theories has <u>not</u> influenced the development of feminist theory?
    A) political economy of aging             B) symbolic interactionism
    C) social exchange                        D) social constructionism
    Answer: C
    *Diff: 2*        *Page Ref: 324*

20) Recent efforts to integrate postmodern theory into gerontology reflect a concern among some feminist theorists to:
    A) focus more on older women
    B) support positivist approaches to feminist research
    C) challenge research practices based on old beliefs and assumptions
    D) challenge clinicians who always view older women as victims

Answer: C
*Diff: 3       Page Ref: 325–326*

21) Life course capital recognizes both the exchange of resources across the life course and:
    A) the adjustments older adults make as they age
    B) the extent to which age norms are enforced
    C) the persistent inequalities in our society
    D) the pattern of role discontinuity older adults

Answer: C
*Diff: 3       Page Ref: 320*

22) The phrase "act your age" is an example of society enforcing:
    A) role discontinuity                    B) age stratification
    C) disengagement                         D) age norms

Answer: D
*Diff: 2       Page Ref: 307*

23) The second transformation in theoretical development in gerontology took place:
    A) in the 1960s        B) in the 1970s        C) in the 1980s        D) in the 1990s

Answer: C
*Diff: 2       Page Ref: 320*

24) An example of role loss that older adults commonly face is:
    A) retirement                            B) movement to a nursing home
    C) elder abuse                           D) the returning home of adult children

Answer: A
*Diff: 2       Page Ref: 308*

25) When a older adult is seen as having dementia, because they lost their car keys; whereas, a younger ignored adult who loses their car keys is seen as being distracted, the older adult is being:
    A) disengaged          B) labeled          C) ridiculed          D) socialized

Answer: B
*Diff: 2       Page Ref: 313–314*

26) The early social gerontological theories focused on how well older adults adjust to aging.
    Answer: TRUE
    *Diff: 1       Page Ref: 306*

27) Disengagement theory has been supported by recent empirical research.
    Answer: FALSE
    *Diff: 2       Page Ref: 310*

28) The early social gerontological theories addressed both individual and environmental factors that affect people's adjustment to aging.
    Answer: FALSE
    *Diff: 2       Page Ref: 304*

29) Structural lag occurs when social structures, such as work and education, are not congruent with the changes in the aging population and older people's lives.

Answer: TRUE
*Diff: 1      Page Ref: 316*

30) The symbolic interactionist perspective was one of the first social gerontological theories to consider the impact of the environment on older people's behavior.

Answer: TRUE
*Diff: 1      Page Ref: 313*

31) One of the implications of the political economy perspective is the need to develop more services that address structural inequities in our society.

Answer: TRUE
*Diff: 2      Page Ref: 318–319*

32) The life course perspective takes account primarily of individual personality changes with age.

Answer: FALSE
*Diff: 1      Page Ref: 319*

33) The widespread availability of models of productive aging help facilitate socialization into old age.

Answer: FALSE
*Diff: 3      Page Ref: 322*

34) Age stratification theory has been useful in explaining how older adults in most societies are discriminated against, because of their position in social structures.

Answer: FALSE
*Diff: 2      Page Ref: 315*

35) Social phenomenologists and constructionists differ from earlier theories by their focus on the subjective meaning of old age.

Answer: TRUE
*Diff: 2      Page Ref: 321*

36) Aging results in a shift in opportunity structures, so that older adults benefit from their increased resources to exchange for benefits during retirement.

Answer: FALSE
*Diff: 2      Page Ref: 317*

37) Both feminist and humanistic approaches toward understanding old age are examples of critical theory.

Answer: TRUE
*Diff: 1      Page Ref: 322*

38) Feminism addresses primarily the individual life experiences of women as they age.

Answer: FALSE
*Diff: 1      Page Ref: 324*

39) The symbolic interactionist view of aging takes account of the meaning of older people's activities within the larger environment.

Answer: TRUE
*Diff: 1      Page Ref: 313*

40) Social exchange theory explains how older people disengage from society because it is beneficial to them and to society.

Answer: FALSE
*Diff: 1*      *Page Ref: 316*

41) Every society conveys age norms through _____, the lifelong process of learning new roles, relinquishing old ones and becoming integrated into society.

Answer: socialization
*Diff: 1*      *Page Ref: 308*

42) _____ occurs when social structures can not keep pace with the changes in population and individual lives.

Answer: Structural lag
*Diff: 1*      *Page Ref: 316*

43) People born in the same time period who share a common history and environmental past, present and future are called a _____.

Answer: cohort
*Diff: 1*      *Page Ref: 315*

44) Which theory is based on Havinghurst's analyses of the Kansas City Studies of Adult Life?

Answer: Activity Theory
*Diff: 3*      *Page Ref: 309*

45) According to the _____ perspective, what is considered to be old age varies with the economic, cultural, historical, and societal context in which aging occurs.

Answer: social constructionist
*Diff: 2*      *Page Ref: 320*

46) Present the key points about continuity theory.

Answer: Continuity theory argues that individuals tend to maintain a consistent pattern of behavior as they age, substituting similar types of roles for the ones lost and maintain typical ways of adapting to the environment. In the absence of illness, individuals do not change dramatically as they age.
*Diff: 2*      *Page Ref: 312*

47) In what ways does social exchange theory challenge activity theory and disengagement theory?

Answer: Social exchange theory argues that social withdrawal happens, not because of system needs or individual choice, but because of unequal exchanges between older adults and other members of society.
*Diff: 2*      *Page Ref: 316*

48) Contrast disengagement theory and activity theory.

Answer: Whereas activity theory focuses on the individual and how the individual attempts to maintain a similar level of activity as one had in middle age, disengagement theory places more emphasis on the system and how individuals adapt to the needs of the system by withdrawing because of the loss of roles.
*Diff: 3*      *Page Ref: 310*

49) Apply a symbolic interactionist perspective to aging.

Answer: The symbolic interactionist perspective of aging argues that the interactions of such factors as the environment, individuals, and their encounters in it can significantly affect the kind of aging process people experience. It emphasizes the importance of considering the meaning of an activity for the individual concerned.

*Diff: 3*     *Page Ref: 313*

50) Identify the four goals of a critical gerontology approach.

Answer: The four goals of a critical gerontology approach are:

1. to theorize subjective and interpretive dimensions of aging

2. to focus not on technical advancement but on praxis (active involvement in practical change)

3. to link academics and practitioners through praxis

4. to produce "emancipatory" knowledge or a positive vision of a "good old age"

*Diff: 3*     *Page Ref: 322–323*

# Chapter 9  The Importance of Social Supports: Family, Friends, Neighbors, and Communities

1) Strong social supports contribute to:
   A) successful aging              B) higher mortality risk
   C) slower recovery from illness  D) greater use of formal services

Answer: A
*Diff: 1      Page Ref: 334*

2) During the 20th century, the number of multigenerational families in the United States:
   A) has decreased
   B) has increased
   C) has remained the same
   D) has resulted in more siblings in each generation

Answer: B
*Diff: 2      Page Ref: 337*

3) Fewer people within each generation are able to provide care for family members because of:
   A) an increase in fertility that necessitates more care to be aimed at children
   B) the increase of women entering the paid workforce in the past 50 years
   C) declining family dissolutions, such as through divorce
   D) a shift in age structure from a beanpole to a pyramid

Answer: B
*Diff: 2      Page Ref: 337*

4) Marital satisfaction is lowest:
   A) among the recently married (during young adulthood)
   B) during child-rearing years including middle age
   C) in the later years
   D) among those experiencing the empty nest

Answer: B
*Diff: 2      Page Ref: 343*

5) Researchers have found that the best predictor of life satisfaction in old age is:
   A) age                          B) health status
   C) work vs. retirement status   D) marital satisfaction

Answer: D
*Diff: 3      Page Ref: 343*

6) During the elderly years (65+):
   A) more women remarry than men   B) as many men remarry as women
   C) more men remarry than women   D) none of the above

Answer: C
*Diff: 2      Page Ref: 344*

7) Which of the following have been identified as possible challenges to grandparents raising their grandchildren?
   A) social isolation             B) concern about their own health
   C) loss over retirement plans   D) all of the above

Answer: D
*Diff: 2      Page Ref: 360*

8) Which statement best describes divorce and remarriage in old age?
   A) The percentage of older persons who are currently divorced is about the same as it was thirty years ago.
   B) For older persons the likelihood of remarriage is smaller than remarriage for younger age groups.
   C) Divorce in old age improves the economic status of men and women.
   D) Divorce results in greater contacts with adult children.

   Answer: B
   *Diff: 2*      *Page Ref: 344*

9) Older gays and lesbians, compared to their heterosexual peers:
   A) are less likely to plan for their future security
   B) tend to build a "surrogate family"
   C) have lower self-esteem
   D) maintain strong ties with their families of origin

   Answer: B
   *Diff: 2*      *Page Ref: 345–348*

10) Sibling relationships in old age:
   A) remain as close or distant as they were in mid-life
   B) are closer between brothers
   C) are closer between sisters
   D) result in more caregiving for frail siblings

   Answer: C
   *Diff: 2*      *Page Ref: 349*

11) Studies of relationships between adult children and their older parents indicate:
   A) most older parents see an adult child frequently
   B) most parents do not live geographically near to any of their children
   C) most older parents are alienated from their children
   D) most older parents rarely see their children

   Answer: A
   *Diff: 2*      *Page Ref: 351*

12) Older people who never married and are without children, and thus do not have adult children to care for them:
   A) generally are more destitute than those with children
   B) usually develop other support systems and turn to others for help
   C) are much happier because children tend to let down their parents
   D) generally experience much worse health

   Answer: B
   *Diff: 2*      *Page Ref: 350*

13) The flow of support between older persons and their adult children is generally:
   A) unidirectional, with children providing housing for their parents
   B) unidirectional, with parents continuing to help their adult children financially and emotionally
   C) reciprocal exchanges financially, emotionally, and in providing care
   D) nonexistent, especially among urban families

   Answer: C
   *Diff: 2*      *Page Ref: 352*

14) Intergenerational transfer of financial support is most likely to occur:
   A) from adult child to elderly parent
   B) from son to elderly parent
   C) from elderly parent to unmarried adult child
   D) from elderly parent to developmentally disabled adult child

   Answer: D
   *Diff: 2      Page Ref: 352*

15) The changing demographic patterns of the United States have also affected the grandparenting role, such that:
   A) older adults today have more grandchildren than earlier cohorts
   B) more older persons are experiencing the grandparent role than in the past
   C) there is less contact between grandparents and grandchildren than in the past
   D) grandfathers and grandmothers spend equal time with their grandchildren

   Answer: B
   *Diff: 2      Page Ref: 352-353*

16) Grandparents who provide custodial care for their grandchildren:
   A) have increased twofold in the last decade
   B) was a more common sight 50 years ago
   C) generally obtain financial help from their adult children
   D) are disproportionately represented by African American women

   Answer: D
   *Diff: 1      Page Ref: 356*

17) Research regarding older adults' relationships with pets:
   A) no benefits have been shown regarding alertness and responsiveness
   B) findings show that pet owners are more likely to be unmarried and living alone
   C) results demonstrate ethnic minority differences in pet ownership patterns
   D) more communication consists of anecdotal acts than empirical studies

   Answer: D
   *Diff: 2      Page Ref: 369-370*

18) The primary factor that affects the frequency of visiting between grandparents and grandchildren is:
   A) geographic proximity
   B) the gender of the grandparent and grandchild
   C) family size
   D) divorce

   Answer: A
   *Diff: 2      Page Ref: 353*

19) In their social relationships in later life, men tend to:
   A) place more value on friendships than women do
   B) be more aggressive about their friendships than women are
   C) depend on their wives for companionship
   D) have a greater need for friends in later life than women do

   Answer: C
   *Diff: 2      Page Ref: 365*

20) In recent years, ethnic minority families have experienced the following:
    A) increasing filial responsibility over time
    B) weakening of the extended family in urban settings
    C) less stress from caregiving than Caucasian families
    D) decreased likelihood of multigenerational family households

    Answer: B
    *Diff: 2*      *Page Ref: 340*

21) Intergenerational programs that link older people with youth in need and young families are:
    A) rapidly growing          B) growing slowly
    C) declining slowly          D) nonexistent

    Answer: A
    *Diff: 1*      *Page Ref: 367*

22) Studies of older adults' relationships with pets tend to be:
    A) at least 10-years-old      B) rigorous empirical studies
    C) anecdotal studies          D) interviews with men only

    Answer: C
    *Diff: 1*      *Page Ref: 369*

23) The majority of men over age 65 are:
    A) married                    B) single/never married
    C) divorced                   D) widowed

    Answer: A
    *Diff: 1*      *Page Ref: 341*

24) Most women view the "empty nest" as:
    A) depressing                 B) an unhappy condition
    C) an opportunity for new activities    D) a reason for divorce

    Answer: C
    *Diff: 1*      *Page Ref: 343*

25) A grandparent who feels close and affectionate to grandchildren without taking on a
    particular role is expressing:
    A) the companionate style of grandparenting
    B) the remote style of grandparenting
    C) the involved style of grandparenting
    D) the authoritative style of grandparenting

    Answer: A
    *Diff: 3*      *Page Ref: 354*

26) Women consistently experience increased levels of marital satisfaction over time than do men.
    Answer: FALSE
    *Diff: 1*      *Page Ref: 343*

27) Childless older adults with health problems tend to be more isolated than other older people.
    Answer: TRUE
    *Diff: 2*      *Page Ref: 350*

28) Divorce in later life is decreasing.
    Answer: FALSE
    *Diff: 1*      *Page Ref: 344*

29) Older men are more likely to be married than are older women.

Answer: TRUE
*Diff: 1        Page Ref: 341*

30) Older women who are divorced have a lower desire to remarry than those who are widowed.

Answer: FALSE
*Diff: 1        Page Ref: 344*

31) The majority of older individuals live alone.

Answer: FALSE
*Diff: 1        Page Ref: 363*

32) Among siblings in old age, sisters are more likely to maintain family ties than are brothers.

Answer: TRUE
*Diff: 1        Page Ref: 349*

33) Most studies indicate that the majority of American adult children reject the norm of filial responsibility.

Answer: FALSE
*Diff: 2        Page Ref: 351*

34) Older parents in the United States are far more likely to receive financial help from their adult children than to assist their children.

Answer: FALSE
*Diff: 2        Page Ref: 352*

35) Multigenerational households tend to be more prevalent among ethnic minority families compared to Caucasian families.

Answer: TRUE
*Diff: 2        Page Ref: 340*

36) The majority of older people are grandparents and see a grandchild at least once a month.

Answer: TRUE
*Diff: 2        Page Ref: 353*

37) Friends are often a more important source of emotional support than family in old age because they are chosen.

Answer: TRUE
*Diff: 2        Page Ref: 364*

38) Overall, older gays and lesbians report low self-acceptance and self-esteem.

Answer: FALSE
*Diff: 2        Page Ref: 347*

39) Older parents generally have infrequent telephone or e-mail contact with their adult children, and only once- or twice-yearly face-to-face contact.

Answer: FALSE
*Diff: 2        Page Ref: 351–352*

40) The majority of custodial grandparents are female, married, and live in the South.

Answer: TRUE
*Diff: 2        Page Ref: 356*

41) _____ describes a situation where geographic separation does not weaken socioemotional bonds.

Answer: intimacy at a distance
*Diff: 3      Page Ref: 352*

42) The style of grandparenting where grandparents live close by and often take on parent-like responsibilities is called _____.

Answer: involved style
*Diff: 2      Page Ref: 354*

43) _____ refers to the placement of children with relatives by the state.

Answer: Formal kinship care
*Diff: 2      Page Ref: 357*

44) _____ are non-family members older adults may turn to because of their concern, interest and understanding.

Answer: natural helpers
*Diff: 2      Page Ref: 365*

45) Children who leave home and then return, often for financial reasons are called _____.

Answer: boomerang children
*Diff: 3      Page Ref: 343*

46) Explain marital satisfaction among older adults.

Answer: It is U-shaped. It is high among those recently married, lower during childrearing years and then higher in the later stages. Late stage satisfaction may be due to children leaving the home and an equalization of the division of labor in the home.
*Diff: 2      Page Ref: 343*

47) To what extent does divorce impact marriages among older adults?

Answer: An increasing proportion of older adults are divorcing and 9% of older adults who are divorced has doubled since 1970. Rates are higher among ethnic minority elders.
*Diff: 2      Page Ref: 344*

48) Characterize sibling relationships in old age.

Answer: The sibling relationship in old age is characterized by a shared history, egalitarianism, and increasing closeness. Sisters are more likely than brothers to have frequent contact.
*Diff: 2      Page Ref: 349*

49) Name and define the five styles of grandparenting and give an example of each.

Answer: The five styles of grandparenting are companionate (close and affectionate without taking on a particular role), remote (less involved, perhaps due to geographic distance), involved (assumes parent-like responsibilities in response to a family crisis), individualized (closer than remote, but does not contribute substantially to the lives of grandchildren) and authoritative (extensive support, perhaps assuming parental responsibilities).
*Diff: 2      Page Ref: 354*

50) Discuss the role of great-grandparenting and the two styles of performing this role.

Answer: The role of great-grandparenting is becoming more frequent. The two styles of grandparenting relate to geographic distance where one is geographically close and one is remote. Remote great-grandparenting usually involves occasional and ritualistic contact. Close great-grandparents have frequent opportunities for physical and emotional closeness and are involved.

Diff: 2        Page Ref: 361

# Chapter 10  Opportunities and Stresses
## of Informal Caregiving

1) The vast majority of older persons:
   A) with three or more limitations in daily activities (ADLs) live in the community
   B) receive services by paid care-givers
   C) live in nursing homes
   D) live with their children

   Answer: A
   *Diff: 1      Page Ref: 385*

2) The "sandwich generation" refers to:
   A) the young adult generation who feels sandwiched between their parents' and their own
   B) middle-aged men sandwiched between the role of caregiver and wage earner
   C) middle-aged women caring for their parents and children
   D) young women worried about young children and careers

   Answer: C
   *Diff: 2      Page Ref: 396*

3) Evidence for shifts in filial piety among ethnic minorities includes:
   A) increased use of services for support among older Asian Americans
   B) increasing proportions of older African Americans using nursing homes
   C) decreasing proportions of older African Americans using nursing homes
   D) increased rates of depression among Latino caregivers

   Answer: B
   *Diff: 3      Page Ref: 397–398*

4) Which demographic and social changes are intensifying demands on families to provide more complex care?
   A) rapid growth of the oldest-old with acute illnesses
   B) increased nuclear family structures
   C) declining racial and economic inequities
   D) more women employed outside the home

   Answer: D
   *Diff: 2      Page Ref: 387*

5) Male caregivers of frail elders:
   A) constitute about the same percentage of caregivers as do females
   B) feel as psychologically responsible as female caregivers
   C) face multiple demands like females
   D) are less likely to give up jobs than females

   Answer: D
   *Diff: 2      Page Ref: 393–394*

6) Which of the following ethnic groups is <u>least</u> likely to report stress, burden and depression in the caregiver role?
   A) Hispanic caregivers                 B) African American caregivers
   C) Asian American caregivers           D) Caucasian, non-Hispanic caregivers

   Answer: B
   *Diff: 2      Page Ref: 397*

7) When compared with their white counterparts, African American and Latino caregivers tend to be:
    A) more likely to have physical health problems
    B) more likely to be spouses
    C) more likely to have alternative caregivers to assist them
    D) as likely to be economically disadvantaged

Answer: A
*Diff: 2*      *Page Ref: 397*

8) The following have been found to be helpful for the family caregiver's self-care and well-being:
    A) setting limits to the older relative's demands
    B) remaining isolated from other relatives
    C) high levels of interaction with other family members
    D) using formal support services

Answer: A
*Diff: 3*      *Page Ref: 389*

9) Caregiver stress is increased by:
    A) severity of the care receiver's disease          B) availability of formal services
    C) living with the care recipient                    D) cognitive status of care receiver

Answer: C
*Diff: 3*      *Page Ref: 388*

10) Short-term interventions to support caregivers:
    A) are rare
    B) require the expertise of geriatric mental health workers
    C) are most effective if focused on relieving subjective burden
    D) have not been proven to relieve burden

Answer: D
*Diff: 2*      *Page Ref: 404*

11) Elder abuse on the part of a caregiver includes:
    A) verbal threats
    B) misuse of the older person's money or property
    C) physical abuse
    D) all of the above

Answer: D
*Diff: 1*      *Page Ref: 407*

12) Which of the following is <u>least</u> likely to cause family members to abuse their elderly relative?
    A) caregiver stress
    B) dementia of the care recipient
    C) unequal power relationships between caregiver and care recipient
    D) living together in the same house

Answer: D
*Diff: 2*      *Page Ref: 411*

13) Elder abuse is:
  A) often concealed by the elderly care recipient
  B) reported in high numbers to adult protective services
  C) screened with an easily administered questionnaire
  D) prosecuted in the majority of cases

Answer: A
*Diff: 2*     *Page Ref: 412–413*

14) Elder self-neglect is <u>least</u> likely to be associated with:
  A) attention-seeking            B) cognitive impairment
  C) depression                   D) alcohol abuse

Answer: A
*Diff: 2*     *Page Ref: 409*

15) Financial abuse refers primarily to:
  A) physical abuse
  B) emotional abuse
  C) economic exploitation
  D) violation of an older person's legal rights

Answer: C
*Diff: 2*     *Page Ref: 407*

16) A major problem faced by adult protective services when investigating cases of elder abuse is:
  A) lack of evidence about the case
  B) lack of cooperation among agencies
  C) too many community options for referring the elder
  D) inadequate finances of the elder

Answer: B
*Diff: 2*     *Page Ref: 413*

17) It is estimated that _____ percent of older adults are abused by someone with whom they share housing.
  A) 70–80          B) 50–60          C) 20–30          D) 0–10

Answer: D
*Diff: 3*     *Page Ref: 408*

18) The group that is at greatest risk of elder abuse is:
  A) wealthy widowed women
  B) oldest-old women
  C) men and women who are physically disabled
  D) people in long-term marriages

Answer: B
*Diff: 2*     *Page Ref: 411*

19) Which of the following variables is <u>least</u> predictive of an older person's move to a nursing home?
  A) perceived burden of the caregiver     B) negative interpersonal dynamics
  C) disease symptoms of the elder          D) severity of the disease

Answer: C
*Diff: 2*     *Page Ref: 414–415*

20) Which of the following is not a part of caregiver assessment?
   A) assesses financial resources needed for caregiving
   B) validates the family's experiences
   C) gives the family a defined role in the treatment process
   D) reduces risks to caregivers' well-being

Answer: A
*Diff: 2      Page Ref: 403*

21) An example of a physical problem attributed to caregiver stress would be:
   A) sleep disorders and exhaustion          B) work absenteeism
   C) social isolation                        D) direct costs of care

Answer: A
*Diff: 1      Page Ref: 389*

22) Strained social and family relationships is an example of what type of caregiver stress?
   A) emotional          B) financial          C) physical          D) biological

Answer: A
*Diff: 1      Page Ref: 390*

23) An example of financial caregiver stress would be:
   A) missed opportunities in one's career    B) increased morbidity
   C) worry and anxiety                        D) grief and loss

Answer: A
*Diff: 1      Page Ref: 389*

24) Withholding or improper administration of needed medication would be an example of which type of elder mistreatment?
   A) physical                          B) medical
   C) material                          D) violation of rights

Answer: B
*Diff: 1      Page Ref: 407*

25) Who is least likely to turn to formal services for caregiving?
   A) women                             B) ethnic minorities
   C) men                               D) both A and B

Answer: D
*Diff: 1      Page Ref: 404*

26) Because families are so busy, agencies and facilities are the major providers of long-term care to older adults with chronic illness.

Answer: FALSE
*Diff: 1      Page Ref: 385*

27) Adult daughters typically provide more direct care for their older parents than do adult sons.

Answer: TRUE
*Diff: 2      Page Ref: 393*

28) The average female caregiver of an older adult is a full-time homemaker.

Answer: FALSE
*Diff: 2      Page Ref: 386*

29) From a feminist perspective, women predominate caregiving because they are socialized to be caregivers and because society devalues women's paid and unpaid work.

Answer: TRUE
*Diff: 3       Page Ref: 393*

30) Ethnic minority caregivers more frequently turn to formal services for help than do their white counterparts.

Answer: FALSE
*Diff: 2       Page Ref: 397*

31) Family caregivers tend to experience the stress of emotional burdens more than financial or physical care burdens.

Answer: TRUE
*Diff: 2       Page Ref: 390*

32) Most family caregivers make extensive use of formal services to assist them with their care tasks.

Answer: FALSE
*Diff: 2       Page Ref: 403*

33) Researchers have found that caregivers of color perceive less subjective burden from their roles than do Caucasian caregivers.

Answer: TRUE
*Diff: 2       Page Ref: 397*

34) The stress of caregiving is the major factor contributing to instances of elder abuse.

Answer: FALSE
*Diff: 2       Page Ref: 411*

35) A caregiver's subjective burden is less salient than objective burden or actual tasks performed.

Answer: FALSE
*Diff: 2       Page Ref: 388*

36) The role of caregiver continues even after the older adult moves to a long-term care facility.

Answer: TRUE
*Diff: 2       Page Ref: 415*

37) Instances of self-neglect are clear cut and require professional intervention to keep the older person safe.

Answer: FALSE
*Diff: 2       Page Ref: 409*

38) The most frequent caregiving pattern is between partners.

Answer: TRUE
*Diff: 2       Page Ref: 394*

39) The Family and Medical Leave Act offers job protection to all workers in the private sector who must take short-term leave for family caregiving.

Answer: FALSE
*Diff: 2       Page Ref: 401*

40) Older people who are mentally competent have the right to remain in their homes, even if they are at risk.

Answer: TRUE
*Diff: 2      Page Ref: 409*

41) _____ refers to the daily physical demands and behavioral phenomena of caregiving.

Answer: Objective burden
*Diff: 2      Page Ref: 388*

42) _____ includes harmful or hurtful conduct that is willfully inflicted upon an older person.

Answer: Elder mistreatment
*Diff: 2      Page Ref: 407*

43) _____ occurs when the older adult engages in behavior that threatens his or her safety, even though he or she is mentally competent and understands the consequences of decisions.

Answer: Self-neglect
*Diff: 1      Page Ref: 409*

44) The _____ is the part of the Older Americans Act that extends services to caregivers of older adults.

Answer: National Family Caregiver Support Program
*Diff: 2      Page Ref: 401*

45) _____ is planned for emergency short-term relief to caregivers from the demands of ongoing care.

Answer: Respite care
*Diff: 2      Page Ref: 405*

46) Discuss the costs and benefits of informal care for society and for informal caregivers.

Answer: For society informal caregiving reduces the financial burden on society while for the individual it may lead to physical (poor health outcomes), financial (direct and indirect costs) and emotional costs (anxiety, worry, feeling alone), but can also result in finding personal meaning in the role and in life, which can enhance caregiver well-being.
*Diff: 2      Page Ref: 388–390*

47) Discuss women as caregivers using the feminist theory perspective.

Answer: Women predominate as caregivers because they are socialized to be carers but also because society devalues women's reimbursed responsibilities in the home and their paid work through employment.
*Diff: 2      Page Ref: 393*

48) Discuss the warning signs of elder abuse and neglect.

Answer: Warning signs include depression, fear, discrepancies in psychosocial and medical history, vague explanations of illness or injuries, the illness is not responding to treatment and frequent visits to the emergency room, especially for unexplained injuries and illnesses.
*Diff: 2      Page Ref: 411*

49) What are the characteristics of elder abusers that reflect power inequalities?

Answer: The abuser is frequently male, dependent on the elder for housing, finances or other services, and experiencing mental illness, substance abuse, a history of problem behaviors and a lack of empathy for those with disabilities.
*Diff: 2      Page Ref: 411*

50) Outline the two federal policy initiatives, the Family and Medical Leave Act of 1993 and the National Family Caregiver Support Program of 2000, aimed at supporting families.

Answer: The FMLA provides up to 12 weeks of unpaid leave for family care (e.g., birth of a child, adoptions, care for an immediate family member) for employees who work for companies with 50 or more employees. The NFCSP provides services for caregivers and is funded by the Administration on Aging. Priority for the NFCSP is given to low income, older caregivers and those giving care to persons with developmental disabilities.

*Diff: 2*      *Page Ref: 401–402*

# Chapter 11  Living Arrangements and Social Interactions

1) Which of the following theories represents the first model of P–E congruence?
   A) Murray's theory of needs and press are not relevant to theories of person–environment fit.
   B) Lewin's field theory
   C) Lawton's and Nahemow's Competence model
   D) Lawton's environmental press model

   Answer:  A
   *Diff: 3        Page Ref: 430*

2) The competence model can best be applied to:
   A) an early–stage Alzheimer's patient
   B) an older person with arthritis and vision problems
   C) a healthy 65–year–old
   D) both A and B

   Answer:  D
   *Diff: 2        Page Ref: 431*

3) Compared to their urban counterparts, elders in suburban communities:
   A) have lower incomes                           B) are more likely to live alone
   C) report to be in better functional health     D) have adequate transportation

   Answer:  C
   *Diff: 2        Page Ref: 432*

4) The primary disadvantage of suburban living for older adults is:
   A) most elders are poorer than younger residents
   B) difficult access to health and social services
   C) most elders live alone
   D) their functional health is worse than among urban elders

   Answer:  B
   *Diff: 2        Page Ref: 432*

5) Compared to younger age groups, people over age 65 are _____ likely to move to a different community and _____ likely to change housing types within the same community.
   A) less/more          B) less/less          C) more/more          D) more/less

   Answer:  A
   *Diff: 2        Page Ref: 434*

6) In a national survey by AARP, the percentage of people who endorsed the survey question "I'd like to stay in my home and never move":
   A) decreased from ages 65 to 85+
   B) remained essentially the same for ages 65 to 85+
   C) increased from age 65 to 85
   D) increased from age 65 to 75, then declined

   Answer:  C
   *Diff: 3        Page Ref: 435*

7) Regarding neighborhood living:
   A) most older persons, in general, are satisfied with their neighborhood
   B) most older persons, in poorer neighborhoods, are dissatisfied with their neighbors
   C) most elders prefer living near their families
   D) neighbors can replace families as support systems

Answer: A
*Diff: 3     Page Ref: 437*

8) The group that experiences the highest rates of robbery is the age group:
   A) 16 to 19          B) 25 to 34          C) 50 to 64          D) 65 and older

Answer: A
*Diff: 2     Page Ref: 437–438*

9) Among all older Americans, those most likely to be a victim of violent crimes are:
   A) elders with the highest incomes          B) elders with the lowest incomes
   C) those who own their homes                D) white women

Answer: B
*Diff: 2     Page Ref: 438*

10) Older people are most likely to be victims of:
   A) robbery                                  B) violent crime
   C) purse snatching/pick pocketing           D) fraud and con games

Answer: D
*Diff: 2     Page Ref: 439*

11) A person aged 65–74 with income > $40,000, and in a rural community is most likely to live:
   A) in a nursing home                        B) in a rental home
   C) in his/her own house                     D) with his/her own children

Answer: C
*Diff: 3     Page Ref: 440*

12) The subgroup of older adults who are most likely to enter a nursing home directly from a hospital is:
   A) the oldest-old                           B) women
   C) African Americans                        D) Caucasians

Answer: C
*Diff: 2     Page Ref: 447*

13) Reverse mortgages are most useful for elders who:
   A) still owe a lot on their home
   B) have high equity and a low mortgage
   C) plan to move soon to a long-term care facility
   D) have a high mortgage remaining on their home

Answer: B
*Diff: 2     Page Ref: 441*

14) Elders who reside in assisted living:
   A) tend to be in the young-old range
   B) overwhelmingly have Alzheimer's disease
   C) are less frail than was intended by this type of housing
   D) are likely to need assistance with bathing

Answer: D
*Diff: 1     Page Ref: 450*

15) "Aging in place" refers to elders who:
   A) prefer to remain in their own homes
   B) prefer to die in a congregate care facility
   C) age by remaining inactive and uninvolved
   D) show early signs of aging

Answer: D
*Diff: 1     Page Ref: 436*

16) Continuous care retirement communities are most attractive to:
   A) very frail elders
   B) couples with financial resources and some health problems
   C) couples in their mid-50s who seek social stimulation
   D) widowed older women of color

Answer: B
*Diff: 2     Page Ref: 443*

17) Which of the following characteristics does <u>not</u> describe the typical nursing home resident?
   A) middle-class white              B) poor white
   C) widowed                        D) ethnic minority

Answer: D
*Diff: 2     Page Ref: 445*

18) Which of the following is <u>not</u> growing rapidly as a long-term care option for frail elders?
   A) nursing homes                  B) assisted living
   C) adult family homes             D) home health care

Answer: A
*Diff: 2     Page Ref: 444*

19) An important advantage of many assisted living facilities over nursing homes is their policy of:
   A) Medicaid waivers               B) negotiated risk
   C) guaranteed lifelong care       D) a medical model of long-term care

Answer: B
*Diff: 3     Page Ref: 450*

20) Home health care has been found to be effective in:
   A) preventing nursing home use altogether
   B) reducing death rates among older people
   C) curtailing the use of hospitals
   D) keeping older people independent

Answer: C
*Diff: 2     Page Ref: 453*

21) Private homes with new technology designed to assist older adults are known as:
   A) smart homes                    B) universal designs
   C) nursing homes                  D) workstations

Answer: A
*Diff: 1     Page Ref: 442*

22) What is the name of the field where gerontologists and engineers work together to create technology to help older adults?
   A) telehealth
   B) gerontechnology
   C) assistive technology
   D) social gerontology
   Answer: B
   *Diff: 1      Page Ref: 456*

23) People over age 50 comprise _____ of the homeless population.
   A) less than 5 percent
   B) about 10 percent
   C) approximately half
   D) almost all
   Answer: B
   *Diff: 1      Page Ref: 461*

24) The gender differential in nursing homes is due to:
   A) women's longer life expectancy
   B) women's greater risk of experiencing chronic illnesses
   C) women's greater likelihood of being married
   D) all of the above
   Answer: D
   *Diff: 2      Page Ref: 445*

25) The most popular modification older adults utilize in their home is:
   A) to install grab bars in the bathroom
   B) to add brighter lights
   C) to replace water faucets with lever handles
   D) to install ramps instead of stairs
   Answer: A
   *Diff: 2      Page Ref: 456*

26) The person-environment perspective is useful in gerontology because it highlights changes in older people's interactions with their environment.
   Answer: TRUE
   *Diff: 2      Page Ref: 430*

27) The majority of all older adults live in urban and suburban communities.
   Answer: TRUE
   *Diff: 2      Page Ref: 431*

28) The majority of older people today live in rental apartments.
   Answer: FALSE
   *Diff: 3      Page Ref: 440*

29) Congregate housing is better for many older people than private houses because of greater opportunities for shared meals and social support.
   Answer: TRUE
   *Diff: 2      Page Ref: 440*

30) National surveys have revealed that fear of crime among older people is consistent with the high levels of crime that they face.
   Answer: FALSE
   *Diff: 1      Page Ref: 437*

31) Assisted living is a feasible housing option for older people of all income levels.

Answer: FALSE
*Diff: 2        Page Ref: 450*

32) Most adult family homes, can serve older people with significant ADL impairments.

Answer: FALSE
*Diff: 3        Page Ref: 452*

33) The proportion of older persons in nursing homes at any one time has declined in the past 20 years.

Answer: TRUE
*Diff: 2        Page Ref: 444*

34) One of the first national efforts aimed at changing the nursing home culture was labeled the Pioneer Network.

Answer: FALSE
*Diff: 2        Page Ref: 448*

35) Medicaid reimbursement rates for adult foster care are one third to one half the rates paid to nursing homes.

Answer: TRUE
*Diff: 1        Page Ref: 452*

36) All fifty states in the U.S. have Medicaid waivers for assisted living.

Answer: FALSE
*Diff: 2        Page Ref: 451*

37) SRO housing is becoming scarcer as an option for low-income older people in urban centers.

Answer: TRUE
*Diff: 1        Page Ref: 461*

38) The young-old are more likely than those aged 75 and older to face all types of crime.

Answer: TRUE
*Diff: 2        Page Ref: 438*

39) Community residential care facilities such as adult family homes are generally not an appropriate setting for older adults with multiple ADL limitations.

Answer: FALSE
*Diff: 2        Page Ref: 449*

40) Future housing that includes universal design features can help people age in place.

Answer: TRUE
*Diff: 1        Page Ref: 456*

41) According to Litwak and Longino, where do a large number of retirees relocate?

Answer: Sunbelt
*Diff: 1        Page Ref: 434*

42) According to the U.S. Census Bureau, _____ percent of the population age 65 and over occupied a nursing home.

Answer: 4.5
*Diff: 2        Page Ref: 444*

43) In which stage of Litwak and Longino's model do older adults relocate because they are facing limitations in their ADLs?

Answer: Stage 2
*Diff: 1*     *Page Ref: 434*

44) What type of housing provides a range of housing, from independent to congregate living?

Answer: continuous care retirement communities
*Diff: 1*     *Page Ref: 443*

45) According to _____ theories of aging, a person is more likely to experience life satisfaction in an environment that is conducive with his or her physical, cognitive, and emotional needs and abilities.

Answer: person-environment
*Diff: 1*     *Page Ref: 429*

46) Explain the foundations of person-environment theories of aging.

Answer: P-E theories of aging focus on the idea that any change in characteristics of either the person or the environment is likely to produce a change in that person's behavior. Murray's theory of personality, that the individual is in dynamic interaction with his/her setting, is an example of this model.
*Diff: 2*     *Page Ref: 430*

47) Discuss Litwak's and Longino's three stage model of migration.

Answer: In stage one the young-old and recent retirees move to the Sunbelt (FL, CA, AZ, TX). In stage two older adults who face a chronic illness or limitations with ADLs may move to a retirement community or an assisted living facility that offers amenities but allows the resident to remain relatively independent. Stage three happens when an older adult faces a disability which requires that the individual move to a nursing home to receive 24-hour skilled nursing care.
*Diff: 3*     *Page Ref: 434*

48) Discuss the advantages of assisted living that have contributed to this type of housing becoming a growing trend.

Answer: Assisted living is touted for its ability to provide older adults, who do not need 24-hour nursing care, assistance with ADLs and is based on a social model rather than a medical model. It is said to provide a more homelike, less institutional setting that encourages active aging.
*Diff: 2*     *Page Ref: 449-450*

49) Outline the key points about the geographic distribution of the older population.

Answer: For example, in the U.S. the older population is more likely to live in metropolitan areas including urban and suburban settings. Older ethnic adults are more likely to live in central cities.
*Diff: 2*     *Page Ref: 431-432*

50) Explain how technology is allowing more older adults to age in place.

Answer: Technology has produced many devices to allow older adults to remain independent and it their homes. Such technology would include levers as door handles, bathrooms with roll-in showers, brighter lighting and pullcords in the bathroom for emergencies. Telehealth allows health information to be transmitted electronically from the patient's home to the physician's office.
*Diff: 2*     *Page Ref: 456-457*

# Chapter 12   Productive Aging: Paid and Nonpaid Roles and Activities

1) Retirement satisfaction is provided by activities that provide:
   A) autonomy                           B) a chance to learn something new
   C) extra spending money               D) both A and B

   Answer: C
   *Diff: 2       Page Ref: 482*

2) The average retirement age in the United States today is _____, compared to age _____ in 1910.
   A) 61.5/74            B) 68.5/65            C) 65/62            D) 60/50

   Answer: A
   *Diff: 2       Page Ref: 478*

3) The timing of retirement is affected by all of the following <u>except</u>:
   A) adequate retirement income         B) family and gender roles
   C) health status                      D) other job prospects

   Answer: D
   *Diff: 2       Page Ref: 480*

4) After age 61, the group most likely to retire early is:
   A) African American women
   B) white women who re-entered work force in their 40s
   C) white men
   D) African American men and women

   Answer: C
   *Diff: 2       Page Ref: 481*

5) The timing of retirement is affected by:
   A) adequate retirement income         B) ethnic minority status
   C) family and gender roles            D) all of the above

   Answer: D
   *Diff: 2       Page Ref: 480*

6) Regarding retirement:
   A) pre-retirement self-esteem generally predicts post-retirement self-esteem
   B) retirement satisfaction is higher for women
   C) health status declines for white men soon after retirement
   D) health status improves after retirement

   Answer: A
   *Diff: 2       Page Ref: 483*

7) The major determinant of retirees' life satisfaction is:
   A) having a spouse who is also retired
   B) financial security and good health
   C) opportunities for part-time employment
   D) opportunities for volunteering

   Answer: B
   *Diff: 2       Page Ref: 482*

8) Pre-retirement planning programs:
    A) are widespread among American companies
    B) are used mostly by low-income workers
    C) help women plan their post-retirement income
    D) are most available to higher income workers
Answer: D
*Diff: 2      Page Ref: 485*

9) To retain older workers, companies may offer the following pre-retirement work option:
    A) working from home                    B) short hours
    C) working any 8 hours during the day   D) all of the above
Answer: D
*Diff: 2      Page Ref: 485, 488*

10) The percentage of men age 65+ who are remaining in the workforce today, compared to the 1950s, is:
    A) higher              B) lower              C) essentially the same
Answer: B
*Diff: 2      Page Ref: 486*

11) Currently the mandatory retirement age in the United States is:
    A) 65          B) 70          C) 75          D) none
Answer: D
*Diff: 3      Page Ref: 491*

12) Most older people who continue to work full-time are concentrated in:
    A) physically demanding jobs    B) service-oriented jobs
    C) high-tech jobs               D) jobs requiring 40-50 hours per week
Answer: B
*Diff: 1      Page Ref: 487*

13) Regarding funding of retirement for most older adults:
    A) home equity is a minor component of assets
    B) private pensions comprise about 20% of income
    C) Social Security provides less than 25% of income
    D) part-time employment provides about 50% of income
Answer: B
*Diff: 2      Page Ref: 491-494*

14) The rates of poverty are highest among older people who are:
    A) single women                 B) single men
    C) married men                  D) married women
Answer: A
*Diff: 2      Page Ref: 499*

15) Leisure can best be defined as:
    A) time spent on vacation           B) any activity which has no obligations
    C) any free time a person can relax D) time spent with family members
Answer: B
*Diff: 1      Page Ref: 501*

16) Rates of volunteerism are <u>highest</u> among older adults who:
   A) have higher income and education
   B) have lower income and are affiliated with a church
   C) are African American women
   D) are widowed

Answer: A
*Diff: 1        Page Ref: 514–516*

17) Regarding religious involvement in old age:
   A) men and women are about equally involved
   B) African Americans and whites are about equally involved
   C) older adults attend religious institutions more than any other age group
   D) religious groups are the most important source of instrumental and emotional support

Answer: C
*Diff: 1        Page Ref: 503–505*

18) Spiritual well-being can generally be characterized by:
   A) achieving a sense of purpose or meaning for one's continued existence
   B) high rates of participation in organized religion
   C) mental well-being
   D) both A and B
   E) both A and C

Answer: E
*Diff: 2        Page Ref: 507*

19) When looking at the political behavior of older people, it is necessary to:
   A) take account of the historical period in which they were raised
   B) use cross-sectional studies
   C) take account of their age
   D) try to isolate age differences

Answer: A
*Diff: 2        Page Ref: 518*

20) The largest and most influential senior organization is:
   A) National Council of Senior Citizens
   B) Gerontological society of America
   C) American Association of Retired Persons
   D) National Council on the Aging

Answer: C
*Diff: 2        Page Ref: 523*

21) Who founded the Grey Panthers?
   A) Elizabeth Kubler-Ross                    B) Maggie Kuhn
   C) President Clinton                         D) the Gerontological Society of America

Answer: B
*Diff: 2        Page Ref: 524*

22) The Gerontological Society of America is an example of a:
   A) professional association                 B) trade association
   C) mass-membership organization             D) political lobbying group

Answer: A
*Diff: 1        Page Ref: 524*

23) The American Association of Retired Persons (AARP) is an example of a:
   A) mass-membership organization          B) trade association
   C) professional association              D) all of the above
   Answer: A
   *Diff: 1        Page Ref: 522-523*

24) Which of the following is <u>not</u> an obstacle to an older adult finding part-time work?
   A) employer policies against employees drawing partial pensions
   B) employer resistance about the additional administrative work and higher health
      insurance cost of part-time older workers
   C) older adults may not be able to find part-time wages at the same level as full-time
      employment
   D) laws forbidding Social Security beneficiaries from working
   Answer: D
   *Diff: 1        Page Ref: 487*

25) Who is more active in voluntary organizations?
   A) older European Americans              B) older Latinos
   C) older African Americans               D) none of the above
   Answer: C
   *Diff: 2        Page Ref: 511*

26) Productivity, a concept broader than paid work, encompasses leisure and recreational
   activities in old age as well.
   Answer: FALSE
   *Diff: 2        Page Ref: 474*

27) Most older adults retire because it is mandatory.
   Answer: FALSE
   *Diff: 2        Page Ref: 491*

28) Contrary to stereotypes, deterioration in mental or physical health does not result from
   retirement.
   Answer: TRUE
   *Diff: 3        Page Ref: 482*

29) Compared with younger people, older adults are more likely to engage in solitary and
   sedentary pursuits during leisure time.
   Answer: TRUE
   *Diff: 2        Page Ref: 502*

30) The pattern of retirement among African Americans and Hispanics tends to resemble the
   pattern among other aging populations.
   Answer: FALSE
   *Diff: 2        Page Ref: 481*

31) The concept of "unretirement" refers to gender-based differences in the retirement experience.
   Answer: FALSE
   *Diff: 2        Page Ref: 484*

32) Fortunately, most middle-aged and young-old adults plan and prepare for their retirement.
   Answer: FALSE
   *Diff: 2        Page Ref: 485*

33) Older workers are more likely to be self-employed than younger workers.

Answer: TRUE
*Diff: 2      Page Ref: 487*

34) Older men are less likely to work part-time than their female counterparts.

Answer: TRUE
*Diff: 2      Page Ref: 487*

35) Social Security is the primary source of income in retirement.

Answer: TRUE
*Diff: 2      Page Ref: 492*

36) Most major employers have restructured the workplace to encourage older adults to work longer.

Answer: FALSE
*Diff: 2      Page Ref: 490*

37) The proportion of older men and women who are employed in the 21st century is smaller than it was in 1950.

Answer: TRUE
*Diff: 2      Page Ref: 486*

38) Elderhostel is an example of a religious organization for older adults.

Answer: FALSE
*Diff: 1      Page Ref: 517*

39) Rates of volunteering are highest among older adults.

Answer: FALSE
*Diff: 2      Page Ref: 514*

40) An older adult can be spiritual without being affiliated with a particular religion.

Answer: TRUE
*Diff: 2      Page Ref: 507*

41) _____ is any activity characterized by the absence of obligation.

Answer: Leisure
*Diff: 1      Page Ref: 501*

42) The median household income of people age 65 and over in 2004 was _____.

Answer: $25,210
*Diff: 2      Page Ref: 491*

43) _____ was enacted in 1974 to strengthen private pensions by being the first comprehensive effort to regulate them.

Answer:      Employment Retirement Income Security Act (ERISA)
*Diff: 2      Page Ref: 495*

44) _____ refers to the higher proportion of poor older women than poor older men.

Answer:      Feminization of poverty
*Diff: 2      Page Ref: 499*

45) Only about _____ percent of the older population receives some type of public assistance, such as Supplemental Security Income (SSI).

Answer: 5
*Diff: 2*　　*Page Ref: 500*

46) Discuss the factors that affect the timing of retirement.

Answer: The factors include:
1. adequate retirement income and/or economic incentives to retire
2. health status, functional limitations and access to health insurance other than Medicare
3. the nature of the job, employee morale and organizational commitment
4. gender and ethnic minority status
5. family and gender roles (whether a partner is working, degree of marital satisfaction)
*Diff: 2*　　*Page Ref: 480*

47) Present a summary of the sources of income older adults may have access during retirement and indicate the percent of total income each represents.

Answer: Older adults' sources of income may include Social Security (39% of seniors' aggregate income), pension (20%), earnings (26%), asset income (13%), and others (2%).
*Diff: 3*　　*Page Ref: 492*

48) A number of older adults live below the poverty line. Discuss the demographic and temporal factors that impact upon poverty rates in later life.

Answer: Poverty rates are affected by gender (older women are the poorest group in the U.S.), ethnic minority status (older African Americans and Latinos have substantially lower incomes than whites), living status (unmarried and living alone have increased poverty rates), and age (over 75 years are especially at risk). Variation also exists in the amount of time individuals live below the poverty line.
*Diff: 2*　　*Page Ref: 499–500*

49) Explain the benefits of religiosity and religious participation for older adults.

Answer: The benefits of religiosity include enhanced social, psychological and physical well-being and a reduction in mortality rates. Religious participation is associated with decreased prevalence of mental illness such as major depression, anxiety disorders, substance abuse and suicide. More devout members of all religions are usually less afraid of dying than the less devout.
*Diff: 2*　　*Page Ref: 505–506*

50) Present both sides of the ongoing debate about whether age serves as a catalyst for a viable political movement.

Answer: Proponents of the "senior power" model of politics argue that older adults do serve as powerful constituency and a strong subculture, whereas the opponents argue that older adults are not a unified group and may vote and express their political views based on demographic characteristics other than age.
*Diff: 2*　　*Page Ref: 520*

# Chapter 13  Death, Dying, Bereavement, and Widowhood

1) The dying person's bill of rights is best explained as:
    A) the right to receive all necessary treatment
    B) the right to die without pain and with dignity
    C) the right to get the latest life sustaining technology
    D) the right to designate a helper for active euthanasia
Answer: B
*Diff: 2    Page Ref: 546*

2) Palliative care refers to:
    A) using life saving care techniques
    B) the relief of pain and physical symptoms
    C) relating to the patient in a very polite manner
    D) treating the disease aggressively to eradicate it
Answer: B
*Diff: 2    Page Ref: 546*

3) Hospice care:
    A) uses experimental drugs that can cure a very ill person
    B) provides care and support to both the patient and the family
    C) represents a philosophy on how to deal with dying patients
    D) both B and C
Answer: D
*Diff: 2    Page Ref: 549*

4) Regarding the death of siblings:
    A) many social supports exist for the bereaved siblings
    B) sibling bonds often don't last as long as other family relationships
    C) research on the effects of sibling death to the older person is limited
    D) none of the above
Answer: C
*Diff: 2    Page Ref: 579*

5) The "Death With Dignity Act" in the state of Oregon:
    A) allows doctors to withhold life-sustaining procedures from dying patients
    B) allows doctors to help patients within 2 days of a request for assisted suicide
    C) allows family members to assist in the suicide of a dying patient
    D) has resulted in higher rates of illegal use of barbiturates in that state
Answer: A
*Diff: 2    Page Ref: 556*

6) Concerning assisted suicide:
    A) several states such as Alaska, California, and Maine have recently legalized it.
    B) the U.S. Supreme Court forbids physicians from prescribing pain-relievers to dying patients.
    C) the U.S. Supreme Court has explicitly endorsed sedation for the terminally ill.
    D) it is illegal in all 50 states.
Answer: C
*Diff: 2    Page Ref: 560*

7) The state of Oregon:
   A) has the highest in-hospital death rate of any state
   B) has fewer referrals to hospices than other states
   C) has established strict barriers to prescribing narcotics for terminally ill patients
   D) has passed the Intractable Pain Act to ease restrictions on pain control

   Answer: D
   *Diff: 3*    *Page Ref: 561*

8) The right given to a relative to remove life-sustaining procedures to a patient who is dying or in a long coma, and the patient has left no document regarding his/her wishes, is provided by the:
   A) surrogate decision makers statute          B) living will
   C) durable power of attorney                   D) medical power of attorney

   Answer: A
   *Diff: 2*    *Page Ref: 566–567*

9) The authorization for someone to act on behalf of an incapacitated individual with regard to property and financial matters is provided by the:
   A) living will                                 B) durable power of attorney
   C) surrogate decision makers statute           D) medical power of attorney

   Answer: B
   *Diff: 2*    *Page Ref: 567*

10) If a patient is unable to make decisions about his/her medical care, the authorization for someone to act on behalf of that person is provided by the:
   A) living will                                 B) surrogate decision makers statute
   C) durable power of attorney                   D) medical power of attorney

   Answer: D
   *Diff: 2*    *Page Ref: 567*

11) An individual who is appointed by the courts to care for another individual's property and finances because that person can no longer do so is called a:
   A) conservator                                 B) guardian
   C) surrogate decision maker                    D) none of the above

   Answer: A
   *Diff: 2*    *Page Ref: 567*

12) An individual who is appointed by the courts to care for another individual's property, finances, housing, and medical treatment is called a:
   A) conservator                                 B) guardian
   C) surrogate decision maker                    D) none of the above

   Answer: B
   *Diff: 2*    *Page Ref: 567*

13) Grief and mourning are distinguished by the fact that:
   A) "grief" refers to psychological and emotional responses to the death of a loved one
   B) "mourning" refers to individual differences in how grief is expressed
   C) the grief process is usually culturally prescribed; mourning is not
   D) grieving goes through specific, predictable stages

   Answer: A
   *Diff: 1*    *Page Ref: 569*

14) With regard to grief and bereavement:
   A) "anticipatory grief" generally reduces the intensity of the grief process after death
   B) many people never fully cease grieving
   C) older people experience grief more easily than young people
   D) the bereaved experiences more distress if a partner dies at home

   Answer: B
   *Diff: 2      Page Ref: 573*

15) Mourning rituals:
   A) are found in almost every culture
   B) assist with individual expressions of grief
   C) focus on traditional funeral ceremonies
   D) are unique to traditional societies

   Answer: A
   *Diff: 2      Page Ref: 569–570*

16) Regarding the loss of a spouse:
   A) rates of psychological distress are far more frequent among women
   B) grief appears to be more intense when the spousal relationships was unhappy
   C) white women experience it more than women of color
   D) non-white women experience it earlier than their white counterparts

   Answer: D
   *Diff: 2      Page Ref: 574–576*

17) Regarding widowhood and social supports:
   A) more than 20 percent report that they don't have strong social supports
   B) women are more likely than men to use social supports for coping
   C) friendships made during the marital relationship are important sources of support during widowhood
   D) Latina and Asian American widows are less likely to have active support systems than whites

   Answer: B
   *Diff: 2      Page Ref: 577*

18) Concerning life following the loss of one's spouse:
   A) older widowed men are more likely to remarry than older widowed women
   B) older widowed women generally move in with a daughter
   C) older widows call on an expanded circle of friends to care for them
   D) younger widows experience more long-lasting grief reactions than do older women

   Answer: A
   *Diff: 2      Page Ref: 575–577*

19) Widowed men are more likely than widowed women to:
   A) complain of loneliness and make a slower emotional recovery
   B) experience a decline in mental health, morale, and social functioning
   C) experience problems with financial management
   D) both A and B

   Answer: D
   *Diff: 2      Page Ref: 577–578*

20) Widowed women are more likely than widowed men to:
    A) remarry
    B) experience problems with social supports
    C) generally experience more financial hardships
    D) experience reciprocal relationships with all their children and friends

Answer: C
*Diff: 2      Page Ref: 576–577*

21) The five stage model of dying was developed by:
    A) Elizabeth Kubler-Ross          B) Compassion in Dying
    C) the state of Oregon             D) Cicely Saunders

Answer: A
*Diff: 2      Page Ref: 543*

22) A "good death" is characterized by:
    A) adequate control of pain        B) choice about where death occurs
    C) adequate time to say goodbye    D) all of the above

Answer: D
*Diff: 2      Page Ref: 544*

23) Which state is the only state to legalize physician–assisted suicide?
    A) Oregon       B) Washington       C) California       D) Florida

Answer: A
*Diff: 2      Page Ref: 560*

24) Today, approximately _____ of all deaths occur in institutions where aggressive treatment is common and with only a few friends and family present.
    A) 25 percent      B) 50 percent      C) 80 percent      D) 95 percent

Answer: C
*Diff: 2      Page Ref: 540*

25) Which of the following is not one of the five stages of dying?
    A) shock and denial                B) anger
    C) happiness                       D) acceptance

Answer: C
*Diff: 2      Page Ref: 543*

26) Older adults fear the dying process rather than death itself.

Answer: TRUE
*Diff: 2      Page Ref: 541*

27) A dying person must advance through all the stages identified by Kubler-Ross in order to have a "good death."

Answer: FALSE
*Diff: 1      Page Ref: 543*

28) "The right to die" refers to dying with dignity, without pain, and in accordance with one's wishes.

Answer: TRUE
*Diff: 1      Page Ref: 546*

29) "Palliative care" refers to efforts to keep someone alive as long as possible.

Answer: FALSE
*Diff: 1      Page Ref: 546*

30) Hospice care is only available in a patient's home.

Answer: FALSE
*Diff: 1      Page Ref: 549*

31) Advocates of the right to die frequently use the term "hastened death."

Answer: TRUE
*Diff: 2      Page Ref: 554*

32) Withholding or withdrawing unwanted medical treatment for patients close to death is both legal and ethical.

Answer: TRUE
*Diff: 2      Page Ref: 557*

33) Public and professional acceptance of physician-assisted suicide is increasing in general, although still opposed by the American Medical Association.

Answer: TRUE
*Diff: 2      Page Ref: 558*

34) Living wills are an example of advance directives.

Answer: TRUE
*Diff: 2      Page Ref: 562*

35) The majority of older adults have completed living wills.

Answer: FALSE
*Diff: 1      Page Ref: 562-565*

36) Younger and older widows generally experience similar grief processes.

Answer: FALSE
*Diff: 2      Page Ref: 575*

37) Grief is always less when death is not sudden and survivors have been able to anticipate it and prepare for changes.

Answer: FALSE
*Diff: 2      Page Ref: 572*

38) Most families and their older relatives have not discussed whether or not to utilize life-saving technologies.

Answer: TRUE
*Diff: 2      Page Ref: 562*

39) Aggressive pain management is viewed as a viable alternative to assisted suicide.

Answer: TRUE
*Diff: 2      Page Ref: 561*

40) The grief process follows certain stages that mourners must complete to resolve their grief.

Answer: FALSE
*Diff: 2      Page Ref: 543*

41) _____ is not a "place" but a philosophy of, and approach to, care that is offered primarily in the home but also in hospital and nursing home settings.

Answer: Hospice
*Diff: 2      Page Ref: 548–549*

42) In _____, treatment is withdrawn, and nothing is done to prolong the patient's life artificially, such as use of a feeding tube or ventilator.

Answer: passive euthanasia
*Diff: 2      Page Ref: 556–557*

43) The first formal hospice in the world start was _____.

Answer: St. Christopher's Hospice
*Diff: 3      Page Ref: 550*

44) _____ may result from several losses simultaneously, which may intensify and prolong grief.

Answer: Bereavement overload
*Diff: 3      Page Ref: 575*

45) The federal law, _____, require health care facilities that receive Medicaid and Medicare funds to inform patients in writing of their rights to execute advance directives regarding how they want to live or die.

Answer: Patient Self-Determination Act
*Diff: 3      Page Ref: 562*

46) Thoroughly discuss Elizabeth Kubler-Ross' five stages of dying and how has its application changed?

Answer: The fives stages are 1) shock and denial, 2) anger, resentment and guilt, 3) bargaining, such as trying to make a deal with God, 4) depression and withdrawal from others, and 5) adjustment/acceptance. Kubler-Ross implied that a person had to complete each stage before moving on. Now, there is agreement that no typical movement through the stages exists.
*Diff: 1      Page Ref: 543*

47) Present the arguments in favor of and against active euthanasia.

Answer: Proponents of active euthanasia argue it is the right of the individual to choose to die without pain and suffering, while the opponents of active euthanasia argue that it is a slippery slope and would lead to society seeing physician assisted suicide as a solution to social problems faced by the poor, persons of color or individuals with disabilities.
*Diff: 3      Page Ref: 558*

48) List the legal option an individual would want to consider when making end-of-life care decisions.

Answer: Documents that address end-of-life care decisions include advance directives (oral/written instructions regarding end-of-life care), living will (the most common type of advance directive), durable powers of attorney (authorizing someone to act on behalf of another regarding financial matters), and medical powers of attorney (authorizing someone to act on behalf of another regarding financial and medical matters). Also the individual would want to consider naming someone as a conservator (financial control), guardian (financial control and control over the person him or herself) or surrogate decision maker (a proxy decision maker).
*Diff: 3      Page Ref: 566–567*

49) Explain the six-R process of mourning.

Answer: The six-R process of mourning includes recognizing and accepting the reality of the loss, reacting to the pain of separation including weeping and articulating feelings of guilt, reminiscing through telling memories, relinquishing old attachments, readjusting to one's environment and adopting to new roles/forming a new identity, and reinvesting in new personal relationships rather than remaining tied to the past.

*Diff: 2*        *Page Ref: 571*

50) Discuss the features of hospice and its history.

Answer: Hospice, which is not necessarily a "place", but a philosophy, is a manner of caring for the terminally ill. An example of a key feature of hospice is that palliative care is primary and pain management is one of the main goals. Other characteristics include focus on quality of life, service available 24 hours a day/7 days a week if needed, support for the family, psychological, social, and spiritual counseling, collaboration among providers, a multidisciplinary team, use of volunteers, inpatient care, and bereavement counseling. The first hospice, St. Christopher's Hospice, started in Great Britain in 1967.

*Diff: 2*        *Page Ref: 548*

# Chapter 14   The Resilience of Elders of Color

1) The poorest group among older adults is:
    A) African American men               B) white men
    C) all older women                 D) older women of color

Answer: D
*Diff: 2      Page Ref: 591*

2) Which of the following is <u>not</u> true for people of color in the United States?
    A) Their median age is lower than for whites.
    B) They experience more economic and health problems.
    C) They have proportionately more young than among whites.
    D) Their social support systems are weaker than whites.

Answer: D
*Diff: 2      Page Ref: 590*

3) Structural barriers to health care use shared by ethnic minority elders includes:
    A) discrimination by service providers      B) geographic distance of services
    C) lack of transportation              D) all of the above

Answer: D
*Diff: 3      Page Ref: 626*

4) The mortality crossover effect occurs:
    A) for women after age 55           B) for men after age 65
    C) for people of color after age 75      D) for people of color after age 85

Answer: C
*Diff: 2      Page Ref: 596*

5) The ethnic minority population that forms the smallest percentage of the total population age 65 and over is:
    A) African Americans           B) Asian Americans/Pacific Islanders
    C) American Indians             D) Hispanic Americans

Answer: C
*Diff: 1      Page Ref: 594*

6) Which of the following statements describing African American elders is <u>false</u>?
    A) They are poorer than whites.
    B) They are not as healthy as whites.
    C) Their life expectancy at birth is as long as whites.
    D) They are less likely to be married than any other ethnic group

Answer: C
*Diff: 2      Page Ref: 599–600*

7) A major source of social and emotional support for African Americans, outside of family, is:
    A) the federal government          B) senior centers
    C) the church                 D) self-help groups

Answer: C
*Diff: 2      Page Ref: 605*

8) Compared to their white counterparts, older African Americans experience twice the rate of:
    A) diabetes mellitus                          B) depression
    C) suicide                                    D) osteoporosis

Answer: A
*Diff: 2        Page Ref: 601*

9) Differences between whites and African Americans in life expectancy at age 75 are:
    A) greater than differences in life expectancy at birth
    B) less than differences in life expectancy at birth
    C) about the same as life expectancy at birth
    D) due to higher infant mortality among whites

Answer: B
*Diff: 2        Page Ref: 599*

10) Comparative studies between older whites and older African Americans have found that older African Americans have:
    A) fewer three or four-generation households
    B) lower frequency of family-based households with adult children
    C) more extended families
    D) less social support from extended family

Answer: C
*Diff: 2        Page Ref: 604*

11) A major reason that some Hispanics do not seek out social services such as Social Security or Medicare is:
    A) their relatives provide all the assistance they need
    B) they may have been illegal immigrants
    C) they do not want assistance
    D) they expect the service system to seek them out

Answer: B
*Diff: 2        Page Ref: 608*

12) Compared to non-Hispanic whites, elders in Hispanic families have traditionally:
    A) played only a minor role in child-rearing
    B) been ignored by younger members
    C) received more respect from young members
    D) had little influence in family decision-making

Answer: C
*Diff: 2        Page Ref: 610*

13) The predominant group within the Hispanic population of the United States comes from:
    A) Mexico              B) Puerto Rico          C) S. America          D) Cuba

Answer: A
*Diff: 2        Page Ref: 606*

14) Use of health services is lower among many Hispanic American subgroups than among whites and African Americans. Which of the following variables is <u>least</u> likely to be a barrier to health service use?
    A) language barriers                          B) illegal entry to the United States
    C) distrust of the medical system            D) lack of health service need

Answer: D
*Diff: 2        Page Ref: 610*

15) Compared to their non-Hispanic Caucasian counterparts, Hispanic elders:
   A) are more likely to live in a nursing home
   B) are more likely to be institutionalized after age 75
   C) have higher death rates from cervical and uterine cancer
   D) view themselves as younger despite limitations in ADLs
   Answer: C
   *Diff: 3      Page Ref: 609–610*

16) Asian American/Pacific Islander elders have long been underserved by mainstream social and health services because:
   A) they have so few problems
   B) they face more language barriers
   C) they are primarily women
   D) they are financially better off than other ethnic minority groups
   Answer: B
   *Diff: 2      Page Ref: 621*

17) Asian American elders differ from other ethnic minority groups in that:
   A) they are primarily third generation immigrants
   B) there are proportionately more women than in other ethnic groups
   C) there are proportionately more men than in other ethnic groups
   D) they overutilize social and health services
   Answer: C
   *Diff: 2      Page Ref: 619–624*

18) The least amount of data is available about the status of:
   A) African American elders                    B) Hispanic American elders
   C) American Indian elders                      D) Asian American elders
   Answer: C
   *Diff: 2      Page Ref: 611*

19) Older American Indians are less likely to use health services than their white counterparts. Barriers include all of the following <u>except</u>:
   A) belief in and practice of traditional medicine
   B) mistrust of mainstream medical providers
   C) IHS focus on youth and families
   D) use of direct communication styles
   Answer: D
   *Diff: 2      Page Ref: 613–614*

20) Which of the following factors would <u>not</u> serve to increase the utilization of social and health services by older persons of color?
   A) increased numbers of bilingual and bicultural staff
   B) services that build upon and respect cultural values and community strengths
   C) centralized services for all ethnic minorities to use
   D) free transportation provided to services
   Answer: C
   *Diff: 2      Page Ref: 628*

21) The largest group of older Asian/Pacific Islanders have ancestry originating in:
   A) China            B) Japan            C) Korea            D) India
   Answer: A
   *Diff: 2      Page Ref: 618*

22) The study of the causes, processes, and consequences of race, national origin, and culture on individual and population aging is called:
   A) ethnogerontology
   B) geriatrics
   C) telogerontology
   D) the double jeopardy hypothesis

Answer: A
*Diff: 2      Page Ref: 596*

23) Elders who are Asian/Pacific Islanders have lower rates of western health service utilization because:
   A) they have fewer chronic diseases when compared with their majority group peers
   B) of sociocultural barriers to health care
   C) of traditional values, such as reliance on family and friends
   D) all of the above

Answer: D
*Diff: 2      Page Ref: 621–623*

24) Today, ethnic minorities comprise _____ of the population over age 65.
   A) 2 percent
   B) 17 percent
   C) 25 percent
   D) 38 percent

Answer: B
*Diff: 2      Page Ref: 593*

25) Health care for American Indian elders who life on reservations is provided by:
   A) Indian Health Service
   B) Bureau of Indian Affairs
   C) National Institute of Health
   D) none of the above

Answer: A
*Diff: 2      Page Ref: 615*

26) Among all ethnic/racial groups in the United States, poverty rates are highest for African American elders, least for whites.

Answer: FALSE
*Diff: 2      Page Ref: 590*

27) By the year 2050, people of color will represent the numerical majority in most parts of the United States.

Answer: TRUE
*Diff: 2      Page Ref: 593*

28) By the year 2050, more than 50 percent of the older population will be comprised of elders of color.

Answer: FALSE
*Diff: 3      Page Ref: 593*

29) The Bureau of Indian Affairs has upheld and supported the traditional roles of American Indian elders.

Answer: FALSE
*Diff: 2      Page Ref: 616*

30) Cancer survival rates are lower for American Indians than for any other ethnic or racial subgroup in the United States.

Answer: TRUE
*Diff: 2      Page Ref: 613*

31) Service utilization can be increased if the agencies providing these services adhere to the cultural integrity of the elder's lifestyles.

Answer: TRUE
*Diff: 2      Page Ref: 627*

32) The racial minority crossover phenomenon refers to findings that the death rate for people of color who are age 75 and over is lower than for whites age 75 and over.

Answer: TRUE
*Diff: 2      Page Ref: 596*

33) African American elders are more likely than whites to live with a family member other than a spouse.

Answer: TRUE
*Diff: 2      Page Ref: 604*

34) Studies clearly demonstrate a higher incidence of suicide among American Indians than for other ethnic minorities.

Answer: FALSE
*Diff: 2      Page Ref: 616*

35) Chronological age is probably the worst way to identify the need for services among older American Indians.

Answer: TRUE
*Diff: 2      Page Ref: 614*

36) Asian American/Pacific Islander elders are increasingly less likely to live in extended family arrangements.

Answer: TRUE
*Diff: 1      Page Ref: 624*

37) Barriers to service utilization can be conceptualized as primarily due to cultural factors.

Answer: FALSE
*Diff: 2      Page Ref: 625*

38) The proportion of people aged 65 and older among ethnic minority groups will increase more than among whites in the 21st century.

Answer: TRUE
*Diff: 1      Page Ref: 594*

39) As compared to Anglos, Hispanics are most likely to live in 3- or 4-generational households.

Answer: TRUE
*Diff: 2      Page Ref: 610*

40) Older American Indian elders who live in urban areas tend to have better health than those on reservations.

Answer: TRUE
*Diff: 2      Page Ref: 612*

41) The fact that people of color experience poorer health and higher death rates than whites at all ages until very old age is known as the _____.

Answer: crossover effect
*Diff: 2      Page Ref: 596*

42) Latino caregiving within the family is influenced by the cultural value of _____, respect for people by virtue of age, experience or service.

Answer: respecto
*Diff: 3*        *Page Ref: 610*

43) _____ refers to the relationship between aged parents and the oldest son who provides care for them and in turn inherits their wealth.

Answer: Law of primogeniture
*Diff: 3*        *Page Ref: 624*

44) The two federal agencies which are responsible for collecting data regarding American Indians are the Indian Health Service and the _____.

Answer: Bureau of Indian Affairs
*Diff: 3*        *Page Ref: 611–612*

45) _____ includes foster parents or children who function in the absence of blood relatives or when family relationships are unsatisfactory.

Answer: Fictive kin
*Diff: 2*        *Page Ref: 604*

46) Discuss the components of the term "ethnicity."

Answer: Ethnicity involves three components:
   1. sense of peoplehood evolved from a group's common ancestry and history
   2. social status that can determine how people eat, work, celebrate, care for each other, and die
   3. informal social support systems
*Diff: 2*        *Page Ref: 591*

47) Explain the patterns shared across populations of color in regard to cumulative disadvantages, centrality of kin, and chronic illness.

Answer: In terms of cumulative disadvantages elders of color may have limited resources throughout their lives to meet their health care needs. In terms of the centrality of kin, elders of color tend to have a preference for in-home services. In terms of chronic illness elders of color may be recognized as old prior to chronological age.
*Diff: 2*        *Page Ref: 597–598*

48) Select one ethnicity discussed in the text (older African Americans, older Latinos, older American Indians, or older Asian/Pacific Islanders) and write a thorough essay on the economic, social and health status of elders of your selected ethnicity.

Answer: Answers will vary greatly.
*Diff: 3*        *Page Ref: 599–625*

49) Given the diverse cultures and background of older Americans, what are implications of this diversity for social services and health care?

Answer: Cultural competence is crucial as service and health care providers need to be aware of the many needs and cultural values of their patients. It has become important to reduce social inequities between elders of minority and dominant groups. Health promotion initiatives targeted to older whites may not be appropriate for populations of color.
*Diff: 2*        *Page Ref: 625*

50) Discuss the barriers to older adults utilizing social services and health care.

Answer: Cultural and economic barriers to service utilization include cultural isolation, stigma of using services, confusion, anger at, and fear of healthcare providers and hospitals, lack of trust and faith in the efficacy of service professionals, lack of knowledge of services, and interest in complementary alternative medicine. Structural barriers within the service system include elimination of some public benefits to legal immigrants, lack of ethnic-appropriate services, discrimination, inaccurately translated assessment instruments, geographic distance, lack of transportation, and staff that are not bilingual and insensitive to ethnic differences.

*Diff: 2*     *Page Ref: 626*

# Chapter 15  The Resilience of Older Women

1) From a feminist perspective, many of the problems faced by older women can be understood as:
   A) the result of individual differences
   B) an outcome of their socialization
   C) due to gender-based differences in power and privilege
   D) cohort differences in family and societal roles

Answer: C
*Diff: 3      Page Ref: 640*

2) Major determinants of older women's life satisfaction and their perceived quality of life are:
   A) financial resources
   B) comparisons to the lives of others
   C) accessing medical care and cost of medical care
   D) political activity

Answer: A
*Diff: 3      Page Ref: 642*

3) A divorced woman age 62 and over can receive Social Security upon divorce if:
   A) she had been married at least 10 years prior to the date of divorce
   B) her former husband is age 62 or older
   C) her former husband is drawing Social Security
   D) she fits all three of the above characteristics

Answer: D
*Diff: 2      Page Ref: 646*

4) Federal laws designed to protect spouses of private pension recipients:
   A) cover all pension recipients
   B) do not apply to state government plans
   C) affect women of all ages
   D) cover women who are divorced from pension recipients

Answer: B
*Diff: 2      Page Ref: 650*

5) About what percent of the population aged 65–74 is female?
   A) 35 percent          B) 55 percent          C) 75 percent          D) 95 percent

Answer: B
*Diff: 1      Page Ref: 640*

6) Structural reasons for economic differences between men and women include:
   A) the methods used to calculate Social Security
   B) employment patterns that differ between men and women
   C) women's reduced access to other retirement income
   D) all of the above

Answer: D
*Diff: 3      Page Ref: 643*

7) Women over age 65 comprise _____ percent of the poor older population.
   A) almost 25          B) almost 50          C) over 70          D) over 90

Answer: C
*Diff: 2      Page Ref: 642*

8) Postmenopausal zest:
    A) was coined by Betty Friedan
    B) a renewed sense of living and time for oneself
    C) is a new medical term to describe endocrine problems that occur in menopause
    D) refers to the depression that occurs after menopause

Answer: B
*Diff: 2*     *Page Ref: 657*

9) The primary source of income for older women is:
    A) Social Security                    B) private pensions
    C) SSI                                D) personal savings

Answer: A
*Diff: 2*     *Page Ref: 644*

10) Among older women, the risk of poverty is greatest among:
    A) women of color                     B) never-married women
    C) married women                      D) working women

Answer: A
*Diff: 2*     *Page Ref: 643*

11) Social Security and pension plans in the United States have been most useful in eliminating poverty among:
    A) divorced women                     B) never-married mothers
    C) older African Americans            D) older men and couples

Answer: D
*Diff: 3*     *Page Ref: 645*

12) The issue of caregiving provides an opportunity for feminist researchers to:
    A) control for the effects of gender
    B) recognize the interconnections between women's paid and unpaid work
    C) identify gender variations in the economic status of older persons
    D) both B and C

Answer: B
*Diff: 3*     *Page Ref: 641*

13) Older women's health status is affected most by:
    A) bad health habits during their younger years
    B) adverse effects of marriage
    C) adverse effects of poverty
    D) a lifetime of family caregiving

Answer: C
*Diff: 1*     *Page Ref: 651*

14) Among middle-aged women, the group <u>least</u> likely to have health care coverage is:
    A) divorced women                     B) married women
    C) the poorest in each state          D) middle-class women of color

Answer: A
*Diff: 2*     *Page Ref: 652*

15) Regarding older womens' informal networks:
   A) women respond to stressful events by "fight and flight"
   B) women respond to stressful events by "tending and befriending"
   C) women have larger nonkin networks than men
   D) women call on non-family networks to provide care for them

   Answer: B
   *Diff: 2     Page Ref: 660*

16) Compared to their male counterparts, older women's health status is characterized as follows:
   A) they are healthier
   B) they are more likely to face non-fatal chronic conditions
   C) they experience fewer days of restricted activity and disability
   D) they are less likely to take curative action when they are ill

   Answer: B
   *Diff: 2     Page Ref: 653*

17) The major reason that older women have less access to group health insurance of their own is because they:
   A) are not as healthy as men
   B) visit doctors more often than men
   C) were less likely to be employed when young
   D) can rely upon their husbands' insurance even after a divorce

   Answer: C
   *Diff: 2     Page Ref: 652*

18) Conversion laws have been useful in:
   A) allowing workers to transfer from one insurance plan to another
   B) allowing workers to keep their insurance when changing jobs
   C) adding names of new dependents on health insurance plans
   D) allowing women to remain on their spouse's policy 3 years after divorce or widowhood

   Answer: D
   *Diff: 2     Page Ref: 652*

19) Regarding the use of HRT for the prevention of osteoporosis:
   A) it can increase bone mass in the spine and hips by 3-5% in the first year
   B) benefits to bone mass are not seen after the second year
   C) benefits increase after age 75
   D) long-term use has been deemed safe

   Answer: A
   *Diff: 2     Page Ref: 655*

20) Which of the following statements is <u>false</u> regarding breast cancer and older women?
   A) Medicare does not reimburse mammography screening costs.
   B) Older women are less likely than younger women to get mammography check ups.
   C) Physicians are less likely to refer older women for mammography.
   D) The majority of women with breast cancer are over the age 50.

   Answer: A
   *Diff: 2     Page Ref: 653*

21) Which of the following strategies will <u>not</u> help an older woman prevent osteoporosis?
  A) maintain a lower-than-normal body weight
  B) participate in a weight-bearing exercise program
  C) consuming sardines, dry roasted soybeans or leafy green vegetables
  D) consume calcium supplements regularly

Answer: A
*Diff: 2      Page Ref: 655–656*

22) Which of the following changes in women's health is <u>not</u> physiologically related to menopause?
  A) osteoporosis      B) heart disease      C) hot flashes      D) depression

Answer: D
*Diff: 2      Page Ref: 657*

23) Which of the following regarding older womens' health is <u>not</u> true?
  A) Women generally rate their health as better than men do.
  B) Women have a higher level of functional impairment than men do.
  C) Women who are among the oldest-old tend to self rate their health better than younger-old women.
  D) Women experience more health and mental health difficulties as they age.

Answer: D
*Diff: 1      Page Ref: 655*

24) Which of the following statements is <u>false</u> when describing the social status of older women?
  A) They have fewer chances to remarry than do men.
  B) They have fewer close friends than older men.
  C) They are more likely to be widowed than older men.
  D) Those living alone are in greater need of social and health services.

Answer: B
*Diff: 1      Page Ref: 658–660*

25) Which of the following potential changes in Social Security will most likely benefit older women?
  A) privatizing Social Security
  B) more women entering the workforce after childrearing
  C) earnings sharing plans
  D) enforcing the Family and Medical Leave Act

Answer: C
*Diff: 2      Page Ref: 648*

26) Older women have long been the focus of gerontological research, serving as research subjects in early studies.

Answer: FALSE
*Diff: 1      Page Ref: 641*

27) Recent national and state legislation to increase minimum wage will have more economic repercussions for men across the life course than women.

Answer: FALSE
*Diff: 1      Page Ref: 663*

28) A primary reason for older women's economic vulnerability is that most women did not work consistently for pay throughout their lives.

Answer: TRUE
*Diff: 2*      *Page Ref: 642*

29) An older woman can depend on her husband's pension to support her, even if he dies before retiring.

Answer: FALSE
*Diff: 2*      *Page Ref: 649*

30) The majority of older women and men live with a spouse.

Answer: FALSE
*Diff: 2*      *Page Ref: 658*

31) Most physicians refer their older women patients for mammography, especially since Medicare pays for biennial visits.

Answer: FALSE
*Diff: 2*      *Page Ref: 653*

32) Although women suffer from more chronic health conditions, most of these are not life-threatening.

Answer: TRUE
*Diff: 1*      *Page Ref: 653*

33) Osteoporosis is a concern for older women because of the associated risk of limiting their ADLs.

Answer: TRUE
*Diff: 2*      *Page Ref: 655*

34) Recent studies have provided support for the popular belief that depression and loss of sexual desire result from the normal physiological changes brought about by menopause.

Answer: FALSE
*Diff: 2*      *Page Ref: 656–657*

35) Middle aged women are generally proactive about coping with the effects of menopause.

Answer: TRUE
*Diff: 1*      *Page Ref: 657*

36) Older women of color are more than twice as likely as their white counterparts to live in multigenerational households.

Answer: TRUE
*Diff: 2*      *Page Ref: 658*

37) Compared to men, women have more social resources to draw upon in old age.

Answer: TRUE
*Diff: 1*      *Page Ref: 660*

38) The primary negative consequence of widowhood is low socioeconomic status.

Answer: TRUE
*Diff: 2*      *Page Ref: 659*

39) Attempts to privatize Social Security will hurt older women more than men.

Answer: TRUE

*Diff: 3*     *Page Ref: 646*

40) Fortunately, the economic status of older women in the future will be substantially improved over the current cohort.

Answer: FALSE

*Diff: 2*     *Page Ref: 663*

41) A _____ is a requirement that a wife must agree to her husband's waiving survivor benefits.

Answer: spousal consent requirement

*Diff: 2*     *Page Ref: 650*

42) _____ require insurance companies to allow women to remain in their spouse's group insurance for up to 3 years after divorce, separation, or widowhood.

Answer: Conversion laws

*Diff: 2*     *Page Ref: 652*

43) The average age of widowhood for women is _____ years.

Answer:   59

*Diff: 2*     *Page Ref: 658*

44) One remedy for gender inequalities in life time contribution to Social Security is _____, whereby each partner in marriage is entitled to a separate Social Security account regardless of which spouse is in the paid labor force.

Answer:   earnings sharing

*Diff: 2*     *Page Ref: 648*

45) Women have a _____ incidence of chronic health problems than men.

Answer:   higher

*Diff: 1*     *Page Ref: 653*

46) Why is there a need in gerontology to focus on the needs of older adult women?

Answer: One of the most significant reasons to focus on the needs of older women is that they are the fast-growing section of the population in the United States and the world. Another reason is that gender structures opportunities across the life course, making the aging process and quality of life in older age markedly different for men and women. The problems of aging are increasingly women's problems. We do not know as much about older women because they were nearly invisible in gerontology until the mid 1970s.

*Diff: 1*     *Page Ref: 640-641*

47) Why are older women one of the poorest groups in society?

Answer: Older women are overrepresented in poverty rates due to having fewer resources (reduced access to other retirement income such as private pensions), their work history (having worked fewer years and in lower paying jobs) and the methods used to calculate Social Security (women are disadvantaged by years spent in caregiving and out of the workforce that calculate a zero earning).

*Diff: 2*     *Page Ref: 643*

48) The majority of older women face osteoporosis. How does this affect their ability to perform their ADLs?

Answer: Osteoporosis can lead to more injuries such as bone fractures (especially wrist, spinal and hip fractures), and more days with limited mobility. The threat or actual occurrence of injuries can limit the social world of older women, especially since half of the affected lose the ability to walk independently.

*Diff: 2*      *Page Ref: 655*

49) Summarize the nonmedical approaches to menopause.

Answer: Examples of nonmedical approaches to menopause include hypnosis, exercise, support groups, herbal remedies such as black cohosh roots to reduce hot flashes, kava to reduce mood swings, irritability and stress, and St. John's wort for depression and anxiety, vitamin E for hot flashes, and dietary changes to reduce fats, preservatives, caffeine, alcohol and spicy food while increasing fiber, calcium and soy.

*Diff: 2*      *Page Ref: 656*

50) Why do older women have limited opportunities to remarry?

Answer: The greatest obstacle to remarriage is the overwhelming number of women compared to men in one's later years. Also, they may choose not to remarry, because their marriage was not a positive experience, they now enjoy being on their own, or they do not want to care for an ill or disabled husband.

*Diff: 2*      *Page Ref: 659–660*

# Chapter 16  Social Policies to Address Social Problems

1) Until the 1960s, public policy for older Americans lagged behind other countries because:
    A) our current older population is so small
    B) families have traditionally cared for their older relatives
    C) our culture places a high value on independence and self-reliance
    D) our older population has not needed assistance until recently

Answer: C
*Diff: 1     Page Ref: 674*

2) Since the 1960s, entitlement programs have taken up more and more of the federal budget, so that today they represent _____ percent of federal spending.
    A) 15            B) 30            C) 40            D) 60

Answer: C
*Diff: 2     Page Ref: 675*

3) Most federal programs for children are:
    A) discretionary and means-based        B) categorical (age-based) and universal
    C) direct cash transfers             D) indirect cash benefits

Answer: A
*Diff: 2     Page Ref: 677*

4) Most federal policies that benefit the older population are:
    A) categorical (age-based) and means-tested
    B) categorical and universal for all older people
    C) direct cash transfers on the basis of mean-tests
    D) noncontributory and categorical

Answer: B
*Diff: 3     Page Ref: 677*

5) Supplemental Security Income (SSI) benefits the population on a(n) _____ basis.
    A) direct cash substitute          B) indirect cash substitute
    C) universal                D) non-contributory

Answer: D
*Diff: 1     Page Ref: 678*

6) Which of the following societal values has <u>not</u> influenced the development of public policy for aging Americans?
    A) Individual welfare is the person's own responsibility.
    B) The community should help with individual welfare.
    C) Citizens are universally entitled to have their needs met.
    D) The government should help only as needed.

Answer: C
*Diff: 2     Page Ref: 678-679*

7) The greatest growth of social policies that benefit older people came in the:
    A) 1930s            B) 1960s            C) 1980s            D) 1990s

Answer: B
*Diff: 2     Page Ref: 674*

8) A negative consequence of "compassionate ageism" in American public policy was:
   A) programs that benefit all elders, including healthy and wealthy
   B) inadequate funds remaining for children's programs
   C) emerging stereotypes of older populations as "greedy geezers"
   D) too much funding for low income and minority elders
   Answer: A
   *Diff: 2      Page Ref: 683*

9) During the 1980s and 1990s, American public policies began to reflect a new recognition about eligibility criteria for old-age benefit programs, with greater concern for:
   A) older women                        B) grandparents caring for grandchildren
   C) low-income elders                  D) elderly immigrants
   Answer: C
   *Diff: 2      Page Ref: 684–685*

10) Contrary to public perception, Social Security was designed to be:
   A) an investment program              B) a minimum floor of protection
   C) a sole source of retirement income D) none of the above
   Answer: B
   *Diff: 2      Page Ref: 688*

11) Which of the following is <u>not</u> one of the Social Security Trust Funds?
   A) Old Age and Survivors Insurance    B) Military Personnel Insurance
   C) Disability Insurance               D) Hospital Insurance
   Answer: B
   *Diff: 1      Page Ref: 687*

12) New proposals to privatize Social Security are characterized by:
   A) increased government regulation
   B) expectations that the government will wisely invest Social Security funds
   C) a greater shift toward the philosophy of social insurance
   D) expectations that individuals can invest more wisely than the government
   Answer: D
   *Diff: 2      Page Ref: 692*

13) Which of the following groups would benefit the <u>most</u> if Social Security is privatized?
   A) investment companies               B) federal government
   C) low-income workers                 D) women workers
   Answer: A
   *Diff: 2      Page Ref: 692*

14) Pension plans have helped improve the economic status of many older Americans. They have also resulted in:
   A) eliminating income disparities among groups of older persons
   B) perpetuating inequities between male and female workers
   C) reducing the need for Social Security income for many elders
   D) reducing the need for employee health benefits
   Answer: B
   *Diff: 2      Page Ref: 696–697*

15) The agency responsible for administering the programs and services of the Older Americans Act is:
    A) the Social Security Division        B) the Leadership Council on Aging
    C) the Federal Council on Aging        D) the Administration on Aging

Answer: D
*Diff: 1     Page Ref: 698*

16) Which of the following viewpoints is <u>not</u> advanced by supporters of the intergenerational inequity perspective?
    A) Younger people will not receive fair returns for their Social Security investments.
    B) Older and younger people have both been hard hit by inflation.
    C) Older adults are draining the federal budget.
    D) Children are poorer than older people are.

Answer: B
*Diff: 2     Page Ref: 702*

17) A basic assumption underlying the interdependence of generations framework is that:
    A) older adults are financially better off than other age groups
    B) significant distribution choices must be made about how to pay the costs of an aging society
    C) the younger generation only benefits from Social Security when they live long enough to retire
    D) our society needs to achieve equity or fairness between generations

Answer: B
*Diff: 2     Page Ref: 702*

18) The public policy perspective that views older citizens as a national resource is known as:
    A) the politics of productivity        B) the politics of entitlement
    C) intergenerational inequity        D) interdependence of generations

Answer: A
*Diff: 1     Page Ref: 701*

19) Which of the following does <u>not</u> characterize the politics of the "New Aging"?
    A) an intergenerational perspective        B) the diversity of the older population
    C) an age-based perspective on services        D) a concern for future generations

Answer: C
*Diff: 2     Page Ref: 705-706*

20) Which of the following public policy models of aging is <u>not</u> related to the paradigm of "New Aging"?
    A) interdependence of generations        B) intergenerational equity
    C) politics of diversity        D) politics of entitlement

Answer: D
*Diff: 2     Page Ref: 705-706*

21) Which services are <u>not</u> provided under the Older Americans Act?
    A) in-home services        B) senior center programs
    C) nutrition programs        D) Social Security benefits

Answer: D
*Diff: 2     Page Ref: 698*

22) The first national public benefits act was:
   A) The Social Security Act
   B) The Older Americans Act
   C) The Direct Loan Program of the Housing Act
   D) The Nursing Home Reform Act

   Answer: A
   *Diff: 2      Page Ref: 681*

23) Sixty-four percent of Social Security's benefits are distributed to:
   A) retired workers              B) children
   C) survivor's of deceased workers    D) disabled workers

   Answer: A
   *Diff: 2      Page Ref: 687*

24) Generations United, a coalition which works to reframe policy agendas based on cross-generational needs, was established by:
   A) the Child Welfare League of America    B) the National Council on Aging
   C) the Children's Defense Fund            D) all of the above

   Answer: D
   *Diff: 2      Page Ref: 706*

25) "Old Age and Survivors Insurance" is more commonly known as:
   A) Social Security                    B) Supplemental Security Income
   C) the Older Americans Act            D) Medicare

   Answer: A
   *Diff: 2      Page Ref: 687*

26) The 1960s represented the peak time for developing most of the policies and programs for older people in the United States.

   Answer: TRUE
   *Diff: 2      Page Ref: 674*

27) The Older Americans Act produced many programs for older adults including senior centers, nutrition sites, and adult day care.

   Answer: TRUE
   *Diff: 2      Page Ref: 677*

28) Social policies for older people tend to be residual and incremental in nature.

   Answer: TRUE
   *Diff: 3      Page Ref: 679*

29) SSI is an example of an age-entitlement program.

   Answer: FALSE
   *Diff: 1      Page Ref: 695*

30) The "compassionate" stereotype of older adults as more deserving than other age groups has influenced recent policy developments in aging.

   Answer: FALSE
   *Diff: 2      Page Ref: 705*

31) Eligibility for most policies and programs for older people is determined on the basis of financial need.

Answer: FALSE
*Diff: 2      Page Ref: 677*

32) Social Security and Medicare are the primary causes for the U.S. federal deficit.

Answer: FALSE
*Diff: 2      Page Ref: 685*

33) Development of the aging policy in the United States has been influenced by the contradicting values of individual and social responsibility.

Answer: TRUE
*Diff: 2      Page Ref: 678-679*

34) Privatizing Social Security would benefit all older adults.

Answer: FALSE
*Diff: 2      Page Ref: 693*

35) Privatizing Social Security would negatively impact higher income, unmarried workers.

Answer: FALSE
*Diff: 1      Page Ref: 694*

36) According to proponents of the political economy theory, such as Estes, U.S. policies have benefited older persons more than the young because politicians recognize that older people are more likely to vote.

Answer: FALSE
*Diff: 2      Page Ref: 680*

37) The politics of the "New Aging" includes new alliances across age groups on the basis of common needs.

Answer: TRUE
*Diff: 2      Page Ref: 705-706*

38) Policy-making in the 1990s can be characterized as a process oriented to advancing efficiency and cost containment.

Answer: TRUE
*Diff: 2      Page Ref: 685*

39) Prior to the 1930s only three programs existed which focused on the needs of older adults.

Answer: FALSE
*Diff: 2      Page Ref: 681-682*

40) Proposals to privatize Social Security will benefit all segments of today's working population.

Answer: FALSE
*Diff: 2      Page Ref: 694*

41) Those programs for which spending is determined by ongoing eligibility requirements and benefit levels rather than by annual Congressional appropriations are called _____.

Answer: entitlement programs
*Diff: 2      Page Ref: 677*

42) The Older Americans Act was first funded in _____.

Answer: 1965
*Diff: 2*      *Page Ref: 677*

43) _____ , designated by State Units on Aging, develop and administer service plans within regional and local areas.

Answer: Area Agencies on Aging
*Diff: 2*      *Page Ref: 699*

44) Social Security and Medicare are _____ programs in that benefits are tied to a person's contribution to the system as a paid worker across the life span.

Answer: contributory
*Diff: 3*      *Page Ref: 677–678*

45) The first national public benefits program is _____.

Answer: Social Security
*Diff: 1*      *Page Ref: 681*

46) Discuss the link between social policy and social programs.

Answer: Social policies identify social problems and propose ways to ameliorate them, whereas social programs are visible manifestations of those social policies. Policies for older adults reflect society's definition of how to meet their needs and division of responsibilities between the public and private sectors.
*Diff: 1*      *Page Ref: 676*

47) Trace the history of public policies affecting older adults from the 1930s to today.

Answer: The Social Security Act in 1935 was the first policy enacted that affected older adults. It established the federal government as a major player in the social welfare arena and established older adults as a governmental responsibility. National interest in policies affecting older adults subsided until the 1960s, until the establishment of Medicare, Medicaid and the Older Americans Act in 1965. More recent policies include the 1996 Personal Responsibility Act restricting welfare legislation and the 2003 Medicare Prescription Drug Bill.
*Diff: 3*      *Page Ref: 681–682*

48) Explain how Social Security is currently funded and the arguments in favor of and against privatizing Social Security.

Answer: Currently, Social Security is funded through a trust fund which receives funding from taxing employees and employers. Proponents of privatizing Social Security argue that privatization would give consumers more control, leading to higher benefits and allow participants to pass wealth to survivors in the case of premature death. Opponents argue that privatization would not be cost-effective for low income employees, would have high transition costs and high administrative costs, benefits would have to be cut dramatically for current workers, current workers would be double taxed, there would be no protection from inflation, there is uncertainty in the stock market, most workers are not investor savvy and a fundamental shift from governmental to individual responsibility would result, not resolving Social Security long term financial problems.
*Diff: 3*      *Page Ref: 693*

49) Outline the programs and services provided by the Older Americans Act.

Answer: The Older Americans Act provides a programs and services focused on community planning and services, research and development and training to personnel to provide services to older adults. Specifically this includes: access to services (information, care management), in-home services (homemaker, respite, telephone reassurance), senior care programs (increased emphasis on health enhancement and wellness), nutrition (such as meals on wheels), and legal assistance.

*Diff: 2*        *Page Ref: 698*

50) Contrast the politics of productivity versus the politics of entitlement.

Answer: The politics of productivity argues that older adults are a resource for society and are quite diverse, whereas the politics of entitlement argues that the older population is needy and need to be given resources solely because of age.

*Diff: 2*        *Page Ref: 701*

# Chapter 17   Health and Long-Term Care Policy and Programs

1) An older person's need for long-term care is generally determined by:
   A) the number of medical conditions
   B) the severity of each medical condition
   C) problems in performing activities of daily living
   D) loss of cognitive skills
   Answer: C
   *Diff: 1      Page Ref: 717*

2) Each of the following can provide long-term care services except:
   A) adult day centers            B) senior centers
   C) assisted living facilities   D) private homes
   Answer: B
   *Diff: 1      Page Ref: 717*

3) The average expenditure for all health expenses for the populations 65+ (including acute, chronic, long-term care) is _____ the cost for people under 65.
   A) equal to          B) twice          C) four times          D) six times
   Answer: C
   *Diff: 3      Page Ref: 718*

4) A fundamental assumption characterizing current long-term care services is:
   A) the public provision of services based on age and need
   B) individuals are first responsible for the costs of long-term care
   C) the importance of curing disease
   D) none of the above
   Answer: B
   *Diff: 2      Page Ref: 731*

5) The primary factor underlying escalating health and long-term care costs is:
   A) more people are reaching old age
   B) older people and their families are paying less for care
   C) older people's disproportionate utilization of hospital and physician services
   D) inflation in hospital costs and physicians' fees and the growth of medical technology
   Answer: D
   *Diff: 2      Page Ref: 719*

6) Which of the following health care costs does Medicare not cover?
   A) long-term nursing home care      B) home health care
   C) hospital care                    D) physician visits
   Answer: A
   *Diff: 1      Page Ref: 722*

7) The following groups have benefited from prescription drug reform except:
    A) private insurance companies
    B) affluent elders
    C) low income elders earning less than $12,000 a year
    D) older adults needing approximately $4000 worth of prescription drugs per year

Answer: D
*Diff: 3*      *Page Ref: 733*

8) Medicare is designed to serve:
    A) low-income older adults
    C) older people with chronic disabilities
    B) institutionalized persons
    D) all persons age 65 and over

Answer: D
*Diff: 1*      *Page Ref: 721*

9) Which of the following is true of Medicaid?
    A) It provides coverage for a limited amount of health services.
    B) It offers basic hospital and optional supplementary insurance.
    C) It finances medical care primarily for people receiving public assistance or SSI.
    D) It covers medical care costs for people aged 65+ years of age, and for disabled Social
        Security beneficiaries.

Answer: C
*Diff: 1*      *Page Ref: 735*

10) The largest expenditure from the Medicare Part A budget has generally been for:
    A) home health care
    C) hospital care
    B) skilled nursing care
    D) physician services

Answer: C
*Diff: 2*      *Page Ref: 722*

11) The largest expenditure from the Medicare Part B budget has generally been for:
    A) home health care
    C) hospital care
    B) skilled nursing care
    D) physician services

Answer: D
*Diff: 2*      *Page Ref: 722*

12) Home health care costs are:
    A) mostly covered by Medicare
    B) primarily funded by state and local sources
    C) always lower than nursing home care
    D) publicly funded for skilled and unskilled services

Answer: A
*Diff: 2*      *Page Ref: 723*

13) Older adults qualify for Medicaid in the following ways:
    A) participation in SSI
    B) designation as medically needy
    C) dual eligibility for both Medicare and Medicaid
    D) all of the above

Answer: D
*Diff: 2*      *Page Ref: 736–737*

14) "Medicare Choice" encourages all of the following choices by beneficiaries except:
   A) use of alternative medicine (e.g. homeopathic, chiropractic)
   B) purchase of private insurance
   C) use of HMOs
   D) setting up medical savings accounts

Answer: A
*Diff: 2      Page Ref: 729*

15) Which of the following statements is true about the funding of the current long-term care system?
   A) It provides an integrated and comprehensive system of both community-based and institutional options.
   B) It finances an adequate level of home health care as a way to keep older people in their homes.
   C) It is dominated by institutional care.
   D) It is guided by a national policy on long-term care.

Answer: C
*Diff: 3      Page Ref: 717*

16) The way in which Medicaid is funded means that:
   A) states must comply with federal regulations regarding which services to provide
   B) home health services, skilled nursing facility care and rural health clinics are optional
   C) most older people are covered by Medicaid
   D) it covers the difference between Medicare and out-of-pocket expenses for elders

Answer: A
*Diff: 2      Page Ref: 736*

17) The proportion of nursing home care that is paid by Medicaid:
   A) is lower than the proportion paid by Medicare
   B) is lower than what is paid by private long-term care insurance
   C) is increasing due to population growth
   D) is increasing due to price increases by health providers

Answer: D
*Diff: 3      Page Ref: 736*

18) It has been argued that middle-class Americans assume that Medicaid will pay long-term costs for themselves or their parents if needed. This attitude may:
   A) prevent greater purchase of long-term care insurance
   B) result in overuse of Medicaid
   C) cause rapid spend-down of an elder's assets
   D) result in seeking more costly long-term care options

Answer: A
*Diff: 3      Page Ref: 744*

19) As a whole, health and long-term care services for older people can be characterized by:
   A) the growth of private insurance plans that fill the gaps left by public funding
   B) growing inequities and the creation of a two tier system of care
   C) greater emphasis on better quality of care in hospitals and nursing homes
   D) greater access to high tech diagnostic services for low-income elders

Answer: B
*Diff: 2      Page Ref: 745*

20) What percent of Medicare beneficiaries have no prescription drug coverage at some point each year?

   A) 25%            B) 40%            C) 10%            D) 75%

Answer: B
*Diff: 2     Page Ref: 742*

21) The Program for the All-Inclusive Care for the Elderly (PACE):
   A) focuses on only a small number of frail elders who are eligible for nursing home placement
   B) provides basic Medicare and Medicaid services
   C) combines primary with long term care
   D) all of the above

Answer: D
*Diff: 2     Page Ref: 749*

22) "Medigap" policies fill which of the following gaps in Medicare coverage?
   A) Medicare deductible and co-payments
   B) items and services not covered by Medicare
   C) charges exceeding the amount approved by Medicare
   D) all of the above

Answer: D
*Diff: 2     Page Ref: 742*

23) Medicare's major limitation is its limited coverage of:
   A) health promotion          B) long-term care
   C) acute care              D) home health care

Answer: C
*Diff: 2     Page Ref: 722*

24) Recently, the majority of funding for home health care comes from:
   A) Medicare               B) Medicaid
   C) private health insurance     D) out-of-pocket

Answer: A
*Diff: 2     Page Ref: 724*

25) The number of proprietary home health agencies that are reimbursed under Medicare:
   A) has declined sharply        B) has declined slowly
   C) remained stable over the last 20 years     D) increased dramatically

Answer: D
*Diff: 2     Page Ref: 725*

26) Long-term care refers to a broad range of care for chronic conditions.

Answer: TRUE
*Diff: 1     Page Ref: 717*

27) The need for long-term care will diminish for aging baby boomers because of a decline in chronic conditions compared to previous cohorts of elders.

Answer: FALSE
*Diff: 2     Page Ref: 716-717*

28) Most long-term care services are covered by Medicare.

Answer: FALSE
*Diff: 2     Page Ref: 723*

29) Medicare is more likely to pay for hospital care, while Medicaid is the primary payer of nursing home services.

Answer: TRUE
*Diff: 2*     *Page Ref: 722*

30) Medicare Part B is financed through the Social Security payroll tax.

Answer: FALSE
*Diff: 2*     *Page Ref: 727*

31) Participation rates of eligible older adults are low in Medicaid.

Answer: TRUE
*Diff: 2*     *Page Ref: 736*

32) Home health care has been shown to be preferred by more older people than receiving care in a long-term care facility.

Answer: TRUE
*Diff: 2*     *Page Ref: 723*

33) Older persons comprise a majority of the total users of Medicaid.

Answer: FALSE
*Diff: 2*     *Page Ref: 736*

34) A prospective payment system to limit payments in advance for a general course of treatment applies only to Medicare-reimbursed hospital care.

Answer: FALSE
*Diff: 2*     *Page Ref: 728*

35) Fortunately, Medicare provides adequate health care protection for older Americans.

Answer: FALSE
*Diff: 3*     *Page Ref: 721-722*

36) The number of Medicare beneficiaries enrolled in managed care plans has increased since its inception.

Answer: FALSE
*Diff: 2*     *Page Ref: 747*

37) The goals of the Medicare Plus Choice Plan are cost-savings and quality of care.

Answer: FALSE
*Diff: 1*     *Page Ref: 746*

38) Medicare coverage for mental health is substantially limited compared to that for physical illness.

Answer: TRUE
*Diff: 2*     *Page Ref: 723*

39) Researchers have shown that Medicaid spend-down requirements have been thwarted by many middle-class families.

Answer: TRUE
*Diff: 2*     *Page Ref: 741*

40) Cash and Counseling programs provide older adults with financial advice for long-term planning.

Answer: FALSE
*Diff: 2     Page Ref: 740*

41) Medicare beneficiaries now have supplemental insurance coverage, called _____, to help pay for additional health care costs, especially for the catastrophic costs of intensive care, numerous tests or extended hospitalization.

Answer: Medigap
*Diff: 2     Page Ref: 742*

42) The federal agency that that approves or denies Medicare claims is known as _____.

Answer: Centers for Medicare and Medicaid Services
*Diff: 1     Page Ref: 728*

43) _____ allow beneficiaries to put Medicare dollars into a tax-exempt account to pay for qualified medical expenses.

Answer: Medical savings accounts
*Diff: 2     Page Ref: 729*

44) _____ is a federal and state means-tested welfare program of medical assistance for the poor, regardless of age.

Answer: Medicaid
*Diff: 1     Page Ref: 735*

45) When an individual is eligible for both Medicaid and Medicare, they are said to be _____.

Answer: dual eligible
*Diff: 2     Page Ref: 737*

46) Distinguish the services provided within home and residential care settings with those that are delivered in community-based settings.

Answer: Services provided within home and residential care settings include personal assistance, assistive devices and technological devices. Services delivered in community-based settings include nutrition programs, senior centers, adult day care, respite, hospice and transportation programs.
*Diff: 2     Page Ref: 717*

47) Explain the structural factors that underlie escalating health care costs.

Answer: These structural factors would include the success of modern medical care (e.g. routine use of CAT scans and MRIs), the poor fit between the needs of the population and the funding mechanisms and regulations for these services, the focus on acute care in public financing and the lack of integrated, comprehensive programs and policies for acute and chronic care.
*Diff: 2     Page Ref: 719*

48) Discuss the factors which have led to the growth in Medicare funded home care services.

Answer: The factors include:
1. early hospital discharges have led to a greater need for home care
2. a class action lawsuit led to a more flexible interpretation of definitions
3. the number of for-profit home health agencies has increased dramatically
4. there are isolated instances of Medicare home health agencies not complying with federal standards
5. high-tech home therapy, such as intravenous antibiotics, oncology therapy and pain management

*Diff: 2*　　*Page Ref: 723-725*

49) What measures have attempted to reduce the costs under Medicare?

Answer: A number of measures have attempted to reduce costs under Medicare. Examples would include, diagnostic related groupings (DRGs), a prospective-payment system, Congress passed the Medicare Catastrophic Health Care Act, physician payment reform, and raising the age of Medicare eligibility from 65 to 67 years.

*Diff: 3*　　*Page Ref: 727-729*

50) In what ways might older adults qualify for Medicaid?

Answer: Older adults qualify for Medicaid by:
1. participating in SSI
2. being designated as "medically needy" under state-specific rules
3. nursing home residents with income and assets below a state designated cap
4. dual eligibility

*Diff: 2*　　*Page Ref: 736-737*

NOTES

NOTES

NOTES

# NOTES

NOTES

NOTES

NOTES

NOTES

NOTES

NOTES

# NOTES